Maestros, Dilettantes, and Philistines

American University Studies

Series IV
English Language and Literature
Vol. 103

PETER LANG
New York • Bern • Frankfurt am Main • Paris

Emily Auerbach

Maestros, Dilettantes, and Philistines

The Musician in the Victorian Novel

PETER LANG
New York • Bern • Frankfurt am Main • Paris

Library of Congress Cataloging-in-Publication Data

Auerbach, Emily
    Maestros, dilettantes, and philistines : the musician in the Victorian novel / Emily Auerbach.
        p. cm — (American university studies. Series IV, English language and literature ; vol. 103)
        Bibliography: p.
        1. English fiction—19th century—History and criticism. 2. Musicians in literature.   3. Music and literature—History—19th century.   I. Title.   II. Series.
PR878.M87A84   1989   823'.8'09352—dc19   88-35048
ISBN 0-8204-0926-X   CIP
ISSN 0741-0700

CIP-Titelaufnahme der Deutschen Bibliothek

Auerbach, Emily:
Maestros, dilettantes, and philistines : the musician in the Victorian novel / Emily Auerbach. —
New York; Bern; Frankfurt am Main; Paris: Lang, 1989.
   (American University Studies: Ser. 4, English Language and Literature; Vol. 103)
   ISBN 0-8204-0926-X

NE: American University Studies / 04

© Peter Lang Publishing, Inc., New York 1989

All rights reserved.
Reprint or reproduction, even partially, in all forms such as microfilm, xerography, microfiche, microcard, offset strictly prohibited.

Printed by Weihert-Druck GmbH, Darmstadt, West Germany

To my mother

ACKNOWLEDGEMENTS

I gratefully acknowledge the invaluable assistance of Professor Edward Alexander of the University of Washington, who read portions of this manuscript and of other colleagues--Richard Dunn, Jacob Korg, Todd Bender, Joseph Wisenfarth--who shared with me their thoughts and ideas. I thank the editors of *Papers on Language and Literature* and *The Sphynx* for publishing sections of this manuscript as articles, and I thank the Newberry Library and the University of Wisconsin Graduate School for providing me with fellowships to support research on this topic.

I also wish to thank my husband, Keith Meyer, my children, David, Beth, and Melanie, and my father Robert Auerbach, for their warmth and support. For her years of faithful assistance and encouragement as both reader and reference librarian, I lovingly dedicate this book to my mother, Wanda Auerbach.

Table of Contents

Introduction /   1

Chapter I
From Eighteenth Century Fiddlers to Romantic Maestros /   3

Chapter II
Das Land ohne Musik /   29

Chapter III
Victorian Melodrama: The Musician as Hero or Villain /   53

Chapter IV
From Sentimentalism to Cynicism: The Musicians of Charles Dickens /   75

Chapter V
Satire: The Musicians of William Thackeray /   91

Chapter VI
Nostalgia: The Old-fashioned Musician from Peacock to Hardy /   111

Chapter VII
Towards Realism: The Musicians of George Eliot /   137

Chapter VIII
Conclusion /   181

Bibliography /   192

Introduction

Walter Horatio Pater's remark in 1879 that "*All art constantly aspires to the condition of music*" reflects the pervasive influence of music in the nineteenth century, a century in which composers sought to achieve verbal effects in their music while writers simultaneously brought music into their works through imagery, stylistic effects, and musical characters. Yet despite the wealth of nineteenth century British poems and essays praising the beauty of Aeolian harps and Orphic bards, musical composition in Victorian England was at its nadir and professional musicians were treated with condescension. While nineteenth century Europe could boast of Brahms, Berlioz, Chopin, Schubert, Liszt, Mendelssohn, Rossini, Verdi, and Wagner, England could offer nothing better than the works of Sir Sterndale Bennett and M.W. Balfe. "I blush for my country," wrote one Victorian music critic.

Victorian novelists grew up in a society which regarded the musician with a paradoxical mixture of romantic admiration, Puritan suspicion, and utilitarian contempt. Furthermore, they inherited a wide assortment of literary musicians, from the amateur performers of Austen to the romantic maestros of the German Romantics. Because of the contradictory attitudes towards music in British literature and society, the musician became a rich and complex source of metaphor for the Victorian novelists.

Dickens, Thackeray, Meredith, Hardy, Eliot, and other Victorians devote many pages of their novels to discussions of music and musical characters: foreign composers whose art connotes a world of romantic abandon, simple folk who sing ballads of an earlier, less troubled age, effeminate dilettantes who use music to avoid work, young ladies who prove their marriageability by playing "a little", piano, and stolid middle-class citizens whose attitudes towards the musician epitomize British ignorance, materialism, and xenophobia. To understand fully the discussion of "fiddling" in Thackeray's *The Newcomes*, the ironic allusions to Aeolian harps in Hardy's *Jude the Obscure*, and Casaubon's objections to music in Eliot's *Middlemarch*, one must be familiar with the attitudes towards music in eighteenth and early nineteenth century literature and society. Similarly, Disraeli's melodramatic portrayal of the musician as a member of another race, Dickens' sentimental depictions of singing workers, and Trollope's nostalgic description of an aging cellist become pregnant with meaning if read in the context of the times. To facilitate interpretation, Chapter I surveys notions of music prior to the Victorian period, and Chapter II provides a brief overview of the prevailing attitudes towards the musician in Victorian society, poetry, and prose.

The varied portrayal of the musician in the Victorian novel as a symbol of romance and innocence, a figure of ridicule, an emblem of the past, or a skilled craftsman (Chapters III, IV, V, VI, and VII) reveals the unique blend of melodrama, sentimentalism, cynicism, nostalgia, and realism characterizing the Victorian regard for music. Yet Victorian novelists did far more than reflect the prejudices of their age. For many novelists, most notably Charles Dickens (Chapter IV), William Thackeray (Chapter V), Thomas Hardy (Chapter VI), and George Eliot (Chapter VII), the musician became a powerful vehicle for attacking the state of art in Victorian England. The musicians of these and other Victorian novelists provide a fascinating and unexplored index to the aesthetics of each writer and of the period.

Chapter I

From Eighteenth Century Fiddlers to Romantic Maestros

"I insist upon your neither piping nor fiddling yourself. It puts a gentleman in a very frivolous, contemptible light." Lord Chesterfield, *Letters*

"Music is a higher revelation than all wisdom and philosophy . . . I am the Bacchus who presses out this glorious wine for mankind." Beethoven, *Letters*

In 1749 Lord Chesterfield informed his son that music was an unbecoming pursuit for a gentleman, but by the turn of the century critics hailed music as the model art and viewed the musician as a godlike hero. The difference between eighteenth and early nineteenth century notions of music reflects the dramatic change in attitude towards the function of art and the status of the artist. Victorian novelists inherited the debate between those who regarded the musicians as a mere tradesman who could provide amusement and those who extolled him as a prophetic genius whose art could disclose to man a hidden realm of mystery and beauty. Furthermore, they inherited the argument that had raged through each century over music's role in religious worship.

In his "Song for St. Cecilia's Day" (1687) Dryden asked, "What passions cannot Music raise and quell?" Writers throughout the eighteenth century explored this question and sought to reconcile the contradictory views of music they found in classical myth, the Bible, medieval lyrics, Renaissance works, and Reformation religious tracts.

Early writers saw that the musician's extraordinary ability to move man's emotions made him a powerful figure with the potential for both good and evil. Classical writing includes accounts of inspired musicians such as Orpheus who, as Ovid writes, could move animals and inanimate rocks with his singing and could make "the pale phantoms weep," yet classical myth also warns man of the Sirens' deadly singing. Plato, while granting music's power, recognized its potential for encouraging indolence and banished musicians from his Republic (II: 401). Although Plato's educational scheme included music, a "potent instrument" for imparting grace and harmony, he warned that this art must not be pursued to excess: "the mere musician is melted and softened beyond what is good for him" (III: 289).

In the Bible God is the "Chief Musician" (Psalm 108) and music brings relief to the spiritually oppressed:

> And it came to pass, when the evil spirit was upon Saul, that David took an harp, and played with his hand; so Saul was refreshed, and was well, and the evil spirit departed from him. (1 *Samuel* 16:19)

But in *Revelation* Christ must silence the "harpers, and minstrels, and flute players, and trumpeters" accompanying the Whore of Babylon, and musical instruments are associated with carnal festivities (*Isaiah* 5: 11-12).

From Chaucer's time through the Renaissance it was assumed that music would form a part of a gentleman's education because it promoted order, harmony, and grace. Chaucer's Squire, among other accomplishments, "koude songes make and wel endite." Etiquette books and educational tracts such as Hoby's translation of *The Courtier*, 1561, Ascham's *The Scholemaster*, 1568, Peacham's *The Compleat Gentleman*, 1634, and Milton's *Tractate of Education*, 1644, praised music's ability to improve manners. As Peacham warned, unmusical people "are by nature very ill disposed and of such a brutish stupidity that scare anything that is good and savoureth of virtue is to be found in them."[1] Dramatists expressed similar sentiments, as in Shakespeare's *The Merchant of Venice* (V, i: 83-85, 88):

> The man that hath no music in himself,
> Nor is not moved with concord of sweet sounds,
> Is fit for treasons, stratagems, and spoils. . .
> Let no such man be trusted.

Although medieval and Renaissance writers praised music, they simultaneously castigated its ability to incite evil and regarded professional musicians, or "minstrels," as little more than servants. Skelton (1490?-1529) wrote contemptuously that the music-master Doctor Devyas "commensyd in a cart, / A master, a mynstrell, a fydler, a farte."[2] Ascham's *Scholemaster* repeated the saying "Much music marreth men's manners," and Burton warned in his *Anatomy of Melancholy* that musicians could not only cure melancholy but cause it.3

Reformation writers added a further complaint against music: it detracted from the serious worship of God. The movement by Wycliffe, Calvin, and others to purify the Catholic church included a reform of the type and function of church music. In their quest for a literal interpretation of the Scriptures and a belief in the supremacy of The Word, church reformists insisted that music be subordinate. In the fourteenth century, Wycliffe warned that "oure fleschly peple hath more lykynge in here bodely eris in sich knackynge and tateynge than in herynge of goddis lawe" and claimed that during the singing of a choir "noman schal here the sentence, and alle othere schulhen be doumbe and loken on hem as foolis." Music, Wycliffe admonished, distracted men from sincere religious devotion, hindered an understanding of words, and stimulated carnal passions; furthermore, singing could make "men wery and indisposid to studie goddis lawe for akying of hedis."4 In his *Commentary on the Book of Psalms*, Jean Calvin (1509-64) insisted that frivolous instrumental music was inappropriate for church services:

> . . . if believers choose to cheer themselves with musical instruments, they should, I think, make it their object not to dissever their cheerfulness from the praises of God. But when they frequent their sacred assemblies, musical instruments would be no more suitable than the burning of incense, the lighting up of lamps, and the restoration of the other shadows of the law.

Enjoyment of "mere melody," Calvin added, suited "childish" people such as the Jews, a group "yet weak and rude in knowledge," but such music was no longer necessary for civilized Christians.5

Influenced by Calvin's position on music, George Wither (1588-1667) and other English Puritans ended the use of organ playing and choir music in church and allowed only plain psalm tunes sung in unison. Wither's "For a Musician" complained that "many musicians are more out of order than their instruments" and included an Ode for their benefit:

> . . . What will he gain
> By touching well his lute,
> Who shall disdain
> A grave advice to hear?

> What from the sounds
> Of organ, fife, or lute,
> To him redounds, Who doth no sin forbear?[6]

Although Martin Luther shared many of Calvin's objections to the rituals of Catholicism, he viewed music more leniently. In *Table Talk and Letters* Luther praised the musician as a man of grace and inner harmony: "Music is one of the greatest gifts that God has given us: it is divine and therefore Satan is its enemy . . Whoever is proficient in this art is a good man, fit for all other things."[7] Luther believed that since music was a gift of God the best music possible should be used in church services, and he did not object either to traditional Catholic chanting or polyphonic music.

In Germany, Luther's embrace of music helped create an atmosphere favorable to musical composition, whereas in England the Puritan distrust of music, which led to the dissolution of cathedral choirs during the Protectorate, lingered even under Anglican administrations. It was not that Puritans disliked music, but rather that they recognized its power and feared it would distract man from a rational understanding of God's word.

Eighteenth century English writers continued to debate the nature of music, to rank it with respect to the other arts, and to define the musician's proper role in society. The classical and Renaissance belief in music's healing power persisted. Charles Avison in *An Essay on Musical Expression* (1753) claimed that music fills the mind with "a silent and serene Joy" and fixes "the Heart in a rational, benevolent, and happy tranquillity."[8] Richard Brocklesby's *Reflections on Ancient and Modern Musick* (1749) and John Gilmore Cooper's *Power of Harmony* (1745) are typical in their insistence that music can promote order and temperance. Richard Browne in *Medicina Musica* (1729) expanded Burton's belief in music as a panacea for melancholy, claiming that music could cure spleen ailments and promote moral and physical health.

Music's principal function was in religion, noted Mason, Cowper, Addison, and other eighteenth century writers, for hymns and organ music created a mood of spirituality. Addison wrote that sacred music "raises noble Hints in the Mind of the Hearer, and fills it with great Conceptions" (*Spectator* 405, June 14, 1712). "Devotion," Avison agreed, "is the original and proper End" of music, whereas frivolous secular music "disgusts every rational Hearer, and dissipates, instead of heightening, true devotion."[9]

Although hymns enhanced the service, instrumental music, because of its abstract nature, was a distraction. John Wesley fought against the introduction of instrumental music, "artificial sounds without any words at all," into the service:

> This astonishing jargon has found a place even in the worship of God. It runs through (0 pity! 0 shame!) the greatest part of even our Church Music! It is found even in the finest of our Anthems and in the most solemn parts of our public worship. Let any impartial, any unprejudiced persons say whether there can be a more direct mocking of God.[10]

A popular hymn by Wesley's brother warned:

> Still let us on our guard be found,
> And watch against the power of sound
>   With sacred jealousy,
> Lest haply sense should damp our zeal,
> And music's charms bewitch and steal
>   Our hearts away from Thee.[11]

Methodist hymnbooks reflected this view, as in the preface to the *Select Hymns with Tunes Annexed Designed Chiefly for the Use of the People called Methodists*, 1765: "Above all sing *spiritually*. Have an eye to God in every Word you sing. Aim at pleasing Him more than yourself, or any other Creature. In order to do this, attend strictly to the Sense of what you sing, and see that your Heart is not carried away with the Sound, but offered to God continually."[12]

This religious condemnation of instrumental music led eighteenth century writers, philosophers, and music critics to regard secular music as at best an amusement and at worst an immoral pursuit. In his essay "On Music as an Amusement," eighteenth century philosopher Vicesimus Knox wrote that instrumental music "contributes to imbecility."[13] In 1711 Richard Steele compared instrumental music to nonsense verse in poetry and objected to the serious pursuit of music at the expense of more noble arts:

> Music is certainly a very agreeable entertainment: but if it would take the entire possession of our ears, if it would make us incapable of hearing sense, if it would exclude arts that have a much greater

tendency to the refinement of human nature; I must confess I would allow it no better quarter than PLATO has done, who banishes it out of his commonwealth (*Spectator*, No. 18, March 21, 1710-11).

Music divorced from words seemed meaningless.

To create or enjoy secular music, wrote the poet Cowper, was an improper activity for a man of devotion. In *The Task*, Bk. IV, Cowper warned the congregation to avoid a situation where "all that we design / Is but to gratify an itching ear, / And give the day to a musician's praise." Music was worse than wine, Cowper wrote in a letter, and he lamented that an acquaintance seemed "to have suffered considerably in his spiritual character by his attachment to music." He continues, ". . . wine itself though a man be guilty of habitual intoxication does not more debauch and befool the natural understanding than music--always music, music in season and out of season--weakens and destroys the spiritual discernment."[14] If music was not used to inspire devotion, eighteenth century writers feared, it might incite evil, voluptuous thoughts and immoral behavior.

Even music historians of the period belittled their art as a frivolous pastime. Charles Burney, most notable of eighteenth century music historians, admitted that "music is an innocent luxury, unnecessary, indeed, to existence, but a great improvement and gratification of the sense of hearing." Burney dismissed the importance of his own *History of Music* by noting that "music being, at best, but an amusement, its history merits not, in reading, the labour of intense application, which should be reserved for more grave and important concerns."[15]

The chief use of secular music was to provide domestic recreation. Eighteenth century books on civility and manners linked music with amusements such as gambling and bear-baiting and called it an agreeable diversion.[16] Jeremy Bentham observed: "Prejudice apart, the game of push-pin is of equal value with the arts and sciences of music and poetry. If the game of push-pin furnish more pleasure, it is more valuable than either."[17] For Bentham and other utilitarians at the end of the century, music was an "art of amusement" with little practical worth or societal value.

Since music was regarded as frivolous, irrational, and immoral, it was pronounced less valuable than the other arts; eighteenth century works which ranked poetry, painting, and music placed music lowest in the hierarchy. Locke disparaged music because it was the least connected to ideas and common sense and noted:

> . . . a good hand upon some instruments, is by many people mightily valued. But it wastes so much of a young man's time, to gain but a moderate skill in it; and engages often in such odd company, that many think it much better spared: and I have among men of parts and business, so seldom heard anyone commended or esteemed for having an excellency in music that among all those things that ever come into the list of accomplishments I think I may give it the last place. [18]

Critics also attacked music because of its failure as a mimetic art, as in William Mason's comment that "Music, as an imitative art, ranks so much below Poetry and Painting."[19] In *Essays on Poetry and Music* (1770) James Beattie asked, "What resemblance is there between Handel's *Te Deum*, and the tone of voice natural to a person expressing, by articulate sound, his veneration of the Divine Character and Providence?"; of music he wrote "Strike it off the list of imitative arts."[20] Herbert Schueller concludes in "Literature and Music as Sister Arts: An Aspect of Aesthetic Theory in Eighteenth Century Britain," the relationship between literature and music in the eighteenth century "would better be described as one between mother and daughter than one between sisters."[21] Music's lack of referential quality made it less valuable to a century excited by the promise of scientific experimentation and rational inquiry.

Music was regarded as the lowest art not only by eighteenth century philosophers and critics but by society as well: professional musicians had little more social status than ordinary servants. It was no longer essential for a gentleman to be proficient in music, whereas this was an assumed ability of the Renaissance courtier. Scholes' *Oxford Companion* reports that the Earl of Mornington (d. 1781) had "cool courage" because he was "the first member of the British aristocracy who dared to walk through the London streets openly and unashamedly carrying a violin case."[22] As Bernarr Rainbow observes in *The Land Without Music:*

> Proud disavowal of musical aptitude by the aristocratic male was a circumstance first to become pronounced during the last decade of the 17th century . . . Music fulfilled no useful function, had lost its earlier status as a badge of culture, was, at a time of thriving insularity, increasingly regarded as the preserve of foreigners, and thus appeared demonstrably unsuitable as an element in the

education of a nobleman. There was, we note, no condemnation of music as a form of entertainment--opera enjoyed noble patronage; rather was it a reappearance of the attitude of ancient Rome, where music was performed by slaves for the gratification of patricians. [23]

Composers were under the patronage of a particular nobleman, while performers were regarded as tradesmen, "mere lackeys" equal in status to household servants.[24] A tangible sign of the musician's low social standing was the cord separating him from others at parties; in etiquette books instructions were given for musicians to be seated at the table next to valets and cooks.[25] Musicians frequently *were* servants, because butlers, cooks, and gardeners were often hired "with an eye to their musical abilities."[26]

Music was a barrier to gentility, a sign of low breeding. When the widow Thrale married a singer in 1784, a huge outcry arose against her scandalous behavior, although her first marriage to a wealthy brewer with gonorrhea was perfectly acceptable.[27] Neither Handel nor Clementi was considered a suitable son-in-law. In 1788 Newberry wrote his "Letter to a Young Man on his too Strong Attachment to Singing and Music" in which he warned that music "may tend, which it naturally does, to enervate the mind and make you haunt musical societies, operas, and concerts; and what glory is it to a gentleman, even were he a fine performer, that he can strike a string, touch a key or sing a song, with the grace and command of an *hired* musician?"[28] Similarly, Lord Chesterfield cautioned his son as he visited Venice:

> As you are now in the musical country, where singing, fiddling, and piping are not only the common topic of conversation, but almost the principal objects of attention; I cannot help cautioning you against giving into those (I will call them illiberal) pleasures (though music is commonly reckoned one of the liberal arts), to the degree that most of your countrymen do when they travel in Italy. If you love music, hear it; go to operas, concerts, and pay fiddlers to play to you; but I insist upon your neither piping nor fiddling yourself. It puts a gentleman in a very frivolous, contemptible light; brings him into a great deal of bad company; and takes up a great deal of time, which might be much better employed. Few things would mortify me more, than to see you bearing a part in a concert, with a fiddle under your chin or a pipe in your mouth.[29]

Chesterfield's remarks epitomize the low regard for musicians and echo the popular gibe, "Musicians' heads are as empty as their fiddles."

Unlike the utilitarians, who linked music, poetry, and painting together as "arts of amusement," Chesterfield distinguished music from the other arts and singled it out for his disapproval:

> Sculpture and painting are very justly called liberal arts; a lively and strong imagination, together with a just observation, being absolutely necessary to excel in either; which, in my opinion, is by no means the case of music, though called a liberal art, and now in Italy placed even above the other two: a proof of the decline of that country. A taste of sculpture and painting is in my mind as becoming as a taste of fiddling and piping is unbecoming a man of fashion. The former is connected with history and poetry, the latter, with nothing that I know of but bad company.[30]

Eighteenth century literature reflects this century's view of the musician, for the major writers of the period are relatively silent about the art of music, and musicians in novels consist primarily of young ladies who "go to the instrument." Dr. Johnson and Alexander Pope were notorious for their lack of music appreciation. Dr. Johnson, who exclaimed "All animated nature loves music--except myself!" dismissed music by remarking that "no man of talent, or whose mind was capable of better things ever would or could devote his time and attention to so idle and frivolous a pursuit."[31] Boswell's *Life of Johnson* includes a description of the two men's response to music.

> In the evening our gentleman-farmer, and two others, entertained themselves and the company with a great number of tunes on the fiddle . . Johnson owned to me that he was very insensible to the power of musick. I told him, that it affected me to such a degree, as often to agitate my nerves painfully, producing in my mind alternative sensations of pathetick dejection, so that I was ready to shed tears; and of daring resolution, so that I was inclined to rush into the thickest point of the battle. 'Sir, (said he,) I should never hear it, if it made me such a fool.'

Boswell's reaction suggests that music, despite the many eighteenth century treatises belittling it, remained for many a powerful, moving art form; Johnson's response indicates that music's ability to affect the emotions was distasteful to those priding themselves on common sense, propriety, and industriousness. Johnson labelled music one of the "little things" of life, appropriate for women or for men with nothing better to do.[32]

Like Johnson, Pope was impervious to music's charms. Thomas Busby, an early nineteenth century music historian, includes a section in his work entitled "Pope's Insensibility to Music" in which he reports of Pope that "Handel's finest performances gave him no more pleasure than the airs of any itinerant ballad singer."[33]

It is not surprising that writers so unmoved by music would choose to ignore this art in their works. German literature parallels this: as Schoolfield notes in *The Figure of the Musician in German Literature*, "The amusical age of the Enlightenment produces no literary musicians."[34] In a century which believed good art should mirror life, provide practical instruction, and stimulate devotion, music seemed trivial.

Just as Dr. Burney actively sought to be known as a 'man of letters' rather than a musician, so Beethoven, whose life spanned the transitional period between the eighteenth and nineteenth centuries, was acutely conscious that 'musician' was a pejorative term and referred to himself as a 'tone-poet' engaged in 'dichten'. He reacted against the fettered artistic position of his predecessors and made grand claims for his art and role as artist:

> "When I open my eyes I must sigh, for what I see is contrary to my religion, and I must despise the world which does not know that music is a higher revelation than all wisdom and philosophy, the wine which inspires one to new generative processes, and I am the Bacchus who presses out this glorious wine for mankind and makes them drunken."[35]

Beethoven's defense of music was part of the aesthetic movement in Germany at the turn of the century that ranked music as the supreme art and envisioned the musician as a revolutionary hero. M.H. Abrams in The *Mirror and the Lamp* writes, "The movement of ideas in German criticism in the late eighteenth century cannot be understood without some reference to the discussions of music," for music replaced painting as the dominant metaphor for art.[36]

The German Romantics embraced the very qualities of music which had disturbed eighteenth century critics: its irrational, abstract, and entrancing nature made it attractive to those looking for an art form capable of transporting man beyond empirical experience and a world of ugly mechanism. Herder called music "a new magical language of the feelings"; similarly, Schlegel claimed, "The musician has a language of feeling independent of all external objects," and Novalis, disparaging words, wrote, "The musician takes the essence of his art out of himself and not the slightest suspicion of imitation can befall him."[37]

Critics such as E.T.A. Hoffmann, Schopenhauer, Hegel, Keble, and Wackenroder viewed instrumental music as the ideal art. Music penetrated the soul, transcended temporal and spacial limitations, and suggested a world of spontaneity, innocence, and spirituality. In "Beethoven's Instrumental Music" (1813) Hoffmann called music

> . . . the most romantic of all the arts--one might say, the only genuinely Romantic one--for its sole subject is the infinite. The lyre of Orpheus opened the portals of Orcus--music discloses to man an unknown realm, a world that has nothing in common with the external sensual world that surrounds him, a world in which he leaves behind him all definite feelings to surrender himself to an inexpressible longing.[38]

Instrumental music was the most abstract and therefore the purest form of music because it was liberated from words, which Schopenhauer labelled "a foreign addition, of subordinate value."[39] This view of instrumental music directly reverses eighteenth century thought.

German critics saw Beethoven as the paradigm of the romantic artist because of his revolutionary sympathies, his refusal to become a puppet of the aristocrats, his simultaneous scorn of philistines and love of humanity, his fascination with relating literature and music, his fervent belief in the power of his art to move the masses, and his fidelity to his artistic ideals despite harsh criticism and social ostracism. Beethoven's ability to write the colossal Ninth Symphony while deaf symbolized artistic genius.

The idolization of Beethoven and the conception of music as model art resulted in an abundance of musical characters in German Romantic literature. In *A Muse for the Masses* Conrad Donakowski writes that "The musician, denigrated as almost subrational by some Enlightenment writers, became the archetypal man of talent and subconscious wisdom."[40] The typical Romantic hero-musician is an inspired genius whose religious devotion to his art leads him to reject society and to approach a state of insanity.

Wackenroder's Joseph Berglinger is representative of this figure. Joseph listens to music "with precisely the same reverence as if he had been in church" and reacts to the sounds as to "a spiritual wine"; his yearning towards music is likened to calling to God. He must battle against his eighteenth century father, a doctor who "despised and detested all the arts as servants of extravagant desires and passions and as flatterers of the elegant world" and who "made a determined and serious effort to convert him, from a harmful propensity for an art whose practice was little better than idleness and which catered merely to sensual excess, to medicine, as the most beneficent science and as the one most generally useful to the human race."

Joseph becomes physically ill when deprived of music, but his eventual career as Capellmeister brings him no satisfaction either, for he learns that as a professional musician "he is of no use to the world; less influential than any tradesman." His love of music is destroyed by those who teach him to regard it as a mathematical science. Joseph concludes:

> "Is it not a most absurd idea to make this art one's whole aim and chief business and to imagine a thousand wonderful things about its great effects on human temperament-about an art which, in everyday reality, plays much the same role as card-playing or any other pastime?"

Joseph, of course, dies young, his creative talent wasted on a society unwilling to accept the romantic view of the artist.[41]

Early death and madness are common afflictions of romantic musician figures, for exposure to a realm of such exquisite beauty and divine power makes them unfit to endure life in the ordinary world. The musician, though a heroic bearer of a "mission," seems a victim of his genius and of forces beyond his control. As Schopenhauer wrote (1818), "The composer reveals the inner nature of the world, and expresses the deepest wisdom in a language which his reason does not understand."[42] Hoffmann's Kreisler goes mad and finds composing a painful as well as euphoric process; other musical figures in Hoffmann become alienated from philistine society, tormented by split personalities, and driven to acts of insanity.[43]

Romantics consistently depicted the art of composing and listening to music as an intense religious experience. Goethe's Faust begins to be restored after hearing a medieval Easter carol, and Goethe writes in *Conversations with Eckermann*:

> Music stands too high for any understanding to reach, and an all mastering efficacy goes forth from it, of which, however, no man is able to give an account. Religious worship cannot therefore do without music. It is one of the foremost means to work upon man with effect of *marvel*.[44]

Although the Germans led in championing music and the musician, a similar movement occurred in France and is reflected in works by Balzac, Victor Hugo, and others. Balzac's Gambara, for instance, is "a martyred saint" and "unrecognized Orpheus" whose obsession with music causes "a noble madness." Gambara holds "the key to the language of heaven" and hears "the chorus of angels"; he is offended when he is compared to a poet and launches into rapturous praise of music:

> "It is the art that delves deepest into the soul. Painting shows you only what you see; poetry tells you only what the poet said. Music goes far beyond both: it shapes your thought and wakens your dormant memories . . . Music, and music only, has the power of making us draw upon the life within. The other arts give us but well defined sensations of pleasure."

Gambara dies a begging street musician, a victim of his superior gift.[45]

French writers not only hailed music's link to the supernatural but also its relationship to nature and to pantheistic harmony, a connection which profoundly influenced English Romanticism. Although Rousseau echoed the eighteenth century view of instrumental music as "cold and tiresome," he believed that in man's primitive state, music, speech, and poetry were one; in *Emile*, music is included as part of a natural education. Rousseau praised the musical genius as a man of superior sensitivity:

> The genius of a musician submits the universe to his art . . . if the charms of this grand art leave you tranquil and contented, if you feel no ravishing transports, if you discover nothing beautiful, dare you ask what is *genius*? Vulgar mortal! Profane not the sacred appellation. What would it avail thee to know it,--thou who canst not feel it?[46]

For French and German Romantics alike, music was ideal because of its spontaneity, its link with primitive cultures, and its relationship to the harmonious sounds of the natural world. The musician was pictured as innocent and child-like, for his lack of experience in the ordinary world was an essential ingredient of his artistic temperament. Hegel had written that "musical talent declared itself as a rule in very early youth, when the head is still empty and the motions have barely had a flutter; it has, in fact, attained real distinction at a time in the artist's life when both intelligence and life are practically without experience."[47] Peter Kivy's article "Child Mozart as an Aesthetic Symbol" discusses the Romantics' attraction to the idea of the musical *Wunderkind*, a genius whose talent seemed innate and internal.[48]

Wordsworth and Coleridge, both of Beethoven's generation, were influenced by the European attraction to music as an emblem of natural beauty, innocence, and divine power. Their musicians are frequently drawn from nature: Wordsworth describes the beauty of the skylark's singing ("To a Skylark"), while Coleridge insists on freeing the nightingale from poetic stylization and praises its power as a merry warbler of "delicious notes" ("The Nightingale").

Wordsworth's musicians are not the maestros of German romanticism but the pipers, harp players, and fiddlers of the countryside or of an earlier age. For both Wordsworth and Coleridge, the rustic musician became a metaphor for the native harmony of man freed from the corrupting influence of civilization. Wordsworth's "Power of Music" describes workers listening to a blind street fiddler:

> An Orpheus! An Orpheus!...
> His station is there; and he works on the crowd,
> He sways them with harmony merry and loud;
> He fills with his power all their hearts to the brim--
> Was aught ever heard like his fiddle and him?
> What an eager assembly! what an empire is this
> The weary have life, and the hungry have bliss;
> The mourner is cheered, and the anxious have rest;
> And the guilt-burthened soul is no longer opprest.

Coleridge's "Music" similarly praises the simple music of a county church congregation.

Children are natural appreciators of music: in *The Prelude* Wordsworth notes that as a "babe in arms" he heard the "ceaseless music" of nature, and in "The Nightingale" Coleridge's child, "though capable of no articulate sound," bids the adults to listen to the bird's singing. Music's value lay in its restorative power and ability to return man to a state of innocence and harmony.

For Coleridge and later English Romantics, music symbolized not only natural beauty but supernatural mystery as well. In Coleridge's "Aeolian Harp" God is a musician whose power permeates all nature, which vibrates like harps; in "Dejection: An Ode" the spirit is "strong music in the soul."[49]

Keats similarly moved beyond sensual music to immortal harmony and used music as a metaphor for the divine:

> Heard melodies are sweet, but those unheard
> Are sweeter; therefore, ye soft pipes, play .
>   on;
> Not to the sensual ear, but, more endeared
> Pipe to the spirit ditties of no tone.
>   ("Ode on a Grecian Urn")

Supernatural musicians offer a realm of enchantment and beauty; listening to this music is an exquisite but deadly pleasure. Keats's musician typically is a goddess or fairy whose singing enthralls her lover.[50] The nightingale of Keats's ode is not the merry bird of Coleridge's poem but a dark emblem of death whose song acts as a "dull opiate" luring the speaker away from reality.

Like Keats, Shelley linked music with intoxication and personified the musician as an enchantress.[51] Jean de Palacio in "Music and Musical Themes in Shelley's Poetry" notes that "in Shelley's poetry, Music always is the intimation of something beyond."[52] In "A Fragment: To Music" (1817) music is a "Silver key of the fountain of tears / Where the spirit drinks till the brain is wild." Elsewhere Shelley compares music to an intoxicating wine which thrills the senses:

> I pant for the music which is divine,
>   My heart in its thirst is a dying flower;

>   Pour forth the sound like enchanted wine,
>   Loosen the notes in a silver shower.
>   ("Music")

Shelley repeatedly uses phrases such as "soul-awakening music," "soul-enfolding music," "wondrous music," and "enchanted music" to suggest music's transcendent nature. Such music, when "too intense, is turned to pain" ("With a Guitar, To Jane").

For Thomas Hazlitt and other English Romantic critics, music symbolized passion and mystery. Hazlitt's essays link music with intense emotions, and he notes, "There is a near connection between music and deep rooted passion. Mad people sing." Musicians are those with the greatest sensitivity: "I contend that the person . . . into whom the tones of sweetness or tenderness sink deeper and deeper as they approach the farthest verge of ecstasy or agony, he who has an ear attuned to the trembling harmony, and a heart 'pierceable' by pleasure's finest point, is the best judge of music." Music is "a mistress whose face is veiled; an invisible goddess" who "lifts the soul to heaven."[53]

Hazlitt's discussions of music show a fascination with synaesthesia. He describes Mozart's *Don Giovanni* as

> . . . a kind of scented music; the ear imbibes an aromatic flavor from the sounds. It is like the breath of flowers; the sighing of balmy winds, or the liquid notes of the nightingale wafted to the bosom of the bending rose. We drink in the ethereal sounds, like draughts of earthly nectar. [54]

Shelley's use of music draws on all senses in like manner, as in "The Sensitive Plant":

>   And the hyacinth purple, and white, and blue,
>   Which flung from its bells a sweet peal anew
>   Of music so delicate, soft, and intense,
>   It was felt like an odour within the sense.

This parallels the German Romantics' fascination with synaesthesia: Goethe called architecture "frozen music", and Herder referred to poetry as "the music of the soul."[55] Romantic writers rejected Joshua Reynolds' insistence that "No art can be grafted with success into any other art" (*Discourses*, 1786) because combining the qualities of each art afforded maximum stimulation of the feelings and emotions.

Because poets tried to merge the arts and blend the senses, the term "musician" acquired a broader, more metaphorical application. Wordsworth's Preface to *Lyrical Ballads* discusses "the poet, singing a song," Coleridge refers to Wordsworth's poetry as "Orphic song" (To William Wordsworth"), Shelley's poet is a lute (*Alastor*) or a nightingale singing in isolation (*Defense of Poetry*), and Hazlitt labels poetry "the music of language." The amazing frequency of references to Aeolian harps, the music of the spheres, Orpheus, and nightingales in the works of all the English Romantic poets suggests music's importance to them as a symbol of the infinite and an illustration of art's mysterious beauty.

Although the English Romantics lauded the beauty of their fictional musicians, they scorned the paltriness and pretentiousness of London's professional and amateur musicians. Hazlitt found more to praise in the singing of birds than in contemporary operatic productions, or "artificial" music which encouraged "an atmosphere of voluptuous effeminacy."[56] Coleridge and Byron contrasted their supernatural musicians with inferior performers of London drawing rooms. In "Lines Composed in a Concert Room" Coleridge places the artificial vocalists of London in opposition to the simple musicians of his childhood and the pure sounds of nature:

> Nor cold, nor stern my soul! yet I detest
>   These scented Rooms, where, to a gaudy
>   throng
> Heaves the proud Harlot her distended breast
> In intricacies of laborious song.
>
> These feel not Music's genuine power, nor
>   deign
>   To melt at Nature's passion-warbled plaint;
> But when the long-breathed singer's uptrilled strain
> Bursts in a squall--they gape for
>   wonderment...
>
> O give me, from this heartless scene released,

> To hear our old Musician, blind and grey,
> (Whom stretching from my nurse's arms I
>   kissed)...

Byron mocks "the long evenings of duets and trios" provided by "Miss That or This, or Lady T'Other" who make a "half-profession" of music and perform "to please their company or mother"; he sarcastically refers to "our own most musical of nations" (*Don Juan*, Canto 16, Stanzas xliv-xlv).

Satirical treatment of musicians is not limited to the age's poetry: Jane Austen uses musical scenery in her novels to define characters and to attack English provincialism and vulgarity.

Austen treats the heroine of eighteenth century novels whose charms included the ability to play and sing for social gatherings with merciless irony in novels such as *Pride and Prejudice* and *Sense and Sensibility*. Mary Bennet, "in consequence of being the only plain one in the family," is always eager to display her musical accomplishment, although she "had neither genius nor taste."[57] Elizabeth: though less affected, can only play "a little," and Miss Bingley performs Italian songs with the sole purpose of attracting Mr. Darcy. Austen satirizes the use of art as a means of captivation in her portrayal of Lady Middleton in *Sense and Sensibility*: Lady Middleton's piano music has lain untouched since her marriage, "for her ladyship had celebrated that event by giving up music although by her mother's account she had played extremely well, and by her own was very fond of it."

Austen ridicules the eighteenth century view of music as a pleasant but frivolous pastime by giving it to Mr. Collins, the pompous Anglican minister of *Pride and Prejudice*:

> "If I," said Mr. Collins, "were so fortunate as to be able to sing, I should have great pleasure, I am sure, in obliging the company with an air; for I consider music as a very innocent diversion, and perfectly compatible with the profession of a clergyman. I do not mean however to assert that we can be justified in devoting too much of our time to music, for there are certainly other things to be attended to."

Austen also attacks those who respond inadequately to musical performances. During Marianne's singing in *Sense and Sensibility*, Sir John continues to talk loudly, Lady Middleton only pretends to be enchanted, and Elinor, who "was neither musical, nor affecting to be so," has her thoughts elsewhere. Colonel Brandon's silent appreciation of Marianne's performance contrasts with the others' "shameless want of taste" and "horrible insensibility."

In *Persuasion*, Austen's last novel, music becomes a more prominent metaphor for feelings and taste. Anne Elliot's private and sincere love of music sets her apart from a society full of artistic pretense. Unlike the affected Musgroves, Anne possesses genuine talent and informed enjoyment of music.

This link between music and honest feelings also appears in Gothic and Romantic novels at the turn of the century. The Marchesa in Anne Radcliffe's *The Italian*, 1797, puts off her plans of murder when she hears an organ because the sounds seem to revitalize her deadened conscience. Sir Walter Scott appropriated Shakespeare's device of giving the truth to mad singers: in *Heart of Midlothian*, 1818, Madge Wildfire's songs suggest a world of innocence and beauty lacking in corrupt society.

To be musical became for the nineteenth century an essential proof of one's sensitivity and culture, whereas in the eighteenth century such skill usually indicated one's lack of seriousness. As nineteenth century writers and philosophers redefined art's function, they embraced music as the supreme art. Rather than being an inferior adjunct to literature, music had a suggestiveness and fluidity missing from the other arts. Schopenhauer and others celebrated music's independence from physical reality: music's lack of concreteness made it the model of art for a century wishing for escape and excitement. What better way to react against eighteenth century rationalism, pragmatism, and moral earnestness than to embrace music, "the language of the feelings," the most abstract, amoral, and emotional of the arts? What easier means to leave behind a world of business, machines, and social turmoil than to be transported by the indescribable beauty of sound? Further, music's universal properties appealed to those influenced by the spirit of the French Revolution and the desire to transcend national boundaries.

At first glance, it appears nineteenth century critics, philosophers, and poets appreciated music far more than their eighteenth century predecessors: indeed, the shift in attitude from Samuel Johnson and Lord Chesterfield to Shelley and Hazlitt is truly dramatic. Yet the change to a great extent took place on paper. Because they wished their art to do more than mirror life, Romantic writers sought to achieve musical effects in their works and devoted pages of rhapsodic prose to discussions of, ironically, the inability of words to equal music. The Romantics' metaphorical attraction to music, however, was not always accompanied by a greater understanding or appreciation of actual music. Despite his synaesthetic raptures about music's beauty, Hazlitt wrote criticism which showed he lacked musical training and had narrow, provincial taste. Many Romantic poets were attracted to music not because they appreciated individual composers and compositions but because they were fascinated by the properties of this art form and its implications for their own work. Music, like drugs, could stimulate their imaginations and provoke dream-like reveries and sensual ecstasies. As Eduard Hanslick complained in the middle of the century, the Romantics were absorbed in the pathological, narcotic effect of music:

> Curled up half-asleep in their easy chairs, these enthusiasts let themselves be carried away and rocked to and fro by the pulsation of the sound, instead of considering it with sharpened attention. As it more and more increases, subsides, exalts, or dies away, it transports them into an indefinite state of feeling, which they are so innocent as to consider purely spiritual.[58]

In England in particular, citizens continued to receive little musical education and musicians suffered social slighting, despite the grand metaphorical role of music and the musician in the century's literature.

Victorian writers who sought to bring musicians into their works had many models to choose from among the literary and philosophical works of earlier generations: female performers using music artfully but not artistically, the empty-headed and immoral social outcasts attacked by Lord Chesterfield, supernatural intoxicators luring one into a world of painfully exquisite beauty, simple shepherds piping of a past Golden Age, or passionate Beethovian composers with long flowing hair and visionary eyes.

Chapter I: Notes

1 Peacham's Compleat Gentleman (Oxford: Clarendon Press, 1906; rpt. 1634 ed.), p. 104. Good discussions of music and musicians in periods prior to the 18th century include John Hollander's *Untuning of the Skies*, Leo Spitzer's *Classical and Christian Ideas of World Harmony*, Walter Woodfill's *Musicians in English Society*, and John Stevens' *Music and Poetry in the Early Tudor Court*.

2 "Against a Comely Coistrown," *The Complete Poems of John Skelton*, ed. Philip Henderson (London: J.M. Dent, 1931), p. 121.

3 Roger Ascham, *The Whole Works*, ed. Rev. Giles (London: John Russell Smith 1864), III: 100; Robert Burton, *The Anatomy of Melancholy* (London: Dent, 1621), II: 116 ff. Burton writes that "Musick is a roaring-meg against melancholy, to rear and revive the languishing soul," but he also warns that madrigals and jigs are "pernicious" and cause disease

4 *The English Works of Wyclif*, ed. F.D. Matthew (London: Trubner & Co., 1880), pp. 191 ff.

5 John Calvin, *Commentary on the Book of Psalms*, trans. Rev. James Anderson (Grand Rapids, Mich.: Eerdmans, 1949), I: 539, III: 495.

6 George Wither, "Library of Old Authors," ed. Farr, 1851, in Percy A. Scholes, *The Puritans and Music in England and New England* (London: Oxford University Press, 1934), p. 157.

7 Martin Luther, *Gedanken uber die Musik* (Berlin, 1825), pp. 17-18,, trans. Jacques Barzun, *Pleasures of Music* (N.Y.: Viking Press, 1951), pp. 180-81. See also Luther's letter to Lewis Senfel, Oct. 4, 1530, in which he concludes that "next to theology there is no art equal to music."

8 Charles Avison, *An Essay on Musical Expression*, second ed. (London: C. Davis, 1753), p. 3. While praising music's soothing power, Avison also warns that "the Force of Music may urge the Passions to an excess, or it may fix them on false and improper Objects, and may thus be pernicious in its Effects" (p. 5).

9 Ibid, p. 88.

10 In Bertrand Bronson, "Some Aspects of Music and Literature in the 18th Century," *Music and Literature* (U.C.L.A.: Clark Memorial Library, 1963), p. 47.

See also Eric Routley, *The Musical Wesleys* (N.Y.: Oxford University Press, 1968); Routley concludes, "in music Wesley was a thoroughgoing conservative."

11 Bronson, p. 47.

12 In Reginald Nettel, *The Englishman Makes Music* (London: Dolson, 1952), p. 40.

13 Vicesimus Knox, "On Music as an Amusement," *Essays Moral and Literary*, 9th ed., 3 vols. (London: Charles Dilly, 1878), II: 108.

14 Letter to Rev. John Newton, Sept. 9, 1781, *The Correspondence of William Cowper*, ed. Thomas Wright (N.Y.: AMS Press, 1904), I: 352. Music, Cowper asserts, must be used "with an unfeigned reference to the worship of God, and with a design to assist the soul in the performance of it."

15 Charles Burney, *A General History of Music*, 1789, (N.Y.: Harcourt, Brace, 1935), I: 19.

16 Herbert Schueller, "The Use and Decorum of Music as Described in British Literature, 1700-1780," *Journal of the History of Ideas*, XIII (1953): 79.

17 *Works of Jeremy Bentham* (Edinburgh: William Tait, 1843), II: 253.

18 "Some Thoughts on Education," *The Works of John Locke* (London: Ward, Lock, and Co.), pp. 543-44.

19 *Essays on English Church Music* (York, 1795), in Alfred Einstein, *Music in the Romantic Era* (N.Y.: Norton, 1947), p. 342.

20 James Beattie, "Essay on Poetry and Music as they affect the Mind," *Essays* (Edinburgh: Creech, 1776), p. 441. Beattie adds that "the expression of music without poetry is vague and ambiguous" (p. 465).

21 *Philological Quarterly*, XXVI (July, 1947), 3: 204.

22 Percy A. Scholes, *The Oxford Companion to Music*, 2nd ed. (London: Oxford University Press, 1943), p. 594.

23 Bernarr Rainbow, *The Land Without Music* (London: Novello, 1967), p. 24.

24 Paul Lang, *Music in Western Civilization* (N.Y.: Norton, 1941), p. 720.

25 Schueller, "The Use and Decorum of Music," p. 89.

26 Lang, p. 173.

27 Arthur Losesser, *Men, Women and Pianos* (N.Y.: Simon and Schuster, 1954), p. 261. Dr. Johnson was one of those objecting to the widow Thrale's marriage to a singer.

28 Ibid., p. 260.

29 *The Letters of Philip Dormer Stanhope, Earl of Chesterfield*, ed. Lord Mahon (5 vols., Philadelphia: Lippincott, 1892), I: 276.

30 Ibid., I: 297.

31 *Johnsonian Miscellanies*, ed. G.B. Hill (N.Y.: Harper, 1897), II, 404. Johnson also writes of music, "it excites in my mind no ideas and hinders me from contemplating my own" (II: 103).

32 James Boswell, *The Life of Samuel Johnson* (N.Y.: Modern Library, 1952), pp. 363, 374.

33 Thomas Busby, *Concert Room and Orchestra Anecdotes of Music and Musicians, Ancient and Modern* (London: Clementi, 1825), p. 273.

34 George Schoolfield, *The Figure of the Musician in German Literature* (Chapel Hill: University of North Carolina Press, 1956), p. 3.

35 Ludwig von Beethoven, *Letters, Journals and Conversations*, ed. and trans. Michael Hamburger (N.Y.: Pantheon, 1952), pp. 86-7. Beethoven's remarks are reported by Bettina Brentano in her letter to Goethe, May 28, 1811.

36 Abrams, p. 91.

37 Ibid, p. 93. Quotations are from Johann Gottfried Herders *Kritische Walder*, Pt. IV *Samtliche Werke*, IV, 18; Friedrich von Schlegel, *Vorlesungen uber Philsophische Kunstlehre* (Leipzig, 1911), p. 136; Novalis, *Romantische Welt: Die Fragmente*, ed. Otto Mann (Leipzig, 1939), pp. 297-98.

38 E.T.A. Hoffmann, "Beethoven's Instrumental Music," (1813), in Oliver Strunk, ed., *Source Readings in Music History* (N.Y.: Norton, 1950), p. 566.

39 Arthur Schopenhauer, *The World as Will and Idea*, trans. Haldane and Kemp (London: Routledge & Kegan Paul, 1883; rpt. 1957), III: 233.

40 *A Muse for the Masses: Ritual and Music in an Age of Democratic Revolution*, 1770-1870 (Chicago: Univ. of Chicago Press, 1972), p. 5.

41 *The Remarkable Musical Life of the Musician Joseph Berglinger* (1797), reprinted in Strunk, pp. 750-63.

42 Schopenhauer, *The World as Will and Idea*, I: 336.

43 For a useful discussion of Hoffmann's musical romanticism and the link in his fiction between music and madness, see Ronald Taylor's *Hoffmann* (N.Y.: Hillary House, 1963).

44 Johann Wolfgang von Goethe, *Conversations with Eckermann* (N.Y. : Dunne, 1901), p. 358.

45 *The Novels of Balzac*, trans. Ellen Marriage (Philadelphia: Bevvie, 1949), pp. 367-436.

46 J.J. Rousseau, "Genius," *A Concise Dictionary of Music*, trans. William Waring (London: Murray, 1709), p. 182.

47 Georg Wilhelm Friedrich Hegel, *The Philosophy of Fine Art*, trans F. Osmaston (London: G. Bell & Sons, 1920), I: 37.

48 *Journal of the History of Ideas*, XXVIII (June, 1967): 249-58.

49 Quotations from Wordsworth are from *The Complete Poetical Works of Wordsworth*, ed. Andrew George, Cambridge Edition (Boston: Houghton, 1932); quotations from Coleridge are from *The Complete Poetical Works of Samuel Taylor Coleridge*, ed. E.H. Coleridge (Oxford: Clarendon Press, 1912).

50 Cytherea's "sweet music" enslaves Endymion; La Belle Dame enchants the knight through her "faery's song"; Lamia's delicious song, "too sweet for earthly lyres," sends Lycius into a trance. Quotations from Keats are from *Selected Poems and Letters by John Keats*, ed. Douglas Bush (Boston: Houghton Mifflin, 1959).

51 The veiled Arabian maiden of *Alastor* plays "from some strange harp / Strange symphony"; Cythna's singing in *The Revolt of Islam* causes the youth to swoon in "a dizzy trance"; the faint, "life-dissolving sound" of Rosalind's harp-playing binds Lionel "in aery rings" (*Rosalind and Helen*). Shelley's musicians are non-human: his "unseen" skylark pours forth "a flood of rapture so divine," and his Orpheus produces a "wondrous sound" which nature cannot rival. Quotations from Shelley are from *Poetical Works*, ed. Thomas Hutchinson (London: Oxford University Press, 1970).

52 *Modern Language Review*, 59 (1964): 357.

53 William Hazlitt, *Works*, V,12; XI, 455; V, 296-7.

54 Ibid, V, 364.

55 Goethe, *Conversations with Eckermann*, II: 84; Herder, *Kritische Walder*, Pt. IV, *Samtliche Werke*, IV: 166, in Abrams, p. 93.

56 Hazlitt, XX, 94-6.

57 Quotations from Austen are from the New American Library editions of her novels. An interesting discussion of Austen's treatment of music is Merike Tamm's *Inter-art Relations and the Novels of Jane Austen*, Ph.D. Diss. University of Wisconsin, 1976.

58 Eduard Hanslick, *Music Criticism, 1846-99*, Trans. Henry Pleasants (Baltimore: Penguin, 1950), p. 127.

Chapter II

Das Land ohne Musik

In 1871 the Reverend Hugh Reginald Haweis, nineteenth century theologian, lecturer, world traveller, and musical amateur, published *Music and Morals*, in which he looked back on the Victorian period and sadly concluded, "The English are not a Musical People."[1] Yet the Victorian era saw the introduction of musical education into schools, an increase in the number of concert tickets, musical instruments, and sheet music sold to the public, and a growing effort to disprove continental Europe's scornful denunciation of England as "das Land ohne Musik." Victorian novelists were influenced by the practices and notions of their paradoxically musical and amusical age and by the portrayal of musicians in Victorian prose and poetry.

The eighteenth century belief that music was not a necessary part of a gentleman's education but rather a distraction from it persisted into the nineteenth century; musical education was not a regular part of public schooling until after 1850, so that most Englishmen had little if any knowledge of this art. It was in fact fashionable to boast of a tin ear. Tennyson, poet laureate of the age, wrote, "I know nothing about music, and don't care for it in the least,"[2] and Charles Lamb, claiming "I have no ear," expressed his sentiments in verse:

> Some cry up Haydn, some Mozart
> Just as the whim bites; for my part,
> I do not care a farthing candle
> For either of them, or for Handel.[3]

Foreign musicians touring England mocked the ignorance of their audiences.

The nineteenth century pianist Anton Rubinstein concluded: "Of the German people at least 50% understand music; of the French not more than 16%; whilst among the English--the least musical of peoples--not more than 2% can be found with any knowledge of music . . . their ignorance of music is only exceeded by their lack of appreciation."[4] The composer Josef Wolfl wrote to his publisher in Leipzig, "You won't believe how backward music still is here."[5]

Foreigners had legitimate grievances against English musicians and audiences. As the power of the aristocracy declined in England, audiences at musical events increasingly were composed of middle-class citizens who lacked a cultural education.6 Because audiences still regarded music as a species of entertainment, concerts were treated as social events and British conductors felt free to tamper with foreign compositions in order to make them more 'palatable.'

The bowdlerized versions of Italian operas which appeared at Covent Garden typify England's outrageous treatment of foreign compositions. In 1832, for instance, Rossini's *Mose* was fused with music from Handel's oratorio *Israel in Egypt*. As Harold Rosenthal remarks, "One shudders to think what the juxtaposition of two such essentially different styles of music as those of Handel and Rossini must have sounded like."7 Other operas were altered to suit the needs of the singers or cut to satisfy restless audiences.

Musical abuse was not limited to opera. As Hector Berlioz sarcastically observed following his tour of England, British conductors felt compelled to give Mozart and Beethoven "lessons in Instrumentation."8 Composers complained that English orchestras were out of tune and poorly disciplined. In his essay "Music" in Ward's *The Reign of Queen Victoria: A Survey of Fifty Years of Progress*, 1887, Walter Parratt summarizes the state of music in England at the beginning of the Queen's reign: "It cannot be said that music was flourishing in this country. The art was cultivated without system and criticised without intelligence by the average Englishman."9

The musician was still regarded as a tradesman who could amuse English society but not become an acceptable member of it. Reverend Haweis writes that musicians in England were regarded as "mere purveyors of Pleasure" and concludes his work with a tirade against his age:

> The people understand music to be a pleasant noise and a jingling rhythm; hence their passion for loudness, and for the most vulgar and pronounced melody. That music should be to language what language is to thought, a kind of subtle expression and counterpart of it; that it should range over the wordless region of the emotions, and become in turn the lord and minister of feeling, sometimes calling up images of beauty and power, at others giving an inexpressible relief to the heart by clothing its aspirations with a certain harmonious form--of all this the English people know nothing. And as English music is jingle and noise, so the musician

is the noisemaker for the people, and nothing more. Even among the upper classes, except in some few cases, it has been too much the fashion to regard the musician as a kind of servile appendage to polite society; and no doubt this treatment has reacted disastrously upon musicians in England, so that many of them are or become what society assumes them to be--uncultivated men in any true sense of the word. And this will be so until music is felt here, as it in Germany, to be a kind of necessity--to be a thing without which the heart pines and the emotions wither--a need, as of light, and air, and fire. [10]

It was assumed in the earlier part of the century that musicians were either foreign or female. Hueffer's history of Engish music, 1889, concludes "that the greater portion of musical work in England in the last half-century has been done by foreigners." [11] Burgh's *Anecdotes of Music; Historical and Biographical, in a Series of Letters from a Gentleman to his Daughter* is aimed exclusively at the female sex, those who have need of music as a pastime:

> The Author of the following Sheets is strongly impressed with the idea, that Music is not only a harmless amusement; but, if properly directed, capable of being eminently beneficial to his fair Countrywomen. In many instances, it may be the means of preventing that vacuity of mind, which is too frequently the parent of libertinism; of precluding the intrusion of idle and dangerous imaginations; and, more particularly among the Daughters of ease and opulence, by occupying a considerable portion of time, may prove an antidote to the poison insidiously administered by the innumerable licentious novels, which are hourly sapping the foundations of every moral and religious principle. [12]

Reverend Haweis patronizingly observes that "as a woman's life is often a life of feeling rather than of action . . . we should not deny her the high, the recreative, the healthy outlet for emotion which music supplies." Males could sing or play an instrument in amateur groups but were not expected to become proficient in "this charming science."[13]

Yet the Romantic glorification of music and the musician had begun to counter the legacy of Lord Chesterfield and his contemporaries. The decline in religious faith and the power of the monarchy left a void in England which glorious artistic heroes seemed to fill. Looking for artists who could provide excitement, novelty and glamor, the nineteenth century Englishman was drawn to the dazzling Italian opera singers, child prodigies, eccentric conductors, and virtuoso instrumentalists imported to fill England's vacancy of musical talent.

The English public received virtuoso performers such as Paganini and Liszt cautiously at first (as Hueffer noted, the English waited to see what the newspapers said before forming an opinion), but soon embraced them as technical wizards who cast spells on their audiences. Leigh Hunt paid homage to Paganini as "the pale magician of the bow" who played with "godlike ravishment" and had "dark flowing locks" and "a mournful look--/ Dreary and gaunt."[14] *The Times* concluded that "he forms a class by himself" and described him as "a devotee about to suffer martyrdom," a man with extraordinary capability for eliciting feeling from the audience.[15] William Gardiner, a hosiery manufacturer and amateur musical editor and composer, described Paganini's "fiend-like" performances and marvelled that "when he seizes the violin, it seems that a star descends on him, and inspires him with fire from heaven."[16] Reverend Haweis hailed him as a "supernatural figure" who "seemed to belong to another race, and to discourse in the weird music of another world."[17]

Similarly, Liszt was extolled for "his commanding presence, his noble brow, his flowing white hair"; women in the audience would fight for pieces of horsehair from his piano stool or swoon from excitement when he descended into their midst.[18] Liszt's first appearance in London was at age thirteen, but he eventually abandoned public performances because of his aversion to becoming a drawing-room oddity. Well aware of the public's taste, other conductors and performers continued to exaggerate their eccentricity and to select pieces with spectacular effects. Conductor Jullien had immense mustaches and long hair, and after a performance would sink into a gold armchair behind the podium.[19]

Foreign musicians owed their success in part to their reputations as demonic Don Juans, men who led lives of scandal and intrigue. Tales of Paganini's clandestine crimes and supernatural powers preceded his tours. When Paganini arrived in Paris in 1831 he found lithographs depicting him as a convict in chains and a murderer. One legend maintained that the G-string of his violin, on which he performed dazzling feats of technical virtuosity, was made from the intestines of his murdered wife.[20] In *My Musical Life* Reverend Haweis describes Paganini's eerie death at moonlight and the "ghastly violin music" heard to issue from his coffin.[21]

The public, attracted to these musicians as showmen and romantic figures of glamor, listened to performances with more amazement than appreciation and understanding. In T.B. Macaulay's comments to his sister about Paganini, one detects the superficiality of this fad for foreign virtuosi: "Tonight I go to another musical party at Marshall's, the late M. P. for Yorkshire. Everybody is talking of Paganini and his violin. That man seems to be a miracle. The newspapers say that long streamy flakes of music fall from his string, interspersed with luminous points of sound which ascend the air and appear like stars. This eloquence is quite beyond me" (May 27, 1831).[22]

Foreign musicians not only faced an uneducated English public but occasionally a hostile one. *The Times*, although admitting Paganini was in a class by himself, vehemently protested the high prices he charged: "There can be nothing in his art, a mere instrumental performer, so great a prodigy, as to deserve such a price" (May 19, 1831).[23] Paganini was in fact forced to lower his prices in England because of stubborn opposition. Newspapers attacked him for his avarice and depicted him as subhuman:

> Of monsters in the air or deep
> > Four-footed, furr'd, or finny,
> There's none to be compared at all
> > To Signor Paganini.
> > > (*The Examiner*, June 22, 1831) [24]

Posters were mounted in London warning the public against Paganini: one read, "Do not suffer yourselves to be imposed upon by the Payment of Charges which are well worthy the name of extortion; rather suffer under the imputations of a want of Taste than support any of the tribe of Foreign Music-Monsters, who collect the Cash of this country and waft it to their own shores, laughing at the infatuation of John Bull."[25]

Because so many musicians in England were foreign, they became the targets of English xenophobia and racial prejudice. Englishmen's pride had been hurt by Europe's scorn of their country's artistic culture, and they retaliated by mocking the greed and immorality of foreign performers. In *The Music of Nature* William Gardiner compares foreign performers to scheming cuckoo birds:

> This noted bird is a foreign musician, and, like many others, remarkable for his cunning, as well as his song. They lay their eggs in the nests of other birds, which are no sooner hatched and fed, than the young cuckoo, with lawless strength, bundles out his by other nestlings, and takes complete possession. Thus obtaining bed and board at others' cost, he stays and sings; and having passed the summer with us, bids John Bull adieu, and goes abroad.[26]

An anonymous nineteenth century British writer accompanied his commentary on William Hogarth's painting "The Enraged Musician" with the following diatribe against Italian music:

> Amidst all the follies of the age, there never was a greater one than the immoderate passion of the people for music. Though amusement and recreation are sometimes necessary, yet when carried to excess, they become vicious. Now, so far did the luxury of this kingdom extend at the time when this plate was first published, which was in the year 1741, that Italians (as being supposed to be the greater proficients) were bought over at considerable expense; and the poorest and least skilled among them, who from a want of ability, or a want of means, would not continue in their own country, soon discovering our folly, gathered here in flocks and took possession of the place. When here, they were encouraged, and their wretched abilities looked upon as supernatural; they introduced a new stile of music, which suited well the growing levity of this nation. The noble and elevated was immediately transformed into the trifling and insignificant: and the solemn and majestic sounds of British harmony gave place to the tinkling frippery of Italian sing-song.[27]

Nineteenth century England viewed foreign musicians with a strange mixture of fascination and dread. As in the previous century, music inspired fear because its severance from words made it amoral and elusive, beyond the control of Church or State. Victorians such as Thomas Cooper, a cobbler and choral secretary, felt uncomfortable with their enjoyment of music: "A passion for music is something far above the mere indulgence of feeling. Oh, how easily I could again yield to it! But I dare not. Thank God! we shall have music in heaven."[28] Music's ability to sway the passions threatened to undermine the power of religion. Reverend Richard Clayton's "Oratorios Unsuited to the House of Prayer, and Inconsistent with a Christian Profession," 1842, attacked the inappropriateness of allowing opera singers to take part in sacred musical performances.[29] Edward Baines raised further objections to music in "On the Performance of Military Bands in the Parks of London on Sundays," 1856, by noting that "the strains of martial music cause the pulse to bound, and fire the imagination, and they are wholly out of accordance with the sacred repose of the Sabbath."[30]

Italian opera provoked the strongest reaction because it seemed to symbolize the new decadence and immorality. For many Victorians, Rossini's work epitomized the new style and popular culture while classical German music represented more restrained and culturally sophisticated taste. Reverend Haweis insisted that by using music "simply as a slave to the senses," Italians had produced enervating, unhealthy music which reflected the century's decline in religious faith and morality:

> The German music is higher than the Italians because it is a truer expression and a more disciplined expressions of the emotions . . . In Beethoven all is restrained, nothing morbid which is not almost instantly corrected, nothing luxurious which is not finally raised into the clear atmosphere of wholesome and brisk activity, or some corrective mood of peaceful self-mastery, or even playfulness.[31]

Burgh labeled Rossini one of "those dealers in "*'notes, et rien que des notes,'* whom the tasteless caprice of fashion is constantly importing, like other wonderful and useless exotics, the natural productions of warm and enervating regions."[32]

Cardinal Newman's attempt to reconcile his love of music and his religious faith illustrates Victorian ambivalence towards music. In "Of Knowledge on Theology" Newman praises music as a more ideal art than painting because of its "abstract and unearthly" nature.[33] Newman enthusiastically describes the musician's ability to transcend everyday existence, but he warns against becoming absorbed in this gift:

> If then a great master in this mysterious science [music] throws himself on his own gift, trusts its inspirations, and absorbs himself in those thoughts which, though they come to him in the way of nature, belong to things above nature, it is obvious he will neglect everything else. Rising in his strength, he will break through the trammels of words, he will scatter human voices, even the sweetest, to the winds; he will be borne upon nothing less than the fullest flood of sounds which art has enabled him to draw from mechanical contrivance; he will go forth as a giant, as far as ever his instruments can reach, starting from their secret depths fresh elements of beauty and grandeur as he goes, and pouring them together into still more marvellous and rapturous combinations-- and well indeed and lawfully, while he keeps to that line which is his own; but, should he happen to be attracted, as he well may, by

> the sublimity, so congenial to him, of the Catholic doctrine and ritual, should he engage in sacred themes, should he resolve to do honour to the mass, or the divine office--. . .is it not certain, from the circumstances of the case, that he will rather use religion than minister to it, unless religion is strong on its own ground, and reminds him that, if he would do honour to the highest of subjects, he must make himself its scholar, must humbly follow the thoughts given him, and must aim at the glory, not of his own gift, but of the Great Giver? [34]

The Romantic tone at the beginning of the passage, expressing the glory of music and the musician's attraction to this beauty, is curbed by the reminder that art must not supercede religion.

Newman's contemporary, John Ruskin, disagreed that music was the ideal art, superior to painting. Like many Victorians, Ruskin objected to music because it appealed to the passions rather than to the intellect. Performing musicians were even less admirable than composers because their art was fleeting, did not reflect their character, and seemed little more than a technical skill. In his essay "on the relative dignity of the studies of painting and music, and the advantages to be derived from their pursuit," 1838, Ruskin writes:

> Let us now consider what is necessary to form a musician, and even one who can not only execute, but compose. It requires talent, distinguished talent, -- but of what description? A musical ear? -that is not intellect; and something else, we do not know what to call it, which involves neither thought nor feeling, -- a sensual power, a corporeal property. A musician may be also a great man, and yet I doubt it: for the habit of sensuality in the ear must gradually embrace and swallow up the other faculties; but on the other hand a musician *may* be what he has been, -- a brute in habits, and a bear in manners; an epicure in palate as in ear, a glutton in eating as in hearing; a man of vulgar mind, of mean thought, of debased intellect, -- of no principle. All this a man may be, and yet may be a great musician.

The amorality of music and the separateness of the musician from his work troubled Victorians who wished for art to be moral, respectable. Ruskin hails painting as a superior art because only elevated, cultured minds can create and appreciate it:

> The power of enjoying music is, like the power of distinguishing tastes in food, a naturally implanted faculty; the power of deriving pleasure from painting is either the acquired taste of a cultivated

mind, or the peculiar gift of an elevated intellect. Brutes can enjoy music; mice, in particular, are thrown into raptures by it. . . The power, therefore, of enjoying music, being common to brutes, must be considered inferior to the capability of appreciating painting, which is peculiar to him who was made after the image of God.

Music, Ruskin adds, is an art practiced by Jews; painting an art pursued by gentlemen.[35]

Victorians not only wished to make music morally acceptable but socially useful as well. Influenced by Rousseau's notion that primitive people were naturally harmonious and that music was an important educational tool, Victorians began spreading music among the lower classes. New treatises appeared suggesting that if used properly, music could promote physical health, refine manners, curb criminal behavior, stimulate patriotism, and increase a worker's productivity. As Reverend Haweis foresaw, music had an importany destiny as the "vast civiliser, recreator, health-giver, work-inspirer, and purifier of man's life."[36] In *Land Without Music* Bernarr Rainbow concludes: "Encouraged by the promise of a musical panacea, philanthropists, temperance workers, the clergy, and politicians lent their support in growing numbers to furthering the singing movement. The marked resurgence of popular musical activity in the mid-nineteenth century must thus be considered as much a phenomenon of social reform as anything else."[37]

J. Turner's *Manual of Instruction in Vocal Music*, 1833, concluded that spreading music among the industrial population would "contribute largely to the rooting out of dissolute and debasing habits"; the texts of the songs, he suggested, should be "simple in character, but conveying sentiments of pure and exalted morality." In 1836, W.E. Hickson's lecture on "The Use of Singing as a Part of the Moral Discipline of Schools" maintained that music "has a tendency to wean the mind from vicious and sensual indulgences; and if properly directed, it has a tendency to incline the heart to kindly feelings, and just and generous emotions."[38] The Reverend J.S. Curwen believed that congregational singing could be "the indirect means of aiding worship, temperance, and culture, of holding young men and women among good influences, of reforming character, of spreading Christianity," and he sketched a picture of a working home made beautiful by the sound of music:

"It [music] has been said to 'oil the wheels of life's chariot on this jolty road'. It gladdens, by association of contentment and love, even the poor man's board with truest festive joy. It adorns his cottage home with hues of peace and happiness. It makes 'the dear familiar face' grow, to us all, more beautiful with age. It throws on all things the glow of a cheerful affectionate mind."[39]

Victorians hoped that exposure to music would improve the character of lower-class workers. Singing could elevate their thoughts, provide them with a healthy outlet for their frustrations, and serve as a vehicle for imparting maxims. Herbert Spencer in "On the Origin and Function of Music," 1854, noted that music could make the lower classes more cultured. "Listen to the conversation of a servant girl," he writes, "and then to that of a refined, accomplished lady, and the more delicate and complex changes of voice used by the latter will be conspicuous"; the difference, claimed Spencer, is that the lady had been exposed to music.[40]

A colleague and a relative of Charles Dickens, John Hullah and George Hogarth, made even greater claims for music's social and moral utility. In the Preface to Wilhelm's Singing Method, 1841, Hullah writes:

> One of the chief means of diffusing through the people national sentiments is afforded by songs which embody and express the hopes of industry and the comforts and contentment of household life; and which preserve for the peasant the traditions of his country's triumphs, and inspire him with confidence in her greatness and strength.
> A nation without innocent amusements is commonly demoralised. Amusements which wean the people from vicious indulgences are in themselves a great advantage: they contribute indirectly to the increase of domestic comfort, and promote the contentment of the artizan. . . The songs of any people may be regarded as an important means of forming an industrious, loyal, and religious working class.[41]

Hogarth's *Musical History, Biography, and Criticism*, 1835, similarly focuses on music as a moral force:

> The diffusion of a taste for music, and the increasing elevation of its character, may be regarded as a national blessing. The tendency of music is to soften and purify the mind. The cultivation of musical taste furnishes to the rich a refined and intellectual pursuit, which excludes the indulgence of frivolous and vicious amusements, and to the poor, a *laborum dulce lenimen*, a relaxation from toil, more attractive than the haunts of intemperance.

Hogarth goes on to commend those manufacturers who provide regular musical entertainment for their workers, for "wherever the working classes are taught to prefer the pleasures of the intellect, and even of taste, to the gratification of sense, a great and favourable change takes place in their character and manners." Even those classes "who earn their daily bread by the sweat of their brow may find in music a recreation within their reach, full of innocent enjoyment, and pregnant with moral and social benefits."[42]

These benefits included physical health, increased productivity, and greater tractability. Curwen, Spencer, and Haweis claimed that the exercise of singing helped prevent consumption, headaches, and other ailments. In fact, William Gardiner maintained, the Germans' health could be attributed to their musical activity: "The Germans are seldom afflicted with consumption, nor have I ever known more than one instance of spitting of blood amongst them. This I believe is, in part, occasioned by the strength which their lungs acquire, by exercising them frequently in vocal music, which constitutes an essential part of their education."[43] Curwen suggested that songs such as 'Begone dull sloth' and 'Try again' would teach diligence and persistence. Haweis agreed that music could "stimulate work" and also celebrated its expediency in creating a people who were happy despite their poverty and thus politically "harmless." Music's beauty would make them "forget the hard, persistent images of pain and trouble, and the coarse realism that dampens Joy" and would "save the country millions in poor-rates." Haweis writes condescendingly:

> I am convinced that the influence of music over the poor is quite angelic. Music is the hand-maid of religion and the mother of sympathy . . . Teach the people to sing, and you will make them happy; teach them to listen to sweet sounds, and you will go far to render them harmless to themselves, if not a blessing to their fellows . . . Once get the people together by the power of music, you can mould them; one closed chamber of their minds after another might be unlocked; and were the scheme conducted with ability, and carefully watched, we should soon hail the dawn of a new era of popular enlightenment and genial instruction combined with an almost boundless variety of accessible, innocent, and elevating enjoyment.[44]

One detects in remarks such as these a peculiar mixture of deluded sentimentalism and shrewd political manipulation.

The Victorian zeal for disseminating music to all strata of society created a new market for musical instruments, sheet music, performers, and music-masters. For middle-class citizens, music provided a means of displaying opulence and social status. A prosperous businessman was able to purchase tickets to concerts which had previously been the exclusive prerogative of the aristocracy; attending a concert gave him a chance to mingle with titled Englishmen and assert his social standing. He could also purchase expensive musical instruments as a tangible symbol of his wealth and taste. Arthur Loesser in *Men, Women and Pianos* describes the new demand for pianos in England:

> By 1820 the piano was tending to become a piece of furniture by owning which a lower-middle-class family could appear a shade less lower. . . The pianoforte became a symbol of respectability. . . People, musical or not, bought pianos just as people, religious or not, supported churches: they would have felt somehow indecent had they not. . . To enhance a living room with a carved and shiny pianoforte costing 20 or 100 guineas seemed an easy advance toward leading the more abundant life.[45]

A middle-class Englishman could further advance his standing by procuring an advantageous marriage for his daughter, and music was a means to that end. Though Charles Dickens was sent to a blacking warehouse, his sister Fanny went to the Royal Academy of Music[46]; if a girl acquired "accomplishments" she became a more desirable marriage partner. Suddenly there was a demand for music teachers who could rapidly make females into accomplished performers. Musicians distributed advertisements geared to this new market: Logier advertised that his piano lessons could make "pupils of *ordinary capacity* and *ordinary industry* . . . capable of emulating Corelli, Handel, Haydn, and Mozart!"[47] 'Brilliant but not difficult' was used repeatedly in advertisements for piano music, and virtuosic and operatic pieces were transcribed for amateurs. A review of a piece by Bayer noted, "These variations will fulfill their purpose most surely in the hands of young pianists who would sometimes like to gleam in the tinsel of this art without having to wipe sweat from their brow." Although Hannah More had written of a girl who by age eighteen had practiced 14,400 hours of piano and then married a man who disliked music, such a prospect did not deter the effort of English families to make their daughters into instant artists.[49] Music-making became such a serious part of a woman's day that one London journalist complained, "in families the piano has extinguished conversation and the love of books" (*Connoisseur*, 1846).[50]

For the working classes, public schools introduced new methods of musical instruction aimed at the masses, and employers sponsored bands, choral societies, and lectures on music appreciation. Two popular manuals were Joseph Mainzer's *Singing for the Million* and J. Fetis's *Music on Everyone's Doorstep: Concise Explanation of Everything Needful to Judge this Art and Speak about it without Study*. Between the years 1843 and 1860, 25,000 students attended John Hullah's singing classes and 39,000 copies of "The Messiah" arranged in the easily understood Tonic-Sol-fa system were sold.[51] England relished its mammoth musical events, such as the Handel Festival at the Crystal Palace in 1859 or the performance of thousands of charity children singing annually at St. Paul's.

The Industrial Revolution facilitated the spread of music by allowing inexpensive type-printing of music and the rapid manufacture of instruments with technological advancements. Pianos, organs, and harmoniums multiplied, and instruments became increasingly loud and metallic. Engineers accommodated musicians by gearing the acoustics of new concert halls to larger audiences.

The widespread dissemination of musical instruction created a surplus of dilettanti ready to display their skills to a public anxious to appear cultured. England, determined not to remain "the land without music," had become a nation of amateurs and "the paradise of foreign musicians."[52]

Musicians profited from the surge of musical interest: "Musicians no longer acted as employers or small-scale enterprisers but rather as powerful independent entrepreneurs."[53] Thomas Busby observed in the earlier part of the century that the number of music-sellers in London had increased from twelve to one hundred and fifty.[54] The increased quantity of music sold, taught, and performed led to a decline in quality, so that Englishmen, rather than regarding music with a new esteem, tended to be confirmed in their suspicion of it as a shallow art.

As instruments became more metallic and composers became money-conscious, Victorians developed a nostalgia for the music of past eras and primitive cultures. Beethoven, Mozart, and Handel loomed as giants from the past whose works and personalities could never be equalled by the paltry musicians of nineteenth century England. Reverend Haweis praised Beethoven's reverence for

God and admired him as a legendary figure from an age when art was more sincere and impassioned:

> The person of Beethoven, like his music, seems to have left its vivid and colossal impress upon the age... the rough hair brushed impatiently off the forehead, the boldly arched eyebrows, resolute nose, and firmly set mouth - truly a noble force, with a certain severe integrity, and passionate power, and lofty sadness about it, seeming, in its elevation and wideness of expression, to claim kindred with a world of ideas out of all proportion to our own. [55]

Other nineteenth century writers went back further, rejecting both the emotional music of romanticism and the florid passages of contemporary Italian opera in favor of the pure, simple melodies of the Middle Ages or the disciplined counterpoint of the Baroque period. Critics resisted the idea of progress in music and looked to the past for a nonartificial, harmonious art to counter the onslaught of technological advances and middle-class taste. Pugin not only wanted a return to medieval architecture but favored the revival of Gregorian music.[56] The Reverend Henry Formby, writing in 1847, agreed and believed current musicians were less holy than their predecessors: "The chief authors and singers of Plain Chant upon earth are among the Saints of the Church, who are known to be in heaven, and to intercede for us; on the other hand, the chief authors of harmony and figured music, are not only *unknown* to be in heaven, but in no few instances, to judge from their lives, are under considerable improbability of being ever admitted there."[57] Musical societies such as the Musical Antiquarian Society, Ancient Concerts, Bach Society, Motett Society, and Purcell Club formed in order to promote the music of the past, and there was a renewed interest in older instruments such as the harpsichord.

Victorian music historians were fascinated by the music of ancient Egypt and Greece and by mythological figures such as Orpheus. Hueffer viewed the music of his era as a movement away from simplicity and writes nostalgically that in the first year of the Queen's reign, 1837, "the spirit of modern enterprise and competition had not yet entered the quiet realm of music."[58] There was a revival of interest in Jewish songs, folk ballads, and the music of cultures such as the blacks of America. While the eighteenth century music-historian Burney had dismissed music written before his century as "very uncouth and unmeaning," Victorian historians were sentimental about the ability of 'primitive' peoples to produce music of greater purity and simplicity. Reverend Haweis notes: "The songs that float down the Ohio River [Negro melodies] are one in feeling and character with the songs of the Hebrew captives by the waters of Babylon. We find in them the same tale of bereavement and separation, the same irreparable sorrow, the same simple faith and childlike adoration, the same wild tenderness and passionate sweetness, like music in the night."[59]

Music of other cultures and eras offered an escape from the pragmatism and industrialism of the times and a relief from feelings of depression and ennui. Because it was a foreign art, music seemed exotic, mysterious, and therefore fascinating. *The Musical World*, 1840, observed that singing in a chorus could "cheat the toiling man of his thoughts of ledgers, day-books, and all the troubles of bookkeeping, and ease his weary carcass of its remembances of office desks, high-stools, and pen cramped fingers."[60]

Like many Victorians, John Stuart Mill found music to be therapeutic because it could stimulate deadened feelings and counter the objective, practical vision offered by the utilitarians. When he saw music through the eyes of his Benthamite father, it became a mathematical science; he worried about "the exhaustibility of musical combinations" because "the octave consists of five tones and two semitones, which can be put together in only a limited number of ways." But Romantic music, "so peculiarly the expression of passion," delighted Mill and helped lead him out of the depression he describes in Chapter V of his *Autobiography*:

> The only one of the imaginative arts in which I had from childhood taken great pleasure, was music; the best effect of which (and in this it surpasses perhaps every other art) consists in exciting enthusiasm; in winding up to a pitch those feelings of an elevated kind which are already in the character, but to which this excitement gives a glow and a fervour, which though transitory at its utmost height, is precious for sustaining them at other times.[61]

This excitement came not from the "garrulous" music of Rossini and other modern composers but from "the musing, meditative tenderness, or pathos, or grief of Mozart or Beethoven" in which one feels "the very soul of melancholy exhaling itself in solitude."[62]

Thomas Carlyle's treatment of music is also important to examine because, as George Eliot wrote, "there is hardly a superior or active mind of this generation that has not been modified by Carlyle's writings."[63] Carlyle reflects the attitudes of early Victorian England in his narrow-minded attacks on opera and his praise of music's ability to stimulate work: "Give me the man who sings at his work. He will do more in the same time - he will do it better - he will persevere longer."[64] Yet because Carlyle also was profoundly influenced by Goethe, Fichte, Novalis, Schopenhauer, and other German Romantics, he viewed the musician metaphorically as a hero-prophet whose "inarticulate mystic speech" allowed him to penetrate "the deep, infinite harmonies of Nature and man's soul"; music, writes Carlyle, "brings us nearer to the infinite."[65] In "The Hero as Poet" Carlyle describes music as a vehicle of truth:

> Musical: how much lies in that. A *musical* thought is one spoken by a mind that has penetrated into the *inmost* heart of a thing; detected the inmost mystery of it, namely the *melody* that lies hidden in it; the inmost harmony of coherence which is its soul, whereby it exists, and has a right to be, here in this world. All inmost things, we may say, are melodious; naturally utter themselves in song.[66]

Carlyle's musicians are apocalyptic figures whose music is synonymous with religion. Christ is a prophetic musician:

> Our highest Orpheus walked in Judaea, eighteen-hundred years ago; his sphere-melody, flowing in wild native tones, took captive the ravished souls of men; and, being of a true sphere-melody, still flows and sounds, though now with thousandfold accompaniments, and rich symphonies, through all our hearts; and modulates, and divinely leads them.[67]

Carlyle also used the musician as the symbolic foil of materialists and philistines. Musicians are martyrs who must battle the harsh, grinding noises of mechanism and the shallow "squeaking" of those who, as Ruskin later wrote, "prefer Pop-goes-the-Weasel to Beethoven."[68] In "Signs of the Times" Carlyle writes that the public "grovelled on the plain with no music in the air," for the age is one of clanking Steam Engines and the "mad primeval Discord" of people who "gabble and jibber." Musicians stand in opposition to the utilitarians, such as the reviewer who dismissed music with the remark that three-deckers can not be built out of songs (*Westminister Review*, IV, 1825).[69]

Like the prose writers of the period, Victorian poets held music to be of profound symbolic importance, but they frequently reveal in their works an absence of actual musical understanding and taste. Victorian poets drew on Romantic music imagery - Aeolian harps, piping shepherds, and so on - but their allusions often seem merely stylistic conventions. Arnold's and Tennyson's poems contain no more than the obligatory references to Pan, Orpheus, rustic pipers, and harp-players.

Browning attempted to go beyond this stylistic use of music by describing actual musicians and by employing technical musical terms. Reflecting his age's nostalgia, Browning's poems dwell on composers of the previous century, such as Galuppi, Avison, and Vogler, and he bemoans "today's music manufacture." In place of complicated fugues Browning calls for "the mode Palestrina" ("Master Hugues of Saxe-Gotha"). In "Parleying with Charles Avison" he praises Avison's March for leading him away from "Brahms, Wagner, Dvorak, and Liszt" back to the age of Handel and older instruments.[70]

Although Browning did not share Tennyson's tin-ear and was considered "extraordinarily well educated musically," his poems show a greater passion for music than understanding of it.[71] Newspaper articles in the late nineteenth century exposed his erroneous use of musical jargon, while a contemporary summed up a discussion of Beethoven's quartets with the comment, "The member who talked most and knew least about the subject was, curiously enough, Browning."[72]

Browning's attempts to make his poems "realistic" by using actual musical terms were part of the growing movement in nineteenth century England to describe the arts as scientific phenomena. Although Haweis writes in glowing terms about the composer's mystical powers, he counters this with a chapter entitled "Longevity," in which he disproves the Romantic myth of the artist who dies young by listing ages attained by actual composers. He further attacks Romantic notions of music by insisting that nightingales and larks are not musical: "There is no music in Nature, neither melody nor harmony. Music is the creation of man."[73] William Gardiner subtitled his work on music: "An attempt to prove that what is passionate and pleasing in the art of singing, speaking, and performing upon musical instruments, is derived from the sounds of the animated world." Spencer went further and reduced music to a science whose effects could be analyzed:

> All music is originally vocal. All vocal sounds are produced by the agency of certain muscles. These muscles, in common with those

of the body at large, are excited to contraction by pleasurable and painful feelings. And therefore it is that feelings demonstrate themselves in sounds as well as in movements . . . we find all the leading vocal phenomena to have a physiological basis.[74]

Thus the Victorian approach to music seems a confusion of varying emotions and beliefs. Victorians were attracted to the musician as a figure of glamor and power, yet suspicious of him as a greedy foreigner, an amoral Bohemian, and an effeminate social outcast. They were sentimental about music as a primitive language of emotions and an emblem of the past, yet simultaneously more aware of music's social utility and scientific foundation.

Each Victorian musical treatise contains an extraordinary blend of sentimentalism, cynicism, nostalgia, and realism. In *Music and Morals*, for instance, Reverend Haweis describes Beethoven as a god-like giant whose art is from another sphere, but then insists that the proper effect of Beethoven's music is to create a "clear atmosphere of wholesome and brisk activity." While he attacks English provincialism, he is himself suspicious of the "large number of very low-class foreigners, with foreign habits and very foreign morals" teaching music in England. Haweis sentimentally writes of women's natural propensity for music ("never such a sensitive harp as a woman's soul") but cynically mocks those young ladies who would "trundle through Beethoven's sonatas in the drawing room" or play a little Chopin "by ear."

D.J. Smith writes in "Music in the Victorian Novel" that "The Victorians cultivated music; they pursued it; they pretended to have captured it; but in reality it eluded them. The root of the difficulty was lack of taste."[75] Smith's article, however, fails to elucidate the root of English "lack of taste." Why, in a country teeming with distinguished men of letters, political statesmen, lawyers, and philosophers, were there no musical geniuses who could rank with the talents of Europe? Victorians themselves were baffled and disturbed by their country's amusicality. In part the vacuum existed because music seemed foreign to a country devoted to business transactions, rational inquiry, and industrial progress. Male children in England were discouraged from pursuing musical professions because music seemed trivial, a waste of time needed for more serious, practical pursuits, while females were expected to exhibit only a smattering of musical talent. Further, both Benthamite philosophy and Evangelical religious thought, which

Buckley labels the two most promiment features of Victorianism, looked on secular music with disparagement.[76]

The tension between conflicting views of music and the stark contrast between literary musicians and the actual performers of nineteenth century England provided Victorian novelists with a fruitful source of metaphor. While some novelists did little more than mirror the musical climate of their time, others brilliantly used their countrymen's view of the musician to illustrate and attack the failings of English society.

Chapter II: Notes

1 Reverend Hugh Reginald Haweis, *Music and Morals* (N.Y.: Harper & Brothers, 1871), p. 409.

2 Letter to Huber Parry, reported in Sir Mountstuart Grant Duff, *A Victorian Vintage*, ed. A. Tilney Bassett (London: Methuen & Co., 1930), p. 164.

3 Charles Lamb, "A Chapter on Ears," *Essays of Elia* (N.Y.: A.L. Burt, 1885), p. 46. Lamb's poem is entitled "Free Thoughts on Several Eminent Composers."

4 *Autobiography of Anton Rubinstein* (1829-89), trans. A. Delano (Boston: Little, Brown, and Co., 1890), p. 118.

5 Arthur Loesser, *Men, Women and Pianos* (N.Y. : Simon and Schuster, 1954), p. 251.

6 Edward J. Dent, "Music," in *Early Victorian England, 1830-65*, ed. G.M. Young (London: Oxford University Press, 1934), Vol. II, p. 252.

7 *Two Centuries of Opera at Covent Garden* (London: Putnam, 1956), p. 42.

8 Cited in Henry Raynor, *Music and Society Since 1815* (N.Y.: Schocken Books, 1976), p. 41.

9 Walter Parratt, "Music," in *The Reign of Queen Victoria*, ed. Thomas Humphrey Ward (London: Smith, Elder, 1887), Vol. II, p. 594.

10 Haweis, pp. 410-11.

11 Francis Hueffer, *Half a Century of Music in England, 1837-87* (London: Chapman & Hall, 1889), Preface.

12 A. Burgh, *Anecdotes of Music, Historical and Biographical* (London, 1814), p. vi.

13 Haweis, p. 437.

14 "Paganini," *The Poetical Works of Leigh Hunt* (Boston: Tickner & Fields, 1857), II: 115-17.

15 Jeffrey Pulver, "*Paganini, the Romantic Virtuoso* (London: Herbert Joseph, 1936), p. 240.

[16] William Gardiner, The *Music of Nature* (Boston: Oliver Ditson & Co., 1832; rpt. 1837), p. 217.

[17] Haweis, *My Musical Life*, 1883 (London: Longmans, 1902), p. 339.

[18] Hueffer, p. 86.

[19] Raynor, p. 103.

[20] Ibid., p. 55.

[21] Haweis, *My Musical Life*, p. 387.

[22] Letters to Hannah Macaulay, May 27 and June 8, 1831, *The Letters of Thomas Macaulay*, ed. Thomas Pinney (London: Cambridge Univ. Press, 1974), II: 17, 34.

[23] Pulver, p. 233.

[24] Ibid., p. 251.

[25] Ibid.

[26] Gardiner, p. 230.

[27] Reprinted in William Hogarth, *Marriage a la Mode and Other Engravings* (Lear: N.Y., 1947), Preface.

[28] *The Life of Thomas Cooper, Written by Himself*, (London: Hodder & Staughton, 1879), p. 110.

[29] Cited in Eric Mackerness, *A Social History of English Music* (London: Routledge & Kegan Paul, 1964), p. 189.

[30] Ibid., p. 186.

[31] Haweis, *Music and Morals* p. 59.

[32] Burgh, p. 456.

[33] Newman, "Of Knowledge on Theology," *On the Scope and Nature of University Education*, ed. Wilfrid Ward (London: Dent, 1915), p. 63.

[34] Ibid., pp. 63-64.

[35] John Ruskin, "Essay on the Relative Dignity of the Studies of Painting and Music," (1838) *The Complete Works of John Ruskin* (London: George Allen, 1905), I: 265 ff.

36 Haweis, *My Musical Life*, p. 194.

37 Bernarr Rainbow, *The Land Without Music: Musical Education in England, 1800-1860* (London: Novello, 1967), p. 35.

38 Ibid., pp. 158-59.

39 John Curwen, *Grammar of Vocal Music*, 1843, p. xiv, in Reginald Nettel, *The Englishman Makes Music* (London: Dobson, 1952), p. 112.

40 Herbert Spencer, "On the Origin and Function of Music," *Essays on Education* (London: Dent, 1911), p. 328.

41 John P. Hullah, Preface to *Wilhelm's Method of Teaching, Singing, Adapted to English Use*, 1841, in Nettel, pp. 105-6. See Chapter IV for a discussion of Dickens' acquaintance with Hullah, his librettist, and Hogarth, his father-in-law, and the implications for his novels.

42 George Hogarth, *Musical History, Biography, and Criticism*, 1835, (London: John W. Parker, 1838), II: 273-75.

43 Gardiner, p. 450.

44 Haweis, *My Musical Life*, p. 118.

45 Loesser, pp. 236, 259.

46 William J. Carlton, "Fanny Dickens: Pianist and Vocalist," *Dickensian*, LIII (1957), 133.

47 Loesser, p. 297.

48 Ibid., p. 291.

49 Hannah More, *Strictures on the Modern System of Female Education*, 1799, (Philadelphia: Budd & Bartram, 1800), pp. 71-72. More's *Strictures* protest the general notion of trivial female "accomplishments."

50 Cited in William Weber, *Music and the Middle Class* (N.Y.: Holmes and Meier, 1975), p. 17.

51 Parratt, p. 596.

52 Paul Henry Lang, *Music in Western Civilization* (N.Y.: Norton, 1941), p. 687.

53 Weber, pp. 37-38.

54 Thomas Busby, *Concert Room and Orchestra Anecdotes of Music and Musicians, Ancient and Modern* (London: Clementi, 1825), p. 198.

55 Haweis, *Music and Morals*, pp. 272-73.

56 In Conrad L. Donakowski, *A Muse for the Masses* (Chicago: University of Chicago Press, 1972, p. 224.

57 *Dublin Review*, XXII (March, 1847), 147, in Donakowski, p. 227.

58 Hueffer, p. 9.

59 Haweis, *Music and Morals*, p. 430.

60 Weber, p. 103.

61 John Stuart Mill, *Autobiography*, chapter V, in *Autobiography and Other Writings*, ed. Jack Stillinger, Riverside Edition (Boston: Houghton Mifflin, 1969), p. 87.

62 Mill, "Thoughts on Poetry and its Varieties," *Autobiography and Other Writings*, p. 196.

63 "Thomas Carlyle," in *Essays of George Eliot,* ed. Thomas Pinney (London: Routledge and Kegan Paul, 1963), p. 213.

64 Thomas Carlyle, Cited without documentation in Nettel, p. 201.

65 Carlyle, *Sartor Resartus*, Book III, Chapter V, in *The Works of Thomas Carlyle*, in 30 vols. (N.Y.: Charles Scribners, 1903), I: 116.

66 Carlyle, "The Hero as Poet," *Heroes and Hero-Worship*, Lectures III, in *Works*, V: 83.

67 Carlyle, *Sartor Resartus*, Book III, Chapter viii, in *Works*, I: 210.

68 John Ruskin, "Traffic," *The Crown of Wild Olive*, Lecture II, in *Complete Works*, XVIII: 437.

69 In M.H. Abrams, *The Mirror and the Lamp* (London: Oxford University Press, 1953), p. 302.

70 Quotations from Browning are from *The Complete Poetic and Dramatic Works of Robert Browning* (Cambridge: Riverside Press, 1895).

71 Penelope Gay, "Browning and Music," *Robert Browning*, ed. Isobel Armstrong (Athens, Ohio: Ohio University Press, 1975), p. 211.

72 Charles Villiers Stanford, *Pages from an Unwritten Diary* (London, 1914), in Herbert E. Greene, "Browning's Knowledge of Music," PMLA, LXII (1947), 1096.

73 Haweis, *Music and Morals*, p. 18.

74 Spencer, pp. 316-17.

75 *Kenyon Review*, 25 (Summer, 1963), 517.

76 Jerome Buckley, *The Victorian Temper* (Cambridge, Mass.: Harvard University Press, 1951), p. 9.

Chapter III

Victorian Melodrama: The Musician as Hero or Villain

"Music in England has always been an exotic," wrote Reverend Haweis.[1] Novelists of Haweis' age also viewed music as foreign and mysterious, an art linked with the excitement of the earlier Romantic period and the lure of alien cultures. The melodramatic portrayal of the musician in works by Charlotte Bronte, George Meredith, and representative minor authors such as Elizabeth Sheppard, Benjamin Disraeli, Wilkie Collins, and George du Maurier greatly influenced major writers of the period and indicates that while Victorian novelists were fascinated by the musician as a symbol of romance and power, they lacked a sound understanding of the art of music.

Just as Victorian audiences viewed Paganini with a mixture of adulation and dread, so Victorian novelists regarded the figure of the musician with great ambivalence. For many Victorian novelists, the hero-musician, fervidly devoted to his art, became a metaphor for romanticism itself. Musicality suggested feelings and a susceptibility to beauty, traits threatened with extinction in a materialistic, utilitarian society. Furthermore, the musician's foreignness offered an escape from prosaic Victorianism. Bronte, Sheppard, Disraelii and Meredith portray the musician as a heroic being beyond the pale of Victorian society, one whose "race" is more spontaneous and vibrant.

But to be musical also was to be dangerously potent, suspiciously foreign, and without moral restraint. For Wilkie Collins and George du Maurier, the Italian or Jewish musician became the archetypal figure of evil. The melodramatic portrayal of the musician as either a glamorous hero or sinister villain reveals Victorian emotionalism, race-thinking, and national prejudice.

The Musician as Hero: Charlotte Bronte (1816-55), *Elizabeth Sheppard* (1830-62), *Bejamin Disraeli* (1804-81), *George Meredith* (1828-1909)

In Radcliffe's *The Italian* and other Gothic or Romantic novels, music connotes truth and passionate emotions. Following in this tradition, many Victorian writers wove music into their novels to reveal their characters' emotional depth and inner feelings.

Victorian readers of *Jane Eyre* (1847) were shocked by Bronte's portrayal of Rochester as a hero "who deliberately and secretly seeks to violate the laws both of God and man" (Elizabeth Rigby, *The Quarterly Review*, 1848). Rochester's secrecy, harshness, and unrestrained virility made him satanic and an unfit member of refined society, but for Bronte his character is redeemed by the power and integrity of his passions: as she wrote to W.S. Williams, "Mr. Rochester has a thoughtful nature and a very feeling heart" (Aug. 14, 1848). The sincerity of Rochester's feelings and the intensity of his love show his superiority over the polite, affected, and superficial society represented by Blanche Ingram. To illustrate Rochester's emotional depth and Miss Ingram's shallowness, Bronte presents them as contrasting musicians, and she demonstrates Jane Eyre's sensitivity by describing her response to their performances. Rochester's musical talent and Jane's appreciation establish them as hero and heroine.

When Jane Eyre arrives at Thornfield Hall, she learns from Mrs. Fairfax that Mr. Rochester "has a fine bass voice, and an excellent taste for music" (*Jane Eyre*, ch. xvi).[2] This judgement is confirmed when she hears his 'con spirito' rendition of a Corsair-song:

> 'Now it is my time to slip away,' thought I, but the tones that then severed the air arrested me. Mrs. Fairfax had said Mr. Rochester possessed a fine voice; he did - a mellow powerful bass, into which he threw his own feeling, his own force; finding a way through the ear to the heart, and there waking sensation strangely. I waited till the last deep and full vibration had expired. (xvii)

Later Rochester accompanies himself on the piano, "for he could play as well as sing," and again Bronte emphasizes the "mellow" quality of the music (xxiv). Rochester's musicianship conveys the paradoxical nature of his character: his powerful bass voice, reminiscent of operatic villains, suggests his sexuality and satanism, yet his love of music and heartfelt execution establish him as a character with inner harmony and sympathy. Rochester's singing, like his dark, swarthy appearance, indicates his potency.

Blanche Ingram is also an accomplished musician, but her performances are marred by her self-consciousness and coldness. Jane Eyre notes of Miss Ingram, "She was very showy, but she was not genuine. She advocated a high tone of sentiment; but she did not know the sensations of sympathy and pity; tenderness and truth were not in her" (xviii). Miss Ingram's music reflects this sentimentality:

she "murmured sentimental tunes and airs on the piano" (xviii). Although her voice is "a very rich and powerful one" and "her execution was remarkably good," it is her appearance while playing, not the music, which captures the audience's attention (xvi). Miss Ingram's use of Italian names when speaking to Rochester connects her with the music of Italian opera composers such as Donizetti, whose works symbolized for many Victorian critics art which was dazzling but empty:

> 'Signor Eduardo, are you in voice to-night?'
> 'Donna Bianca' if you command it, I will be.'
> 'Then, signor, I lay on you my sovereign behest to furbish up your lungs and other vocal organs, so they will be wanted in my royal service.'
> 'Who would not be the Rizzio of so divine a Mary?'. .
> Miss Ingram, who had now seated herself with proud grace at the piano, spreading out her snowy robes in queenly amplitude, commenced a brilliant prelude; talking meantime. She appeared to be on her high horse to-night; both her words and her air seemed intended to excite not only the admiration, but the amazement of her auditors; she was evidently bent on striking them as something very dashing and daring indeed.
> 'Oh, I am so sick of the young men of the present day!' exclaimed she, rattling away at the instrument. (xvii)

Bronte's description of Miss Ingram's performance captures her affected pose and her lack of absorption in the music itself ("talking meantime").

In Bronte's artistic hierarchy it is far better to lack accomplishment in music but be moved by its power than to use one's skill in music merely as a means of display. Jane's limited musical talents are established early in the novel when Rochester asks, "Can you play?"

> 'A little.'
> 'Of course: that is the established answer. . . Go then, into the library; take a candle with you; leave the door open; sit down to the piano, and play a tune.'
> I departed, obeying his directions.
> 'Enough,' he called out in a few minutes. 'You play a little, I see, like any other English schoolgirl: perhaps rather better than some, but not well.'
> I closed the piano and returned. (xiii)

Later Rochester denounces Jane as "a little bungler" at the piano, and she admits her deficiency (xxiv). Yet of greater importance, Bronte suggests, is Jane's susceptibility to music's sway over the emotions. As a child Jane cries at the "indescribable sadness" she hears in the ballad Bessie sings in her sweet voice (iii). When Jane rejoins Rochester at the novel's conclusion she requests Rochester to sing for her, knowing it will give them both pleasure. Music forms an integral part of the scene's romantic setting:

> I remembered his fine voice; I knew he liked to sing - good singers generally do. I was no vocalist myself, and; in his fastidious judgment, no musician either, but I delighted in listening when the performance was good. No sooner had twilight, that hour of romance, begun to lower her blue and starry banner over the lattice, then I rose, opened the piano, and entreated him, for the love of heaven, to give me a song...'
> Did I like his voice? he said.
> 'Very much.' (xxiv)

This love of music sets Rochester and Jane apart from a world of deadened feelings and showy exteriors. Bronte's portrait of the mysterious, impassioned musician whose music expresses his inmost soul shows a heavy indebtedness to Gothic and Romantic literature, but her sarcastic expose of Jane's "accomplishments" adds a note of Victorian realism which becomes more pronounced in the works of later novelists.

Six years after the appearance of *Jane Eyre*, Elizabeth Sheppard published *Charles Auchester* (1853), a novel which carried the figure of the hero-musician to its melodramatic extreme. Sheppard, influenced by the Victorian craze for foreign virtuosi, modeled her musical characters after Mendelssohn, Jenny Lind, Berlioz, and other actual musicians, but she made them so glamorous and superhuman that they seem ludicrous to the modern reader.

Sheppard's novel is narrated by Charles Auchester, a youth of extraordinary sensitivity and musical talent. Charles notes, "I was romantic to intensity, even as a boy... I must be a musician, or I should perish" (*Charles Auchester*, chs. xxii, x). Charles can sing before he can talk, like the infants of Coleridge and Wordsworth whose love of music precedes their understanding of words. Charles listens to concerts with feverish appreciation, but learns that he must leave England if he is to receive proper musical instruction: "Certainly it is out of English life in England one must go for the mysteries and realities of existence" (xvii). Only in Germany can he find people truly devoted to the art of music, for "here alone has music its priesthood, and here alone, though little enough here, is reverentially regarded as the highest form of life, subserving to the purposes of the soul"(xxxi)

The novel's focus, however, is not on Charles's musical instruction but on his worship of Chevalier Seraphael, a German-Jewish composer-conductor modelled after Felix Mendelssohn. As the name suggests, Chevalier Seraphael is a godlike hero, and the book becomes little more than an extended eulogy. Sheppard was not alone in her idolization of Mendelssohn: Grove's *Dictionary of Music and Musicians* compared Mendelssohn's face to the Savior's, and critics such as Reverend Haweis regarded him with special reverence:

> Mendelssohn became my patron saint in music. I used to see his face in dreams, transfigured, splendid with inspired thought. He would come to me - smile, and speak kind words. I seemed then to have known him long, his step was familiar, the long tapering fingers of his beautiful white hand . . . - his slight figure, his wavy, sunny hair, his noble forehead, his large gentle eyes beaming with a certain child-like fondness, full of unconscious simplicity, flashing at times with a fire so intense that it seemed to burn into the soul of every man in the orchestra. [3]

Similarly, Sheppard's Seraphael, "that strong immortal," has "beautiful curling hair" and a "god-like head" (xxvii, xxviii). Charles worships him, trembles in his presence, and believes in his purity with religious devotion. He notes of Seraphael, "He is pure and clear, his brow like sun-flushed snow high lifted into light. . the heights of eternity were fore-shadowed in the forehead's marble dream" (xxviii, viii).

Seraphael's music, like his character, is inspiring and heavenly. Charles's experience as he listens to it is like a religious conversion: "his creation did indeed not only first affect me beyond all analysis of feeling, but cause upon me, and through me, a change to pass - did first recreate, expurge of all earthly; and then inspire surcharge with heavenly hope and holiest ecstasy" (xxxiv). Sheppard consistently links music with religion, as did the German Romantics. Charles's sister comments that "music is the highest gift that God bestows, and its faculty the greatest blessing" (i); a singer cries, "God will take care of me. I try to serve Him. None have to answer for themselves as musicians" (xxxiii); and musicians are referred to as the "chosen" or as priests and prophets whose audiences are "the initiated" (xlvii, xxxiv). Yet Sheppard's emphasis is on the musician's morality, purity, and chasteness, on his ability to excite "*holiest* ecstasy." One reason for Mendelssohn's popularity in England was in fact his gentlemanly character and his avoidance of the scandal and intrigue frequently associated with musicians.

When Charles learns that Seraphael is Jewish he is delighted, as he is when he learns of his own Jewish ancestry, for this seems to give proof of the conductor's true musicianship and to link him with a world of wonderful mystery:

> (Charles) "Sir, you are certainly a Jew if you say 'Jehovah' ; I was quite sure of it before, and I am so pleased."
> (Seraphael) "I cannot contradict thee, but I am almost sorry thou knowest there are even such people as Jews."
> "Why so, Sir? pray tell me. I should have thought that you, before all other persons, would have rejoiced over them."
> "Why so, indeed! but because the mystery of their very name is enough to break the head, and perhaps the heart." (xxvii)

Sheppard herself was thrilled to discover one of her ancestors was Jewish for this seemed to link her with an alien world, a culture more "primitive" and therefore more pure, a "race" which, as Edgar Rosenberg notes, seemed to have a monopoly on music.[4] A late Victorian critic, attempting to explain the prevalence of Jewish musicians in literature, noted incorrectly:

> It is evident why there could be no sculptors or painters among the Jews in ancient or medieval times, for well-nigh all the works of art treated subjects of a religious character, and the Jews, with their strict monotheism and the literal interpretation of the second commandment, could naturally pursue none of the plastic arts. Hence, music and poetry were the only channels in which the aesthetic nature among them could develop itself.[5]

A more likely explanation for the association of musicians and Jews is the fact that Victorians regarded both as exotic and somewhat suspect. Furthermore, music seemed an appropriate skill for a people without a country, for it was an art which transcended national boundaries more easily than literature.

Sheppard was familiar with Jewish musicians of earlier novels, such as Sir Walter Scott's *The Surgeon's Daughter* (1827); in a typical passager Scott describes the melodious death of the "Jewess" Zilia:

> She flew to a harpsichord which stood in the room, and while the servant and master gazed on each other, as if doubting whether her

> senses were about to leave her entirely, she wandered over the keys, producing a wilderness of musical talent, until at length her voice and instrument united in one of those magnificent hymns in which her youth had praised her maker, with voice and harp, like the Royal Hebrew who composed it. The tears ebbed insensibly from her eyes which she turned upwards - her vocal tones, combining with those of the instrument, rose to a pitch of brilliancy seldom attained by the most distinguished performers, and then sank into a dying cadences which fell, never again to rise - for the songstress had died with her strain. (*The Surgeon's Daughter*, ch. viii)

Scott's portrait of the weeping musician dying in a burst of passionate song has the same melodramatic tone which Sheppard uses throughout her novel. In the final section of *Charles Auchester*, entitled "The Crown of Martyrdom," Sheppard describes with an alliterative flourish Seraphael's night burial and the heavenly music surrounding his grave: "Distantly, dyingly, till death drank distance up, the music wandered. . . rising up to heaven, from the shores of lands untraversed as that country beyond to grave!" (xlix).

Benjamin Disraeli wrote of *Charles Auchester*: "No greater book will ever be written upon music"[6] Sheppard's flowery discussions of music, however, exhibit little knowledge of musical composition, and the reverential tone she adopts when describing her godlike musicans verges on the absurd.

Disraeli shared Sheppard's fascination with Jews and her belief that their "race" accounted for their exceptional talents. "All is race," wrote Disraeli, "there is no other truth. . . What is individual character but the personification of race?" (*Tancred*, Vol. II, ch. xiv). Disraeli's novels are filled with musical Jews and Italians who are placed in opposition to drab Englishmen.

In *Tancred* (1847), for instance, Disraeli narrates the history of the Baronis, a Jewish-Italian family of artists who are "pure Sephardim, in nature and in name" (IV, xi). The Baroni parents and children are all "great artistes": Baroni excels in the violin and "can play in some fashion upon every instrument;" daughter Adelaide, who has "a voice of the rarest quality . . . Promising almost illimitable power," becomes Europe's foremost *prima donna* and the "Queen of Song;" and brother Michel, a composer, "promises to be the rival of Meyerbeer and Mendelssohn" (IV, viii). Similarly, the Hebrew Laurella daughters "excel in music" and sing with an exotic richness that sends Tancred into a state or synaesthetic ecstasy:

> The glowing sky, the soft mellow atmosphere, the brilliant circumstances around, flowers and flashing gems, rich dresses and ravishing music, and every form of splendour and luxury, combined to create a scene, that to Tancred was startling, as well from its beauty as its novel character. A rich note of Therese Laurella for an instant arrested their conversation. They were silent while it lingered in their ears. (V, vii)

The oriental beauty Eva, an "exotic Jewess," is surrounded by maidens playing on psalters and singing with a wild murmur (IV, viii).

Beautiful music and the mysterious customs of other cultures offered to Disraeli an escape from "the material, sordid, calculating genius of our reign of Mammon," a chance to experience a life other than the English "existence. . .in steamboats and railways" (II, xv, xii). He describes the lure of Judaism in musical terms:

> And when that labouring multitude cease for a while from a toil which equals almost Egyptian bondage, and demands that exponent of the mysteries of the heart, that soother of the troubled spirit, which poetry can alone afford, to whose harp do the people of England fly for sympathy and solace?. . . the most popular poet in England is the sweet singer of Israel. Since the days of the heritage, when every man dwelt safely under his vine and under his fig-tree, there never was a race who sang so often the odes of David as the people of Great Britain. (IV, iv)

"Disraeli," Hannah Arendt writes, "had an admiration for all things Jewish that was matched only by his ignorance of them."[7] Orientalism and Judaism seem that was matched only by his ignorance of them." Orientalism and Judalism seem indistinguishable to Disraeli: his novels abound in phrases such as "Arabs are just Jews on horseback" (*Tancred*, IV, iii). Disraeli's depictions of Jewish musicians show his unfamiliarity with both Judaism and music. In *Tancred* the Baronis seem a family of implausible freaks; Eva and the Laurellas are exotic birds of paradise. Musicianship, Disraeli implies, is not the result of disciplined instruction but a talent which comes naturally to those of other races.

"These Italians are really like the Jews," comments the Duchess of Lenkenstein in George Meredith's *Vittoria*. Meredith, discovering in the Italian national identity the same mystery and passion that Scott, Sheppard, and Disraeli found in the Jewish culture, colors his portrait of the Italian singer Emilia with a romantic glow.

Emilia's musical life is chronicled in both *Sandra Belloni*, 1864, and its sequel *Vittoria*, 1866, as we follow Emilia from England to Italy. We are first introduced to Emilia as she sings in the moonlit woods, an action which seems incongruous "in the nineteenth century, within sixteen miles of London City" (*Sandra Belloni*, Vol. I, ch. i). Her voice is "unearthly" and "divine," and the Brookfield sisters listen with amazement:

> The voice had the woods to itself, and seemed to fill them and soar over them, it was so full and rich, so light and sweet. And now, to add to the marvel, they heard a harp accompaniment, the strings being faintly touched, but with firm fingers. . . Tell me, what opens heaven more flamingly to heart and mind, than the voice of a woman, pouring clear accordant notes to the blue night sky, that grows light blue to the moon? There was no flourish in her singing. All the notes were firm, and rounded, and sovereignly distinct. She seemed to have caught the ear of Night, and sang confident of her charm. It was a grand old Italian air, requiring severity of tone and power. Now into great mournful bellows the voice sank steadfastly. One soft sweep of the strings succeeded a final note, and the hearers breathed freely. . .
>
> "Hush! she will sing again," whispered Adela. "It is the most delicious contralto." Murmurs of objection to the voice being characterized at all by any technical words, or even for a human quality, were heard. (*SB*, I, i)

Throughout, Meredith emphasizes the supernatural quality of Emilia's voice, its resistance to classification or description in mortal terms, its ability to lift the audience beyond their pedestrian existence to a more exalted realm, and its link with the harmony of nature. Emilia sings with "the richness and fulness of passionate blood that marks the modern Italian"; her musical power is "wizardry" (*SB*, I, ii).

Emilia, like the enchantresses of Keats and Shelley, is as emotional, wild, and beautiful as her music. Meredith praises "the peculiar black lustre of her hair, and thickness of her long black eyebrows," and describes her as "a little wild woman to tame" (*Vittoria* ch. xiv). Emilia loves intensely and without restraint, whether it be her music, her English lover, or Italy, the country which personifies for her all the vibrancy and beauty lacking in provincial English life. Her father, a disreputable Italian violinist, was destroyed by the move to England where he was "condemned to serve amongst an inferior race, promoters of discord" (*SB*, I, xxv). Emilia too must leave England if she is to survive as a musician, for at Brookfield she is beset with temptations to forsake her music in favor of wealth, social status, and personal vanity. Only in Italy can she develop her voice to its full potential: "My father says I shall never be so great, because I am half English. It's not my fault. My mother is English. But I feel that I am much more Italian than English. How I long for Italy - like a thing underground . . . The name of Italy is my nightingale" (*SB*, I, vi).

Even in Italys' as we learn in *Vittoria*, Emilia must struggle against becoming a performer of showy music divorced from passion and meaning; only when she combines "her love of her country and devotion to her Art" can she lead "a consummate life" (*V*, xxxi). Meredith makes this clear in the opening scene of *Vittoria* as Vittoria (Emilia) sings for the revolutionary patriots of Italy. The impassioned Corte, who eventually becomes Vittoria's lover and husband, contemptuously dismisses the idea of using a singer to further their cause because of the musician's separateness from national boundaries:

> "Ah! that completes it." Corte rose to his feet with an air of desperation. "We require to be refreshed with quavers and crescendos and trillels! Who ever knew a singer that cared an inch of flesh for her country? Money, flowers, flattery, vivas! but, money! money! money! . . . These singers have no country." (*V*, ii)

Vittoria's first song only confirms Corte's opinion, for she sings correctly but without emotion or meaning: "It was a song of flourishes: one of those beflowered arias in which the notes flicker and leap like young flames. . . Others might have sung it; and though it spoke favourably of her aptitude and musical education, and was of a quality to enrapture easy, merely critical audiences, it won no applause from these men." (*V*, iii). Vittoria's education has only made her adopt the "flourished" style so absent from her unearthly song in the moonlight at the opening of *Sandra Belloni*. But when Vittoria switches to the aria "Italia, Italia, shall be free!" sung with conviction in an impassioned voice, her revolutionary listeners are moved beyond words and are convinced of music's political power.

Vittoria joins the revolutionaries fighting to free Italy from Austrian domination and rejects her silly, sentimental English lover in favor of a zealous Italian fighter. In her native land her voice sounds forth with unparalleled beauty and power; she becomes Meredith's embodiment of Italy's natural beauty: "It was an animated picture of ideal Italia. A virgin who loosens a dove from her bosom does it with no greater effort than Vittoria gave out her voice. The white bird flutters rapidly; it circles and takes its flight. The voice seemed to be as little the singer's own." (V, xx).

The climax of *Vittoria* is Vittoria's triumphant performance in the opera *Camilla*, performed in an incendiary style in flagrant violation of Austrian censorship. The opera itself is a departure from the modern Italian operatic style so offensive to those Victorians looking for high seriousness in art:

> Rocco's music in the opera of *Camilla* had been sprung from a fresh Italian well; neither the elegiac melodious, nor the sensuous-lyrical, nor the joyous buffo; it was severe as an old masterpiece, with veins of buoyant liveliness threading it, and with sufficient distinctness of melody to enrapture those who like to suck the sugarplums of sound. He would indeed have favoured the public with more sweet things, but Vittoria, for whom the opera was composed, and who had been at his elbow, was young, and stern in her devotion to an ideal of classical music that should elevate and never stoop to seduce or to flatter thoughtless hearers. (V, xxi)

The high point of the opera is Emilia's entrance as "Italy" and her stirring performance of "Italia, Italia" to a crowd of listeners sympathetic to the Italian cause and susceptible to the bewitching power of exquisite music. Meredith's rapturous description of Emilia's performance, and of the glory belonging to the romantic artist alone, is filled with poetic imagery and synaesthesia:

> The wonderful viol-like trembling of the contralto tones thrilled through the house. It was the highest homage to Vittoria that no longer any shouts arose: nothing but a prolonged murmur ... The flattery of beholding a great assembly of human creatures bound glittering in wizard subserviency to the voice of one soul, belongs to the artist, and is the cantatrice's glory, pre-eminent over whatever poor glory this world gives ... This is what the great voice does for us. It rarely astonishes our ears. It illumines our souls, as you see the lightning make the unintelligible craving darkness leap into long mountain ridges, and twisting vales, and spires of cities, and inner recesses of light within light, rose-like, toward a central core of violet heat. (V, xx)

Meredith himself seems transported by the *idea* of such music, by the glory of an age or culture which would view the artist not as a mere entertainer but as a powerful medium, a revolutionary hero.

Meredith's celebration of the Italians, Sheppard's adulation of the Jews, and Disraeli's embrace of both exemplify national and racial stereotyping prevalent in nineteenth century England, where Italians and Jews were regarded as foreigners of passionate "blood" and artistic temperament. Climate theories abounded in Victorian England. William Gardiner, for instance, claimed that Italians were more passionate because of the Mediterranean sunshine, while Englishmen were more practical because of their harsher clime:

> For the last one hundred and thirty years we have scarcely produced more than half a dozen singers of first-rate eminence of either sex; while Italy has been pouring into this country a crowd of vocalists.
>
> The humidity of our climate, and the harshness of our language, are the reasons why we have not attained to that excellence for which the Italians have been so justly celebrated.[8]

As Jacques Barzun notes, the climate theory of art is racist because it treats a group of diverse people as if it were one individual possessing a single trait.[9] Victorian novelists not only reflected this racial stereotyping but perhaps reinforced it by portraying Italians and Jews as heroes who were inevitably musical, inevitably passionate.

In contrast to Meredith's innately musical Italian heroine, Emilia, the English characters in *Sandra Belloni* and *Vittoria* are insipid, narrow-minded, and virtually tone-deaf. Meredith introduces numerous figures into his novels as foils to his romantic Emilia and uses their reactions to music to express his contempt of Victorian taste.

The affected Pole sisters of Brookfield embrace music as a vehicle for social advancement; they are, Meredith notes, "scaling society by the help of the Arts" (*SB*, I, 1). Emilia becomes for the Pole sisters nothing more than "a property to acquire, exhibit, and exploit." The Poles similarly treat the British musician, Mr. Purcell Barrett, with condescension and regard him as a pleasant household "pet" (*SB*, I, viii). Barrett's father disinherits him when he learns he plays the organ, an action demonstrating that Lord Chesterfield's view of "fiddling" as a frivolous and unseemly pursuit retained its adherents in Victorian England.

Meredith uses Mr. Pole and Father Wilson to represent the unmusical English public. Pole rejects foreign music in favor of more "manly," down-to-earth singing. "I like glees," he remarks, "good, honest, English, manly singing for me!

Nothing like glees and madrigals, to my mind. With chops and baked potatoes, and a glass of good stout, they beat all other music" (*SB*, I xxv). Father Wilson likewise takes stubborn pride in the music of his own country and tells Emilia, "Furrin songs 's all right enough; but 'Ale is my tipple, and England is my nation! Let's have something plain and flat on the surface, miss!'" (*SB*, I, xi).

Meredith's satirical portraits of his English characters undermine Mr. Purcell Barrett's complacent assertion that "We English are more imaginative than most nations" (*SB*, I, viii). Emilia is patronized, exploited, and rejected as "furrin" by a country too shortsighted and parochial to respect the presence of an artistic genius. Meredith's melodramatic description of Emilia's appearance, adventures, and musical performances suggests that he regarded her as a symbol of romanticism and mystery, an embodiment of those qualities lacking in English life. Although *Sandra Belloni* and *Vittoria* are frequently dismissed by Meredith critics as early works marred by their sentimentalism, Meredith counters his romantic description of Emilia with his cynical expose of English taste. In addition, he seems to mock his own melodramatic portrayal of Emilia by giving her a few realistic flaws, such as a weight problem. Unlike the earlier Chevalier Seraphael, Emilia is not quite divine.

The Musician as Villain: Wilkie Collins (1824-89), George du Maurier (1834-96)

Disraeli's Eva notes in *Tancred* that Englishmen "either worship or despise a Jewess." The two seemingly opposite emotions are in fact closely related. Hannah Arendt observes in *The Origins of Totalitarianism* that both the antisemitic ostracism of the Jew as pariah and the sentimental embrace of him as a *parvenu* stem from the concept of the Jew as outsider.[10] The same race-thinking and national prejudice which led Sheppard, Disraeli, and Meredith to sentimentalize Jews and Italians as superior beings led other novelists, such as Wilkie Collins and George du Maurier, to portray them as villains.

Count Fosco in Wilkie Collins' *The Woman in White*, 1860, typifies the Italian musician-villain. Just as Rochester's musicality makes him both sinister and spiritual, so Fosco's musical talent makes him admirable as well as contemptible.

Fosco is a fat, hypersensitive Italian count with "effeminate tastes and amusements," including music, and a great tenderness for small animals (*The Woman in White*, No. 10). His obesity, like his music, suggests his self-indulgent, sensual nature. Fosco is also a machiavellian spy and traitor, a scheming murderer who lacks all moral scruples. Fosco's musical power is part of his social charm but also part of his demonism, linking him with the decadence and immorality of Italian opera. He sings "with that crisply-fluent vocalisation which is never heard from any other than an Italian throat," and accompanies his performance "with ecstatic throwings-up of his arms, and graceful twistings, and turnings of his head, like a fat St. Cecilia masquerading in male attire" (No. 14). Fosco sings Rossini "in a sonorous bass voice," plays Neapolitan street-songs on the piano, and attends Donizetti's spectacular opera "Lucrecia Borgia" (No. 20, 38).

Unlike the gentle Laura, who plays old melodies of Mozart with tender feeling and taste, and the genial Hartright, who listens "with an innocent enjoyment of the sweet sounds," Fosco plays the music of Italian opera and listens to performances "with a clear, cultivated, practical knowledge of the merits of the composition, in the first place, and of the merits of the player's touch, in the second" (No. 10, 18). To be a natural musician is heavenly, Collins suggests, but to be a cultivated musician is diabolical. Laura's musicality depends on her inner state, so that she plays Mozart with "heavenly tenderness" when happy but unskillfully plays "new music of the dexterous, tasteless, florid kind" when deprived of love (No. 4). Fosco's musicianship is divorced form morality and does not fluctuate: he can plot a murder and play glorious music at the same time. It was precisely this amorality of music which made Victorians uncomfortable with it as an art form. As Reverend Haweis complained in *Music and Morals*, "a musician may be both intemperate and dishonest, and yet may play superbly."[11]

Fosco's performances are frightening and satanic to the non-musical Marian Holcombe:

> He began thundering on the piano, and singing to it with loud and lofty enthusiasm: only interrupting himself, at intervals, to announce to me fiercely the titles of the different pieces of music... The piano trembled under his powerful hands; and the teacups on the table rattled, as his big bass voice thundered out the notes, and his heavy foot beat time on the floor.
>
> There was something horrible--something fierce and devilish, in the outburst of his delight at his own singing and playing, and in the triumph with which he watched its effect upon me, as I shrank nearer and nearer to the door. I was released, at last, not by my own efforts, but by Sir Percival's interposition. He opened the dining-room door, and called out angrily to know what 'that infernal noise' meant. The Count instantly got up from the piano. 'Ah! if Percival is coming,' he said, 'harmony and melody are both

at an end. The Muse of Music, Miss Halcombe, deserts us in dismay; and I, the fat old minstrel, exhale the rest of my enthusiasm in the open air!' He stalked out into the verandah, put his hands in his pockets, and resumed the 'recitativo of Moses,' *Sotto voce*, in the garden. (No. 20)

Collins uses the image of the rattling teacups to suggest the disturbing effect Italian music has on a Victorian society characterized by its propriety and restraint. The same image occurs earlier when the Italian professor Pesca breaks Sarah Hartright's teacups because of his volatile enthusiasm, upsetting Sarah's "insular notions of propriety" (No. 1). The respectable Marian Halcombe reacts to Fosco's thundering music as if she is being raped.

Collins' judgement of Fosco's musicality is ambiguous. On the one hand, Fosco's love of music shows his hedonism and wickedness, but on the other hand, it reveals his cultural superiority to those around him. Collins himself was an avid admirer of Rossini, and he has Fosco defend Italian opera with great eloquence (No. 20). Fosco performs not only the showy arias of light Italian operas but also the profound recitatives of *Moses In Egypt*, a work which, as Fosco justly notes, rivals English oratorios for its emotional depth.

In his description of Fosco's behavior at "Lucrecia Borgia" Collins manages to satirize both the vanity of the Count and the ignorance of the English audience:

> Not a note of Donizetti's delicious music was lost on him. There he sat, high above his neighbours, smiling, and nodding his great head enjoyingly, from time to time. When the people near him applauded the close of an air (as an English audience in such circumstances always *will* applaud), without the least consideration for the orchestral movement which immediately followed it, he looked round at them with an expression of compassionate remonstrance, and held up one hand with a gesture of polite entreaty. At the more refined passages of the singing, at the more delicate phrases of the music, which passed unapplauded by others, his fat hands adorned with perfectly-fitting black kid gloves softly patted each other, in token of the cultivated appreciation of a musical man. At such times, his oily murmur of approval, 'Bravo! Bra-a-a!' hummed through the silence, like the purring of a great cat. His immediate neighbours on either side--hearty, ruddy-faced people from the country, basking amazedly in the sunshine of fashionable London--seeing and hearing him, began to follow his lead. Many a burst of applause from the pit that night started from the soft, comfortable patting of the black-gloved hands. The man's voracious vanity devoured this implied tribute to his local and

> critical supremacy, with an appearance of the highest relish. Smiles rippled continuously over his fat face. He looked about him, at the pauses in the music, serenely satisfied with himself and his fellow creatures. 'Yes! yes! these barbarous English people are learning something from ME. Here, there, and everywhere, I--Fosco--am an influence that is felt, a man who sits supreme!' (No. 30)

Collins attacks English xenophobia by exposing the ignorance of Mr. Fairlie, who "hated a foreigner, simply and solely because he was a foreigner," and Sir Percival, who believes "foreigners are all alike" (No. 8, 20), yet Collins himself is susceptible to such sentiment. Fosco's Italian heritage is an integral part of his villainous nature, and he commits crimes which, as Collins notes in his remarks on *The Woman in White*, are "too ingenious for an Englishman."

The tone Collins adopts when describing his innocent musical heroines (Laura Fairlie; blind Lucilla in *Poor Miss Finch*) and his musical-villain Fosco indicates that he was mystified by music. Practically tone-deaf, Collins loved music but found it beyond his grasp. Just one year after the publication of *The Woman in White* he wrote to the Lehmanns:

> In one respect only, I have been the worse for the delightful party at Halle's--the 'Great Kreutzer Sonata' has upset me about classical music. I am afraid I don't like classical music after all--I am afraid I am not the Amateur I once thought myself. The whole violin part of 'The Great K.S.' appeared to me to be the musical expression of a varying and violent stomach-ache, with intervals of hiccups.[12]

Collins' knowledge of music, his biographers conclude, "was not particularly profound."[13] Perhaps because music eluded him, he portrayed its practitioners with sentimentalism and melodrama.

The belief that some races were naturally musical persisted throughout the Victorian period, culminating in works such as George du Maurier's *Trilby*, 1894. The Jewish musician, treated as an implausible figure of romance by Sheppard and Disraeli, emerges in du Maurier as the archetypal symbol of evil.

Trilby's hero, the artistic Little Billee, has talent because of a "very remote Jewish ancestor" who has given him "just a tinge of that strong, sturdy, impressionable, indomitable, indelible blood which is of such priceless value in diluted homopathic doses" (*Trilby*, Part I). A non-diluted, full-blooded Jew, such as the musician Svengali, however, has a terrifying potency and egregious nature.

To describe Svengali, du Maurier musters an incredible catalogue of invectives and racial slurs. When Svengali is first introduced we see him as:

> ... a tall, bony individual... of Jewish aspect, well-featured but sinister. He was very shabby and dirty, and wore a red beret and a large velveteen cloak, with a big metal clasp at the collar. His thick, heavy, languid, lustreless black hair fell down behind his ears on to his shoulders, in that musicianlike way that is so offensive to the normal Englishman...He went by the name of Svengali, and spoke fluent French with a German accent, and humorous German twists and idioms, and his voice was very thin and mean and harsh, and often broke into a disagreeable falsetto. (Pt. I)

Svengali is poor, offensive, egotistical, "and then he was both tawdry and dirty in his person; more greasily, mattedly unkempt than even a really successful pianist has any right to be even in the best society." Svengali, compared to "a sticky, haunting, long, lean, uncanny, black spider-cat, if there is such an animal outside a bad dream," is "always ready to vex, bully, or torment anybody or anything smaller and weaker than himself--from a woman or a child to a mouse or a fly." Trilby, an innocent English/Scottish girl, regards Svengali as "a dread, powerful demon...an incubus." Du Maurier adds the superfluous afterthought, "he was not a nice man" (Pt. II).

Svengali is "only to be endured for the sake of his music," and in this art he is the unparalleled master (Pt. II). Like Paganini, referred to throughout *Trilby*, Svengali possesses a magical power for producing music unlike anything ever heard before. Even from a simple flageolet Svengali can elicit sounds which surpass the exquisite violin melodies of his swarthy gypsy partner, Gecko:

> ... And it would be impossible to render in any words the deftness, the distinction, the grace, power, pathos, and passion with which this truly phenomenal artist executed the poor old twopenny tune on his elastic penny whistle--for it was little more--such thrilling, vibrating, piercing tenderness, now loud and full, a shrill scream of anguish, now soft as a whisper, a mere melodic breath, more human almost than the human voice itself, a perfection unattainable even by Gecko, a master, on an instrument which is the acknowledged king of all! (Pt. I)

Sensitive Little Billee listens to Svengali with profound delight; he had never heard anything but

> ... "British provincial home-made music--melodies with variations, "Annie Laurie," "The Last Rose of Summer," "The Blue Bells of Scotland!" innocent little motherly and sisterly tinklings, invented to set the company it their ease on festive evenings, and make all-round conversation possible for shy people; who fear the unaccompanied sound of their own voices, and whose genial chatter always leaves off directly the music ceases. (Pt. I)

In contrast to these trivial English tunes, Svengali's masterful renditions of works by Chopin, Schumann, and other Romantic composers transport Little Billee to a sphere of transcendent beauty:

> He had never heard such music as this, never dreamed such music was possible. He was conscious while it lasted, that he saw deeper into the beauty, the sadness of things, the very heart of them, and their pathetic evanescence, as with a new, inner eye--even into eternity itself, beyond the veil--a vague cosmic vision that faded when the music was over, but left an unfading reminiscence of its having been. (Pt. I)

Svengali epitomizes the foreigner: he is "an Oriental Israelite Hebrew Jew," a "German Pole" who speaks "German-Hebrew-French" (VII, I, II). In addition to Svengali, there are other Jews in *Trilby* whose natural musicianship contrasts markedly with the Englishmen around them who, like Lord Witlow, "couldn't tell 'God Save the Queen' from 'Pop Goes the Weasel', if the people didn't get up to stand and take their hats off" (V). Svengali's pupil, Mademoiselle Honorine Cahen, is "a dirty, drabby little dolly-mop of a Jewess" who, however, has "a charming voice and a *natural* gift of singing so sweetly that you forgot her accent" (my italics) (II). The bearded Glorioli, a Spanish Jew who doubles as a wine-merchant and singer, is presented as a vocal equivalent of Paganini or Liszt:

> ...a tall, good-looking, swarthy foreigner came in, with a roll of music in his hands, and his entrance made quite a stir; you heard all round, "Here's Glorioli," or "Ecco Glorioli," or "Voici Glorioli," till Glorioli got on your nerves. And beautiful ladies, ambassadresses, female celebrities of all kinds, fluttered up to him and cajoled and fawned; ... Glorioli stood up on the platform... and from his scarcely parted, moist, thick, bearded lips, which he always licked before singing, there issued the most ravishing sounds that had ever been heard from throat of man or woman or boy!...
>
> Glorioli--the biggest, handsomest, and most distinguished-looking Jew that ever was--one of the Sephardim (one of the

Seraphim!)--hailed from Spain. . . there was no voice like his anywhere in the world, and no more finished singer. (V)

The Jew's musical power can even be transferred. Svengali hypnotizes the tone-deaf Trilby and makes her the instrument for his musical genius. As the innocent Trilby, she couldn't tell one note from the next, but as La Svengali, controlled by the diabolical Jew, she becomes "the apotheosis of voice and virtuosity," the superior of Jenny Lind (VI). Gecko describes the transformation:

> "*There were two Trilbys.* There was the Trilby you knew, who could not sing one single note in tune. She was an angel of paradise
> . . . with one wave of his hand over her--with one look of his eye--with a word--Svengali could turn her into the other Trilby, his Trilby, and make her do whatever he liked. . . That Trilby was just a singing-machine--an organ to play upon--an instrument of music--a Stradivarius--a flexible flageolet of flesh and blood--a voice, and nothing more--just the unconscious voice that Svengali sang with." (VIII)

As La Svengali Trilby sings like "a woman archangel. . . or some enchanted princess out of a fairy-tale." Du Maurier's synaesthetic description of La Svengali's performance of Chopin is reminiscent of Romantic poems on music: "Every single phrase is a string of perfect gems, of purest ray serene, strung together on a loose golden thread!. . . the mellow, powerful, deep chest notes are like the pealing of great golden bells, with a little pearl shower tinkling round-drops from the upper fringe of her grand voice as she shakes it" (VI). The notes she sings are like "velvet and gold, beautiful flowers, pearls, diamonds, rubies--drops of dew and honey; peaches, oranges, lemons!" (VIII) Like Shelley's protagonists who are bewitched by the siren's music, du Maurier's Britishers thirst to hear more of La Svengali's intoxicating bitter-sweet singing. Her "cruelly sweet" voice fills them with an aching, nostalgic yearning, and they experience "sudden exotic warmths, fragrances, tendernessess, graces, depths, and breadths" (VI).

In true melodramatic fashion, Trilby loses her voice when Svengali dies (she is only his tool), but at the sight of his photograph she regains enough power for one final swan-song. Like Scott's Zilia, Trilby dies in a burst of melody. Her performance of Chopin on her death-bed is "the most divinely beautiful, but also the most astounding feat of musical utterance ever heard out of a human throat."

Trilby dies murmuring the chilling words, "Svengali . . . Svengali . . . Svengali!" (VIII).

Du Maurier confesses of himself, "The writer is no musician, alas! (as, no doubt, his musical readers have found out by this) save in his thraldom to music" (VI). His melodramatic characterizations of the musician reflect both this musical ignorance and "thraldom."

Romantic poets and critics had employed music as a metaphor for the supernatural, the ideal realm of nonrepresentational art; for many Victorian novelists, music continued to symbolize this otherworldliness and infinitude. Musicians in Victorian novels frequently seem one-dimensional black or white characters whose heroism or villainy is greatly exaggerated. Rochester, Seraphael, the Baronis, Emilia, Fosco, and Svengali all loom as supra-mortal characters whose music places them beyond the limits of actual experience. Because music seemed foreign to Victorian society, its novelists treated musicians without technical accuracy, realism, or restraint. Melodramatic passages by Sheppard, Collins, and other minor novelists of the period inflated the literary musician to such a ridiculous size that the puncturing wit of cynicism was soon to follow.

Chapter III: Notes

1   H.R. Haweis, *Music and Morals* (N.Y.: Harper Brothers, 1871), p. 410.

2   Because so many editions exist of *Jane Eyre* and other Victorian novels, I have simplified my references by indicating chapter number (and, where appropriate, volume or part number) rather than page number.

3   Haweis, *My Musical Life* (London: Longmans, 1902; written 1883), p. 16.

4   Edgar Rosenberg, *From Shylock to Svengali; Jewish Stereotypes in English Fiction* (Stanford: Stanford Univ. Press, 1960), p. 109.

5   David Philipson, *The Jew in English Fiction* (Cincinnati: Robert Clarke, 1889), p. 128.

6   Letter to Elizabeth Sheppard, in Jessie A. Middleton, Introduction to *Charles Auchester* (London: Dent, 1911), p. vii.

7   Hannah Arendt, *Origins of Totalitarianism* (N.Y.: Harcourt, Brace, and World, 1966), Vol. I, p. 70.

8   William Gardiner, *The Music of Nature* (Boston: Ditson, 1832; rpt. 1837), p. 93.

9   Jacques Barzun, *Race: A Study in Superstition*, Revised ed. (N.Y.: Harper and Row, 1965), p. 81.

10   Arendt, p. 66.

11   *Music and Morals*, p, 79.

12   In Kenneth Robinson, *Wilkie Collins* (N.Y.: Macmillan, 1952), p. 155.

13   Ibid.

Chapter IV

From Sentimentalism to Cynicism:

The Musicians of Charles Dickens

Music suggested not only the excitement of exotic lands but also the enchanting innocence of childhood. For Charles Dickens (1812-70) children and lower class workers who sang and played on rustic instruments seemed untouched by the pragmatic, mechanistic culture around them. By melodramatically depicting Jewish and Italian musicians as superhuman or subhuman, novelists such as Sheppard and Collins may have perpetuated the prejudices of their age; similarly, Dickens' sentimental descriptions of naturally harmonious and musical workers and mistreated children did little to alleviate their plight.

Although Dickens reflected and catered to Victorian sentimentality, he also stood apart from his age and viewed its flaws. As Meredith notes towards the close of *Sandra Belloni*, sentimentalism soon turns to cynicism for the two are brothers. Dickens adds ironic notes to his descriptions of the harmonious poor and uses music to reveal English provincialism, hypocrisy, and greed. Dickens' changing attitude towards his musical characters from his early to his late novels reveals his movement away from Victorian sentimentalism and his increasing belief in the artist's obligation to create socially relevant art.

Not musically proficient himself, Dickens nevertheless had firsthand knowledge of the music and musical criticism of his time. Through his sister, who attended the Royal Academy of Music, he met musicians and heard discussions of music. As I noted in Chapter II, Dickens collaborated with John Hullah, the music master and theorist who believed in spreading music to the masses in order to make them industrious, devout, and harmless. Together they produced a comic opera, *The Village Coquettes*. Dickens' father-in-law, George Hogarth, was music critic for the *Daily News*, a paper Dickens founded in 1846; like Hullah, Hogarth favored using music to refine the manners of the poor and keep them happy with their lot.

Dickens' familiarity with this patronizing encouragement of the lower classes to engage in music, a calculating form of sentimentalism, becomes obvious in two letters he addressed to Hullah concerning music's power to refine women convicted of crimes or prostitution. On December 12, 1847 he wrote Hullah:

> I am actively engaged, for Miss Coutts, in the management of a private establishment (called her home) for the reclamation of certain young women, and for the training of them for colonization.
>
> We want them to learn to sing in parts, on your system ... I am very anxious for the instruction beginning without delay, as I attach immense importance to its refining influence.

The following year Dickens again wrote Hullah, this time to note that further musical study was not necessary for those women:

> Miss Coutts thinks that our young ladies have made sufficient advancement in that scientific kind of instruction which Mr. Bannister communicates--which is better adapted, she holds, to the wants of a superior class of pupils who have not so much work to attend to--and therefore she would desire to terminate that engagement at the expiration of the current quarter . . . and to substitute some female teacher of lower qualifications who could come on Saturday evenings, and sing hymns and so forth, with them. Her wish is, that they should now use what they have learnt in this wise, socially, and turn it to account in their devotion and relaxation rather than they should learn more, as an abstract study or accomplishment.
>
> I state her views, of courses without any admixture of my own.
>
> Faithfully yours always,
> Charles Dickens [1]

Dickens' second letter suggests that he had greater hopes for music's "refining influence" than Miss Coutts, who perhaps discerned that the young women needed more practical aid.

The condescension of Dickens' tone, reflecting that of his librettist and father-in-law, turns to sentimentalism in his fictional portrayal of simple, musical folk: women crooning sweet ballads to their infants, laborers humming as they work, poor children singing with pure, clear voices. Music in Dickens' early novels often symbolizes innocence and beauty, traits threatened with extinction in a materialistic age.

Both Madeline Bray and Little Nell, saintly heroines of *Nicholas Nickleby* (1838-39) and *The Old Curiosity Shop* (1840), have an innate musicality in sharp contrast to the discord and sordidness of their surroundings. Like many Victorians,

Dickens nostalgically viewed older instruments, music, and musicians as emblems of a time of greater poetry and fellowship. He describes Madeline's room with unabashed sentimentalism:

> But how the graces and elegancies which she had dispersed about the poorly-furnished room went to the heart of Nicholas! Flowers, plants, birds, the harp, the old piano whose notes had sounded so much sweeter in by-gone times--how many struggles had it cost her to keep these last two links of that broken chain which bound her yet to home! . . . He felt as though the smile of Heaven were on the little chamber.
>
> (*Nicholas Nickleby*, Vol. II, ch. xiv)[9]

Similarly, Dickens shrouds Little Nell in an angelic and musical mist. In the happiness of her youth, Little Nell sings in her pretty voice; later she hears "music in the air and a sound of angel's wings," and the music of the spheres graces her death: "Waking, she never wandered in her mind but once, and that was of beautiful music which she said was in the air. God knows. It may have been" (*Old Curiosity Shop*, lxxii).

As Lorenzo noted in Shakespeare's *The Merchant of Venice*, unmusical men are "fit for treasons, strategems, and spoils" (V: i, 85). Both Madeline and Little Nell become easy victims of those with evil designs. Arthur Gride, an old lecherous usurer, purchases Madeline as wife and regards her musicianship with crass materialism. He gloats that Madeline "can play the piano, (and, what's more, she's got one,) and sing like a little bird. She'll be very cheap to dress and keep" (*NN*, II, xix). Little Nell and her grandfather are evicted by the monstrous dwarf Quilp (to whom music means subhuman howling) and must lead a wandering life. As a boat transports them away from the peaceful countryside, a drunken, "brutal" boatman demands that Nell sing:

> . . . poor Nell sang him some little ditty which she had learned in happier times . . . to which he was so obliging as to roar a chorus to no particular tune, and with no words at all, but which amply made up in its amazing energy for its deficiency in other respects. (*OCS*, xliii)

The stronger voice drowns out Nell's sweet music as they land at a dirty manufacturing town with chimneys "vomiting forth a black vapor."

Harmony turns to discord throughout *The Old Curiosity Shop*. Generous, simple-minded Kit, whose very name has a musical connotation, is framed for robbery by Quilp and Sampson Brass, a callous lawyer.[10] To make Kit believe he is good-natured, Brass hums with a seraphic smile and tries to appear "like a man whose soul was in the music." The resulting sounds lack harmony, however, because he hums "in a voice that was anything but musical, certain vocal snatches which appeared to have reference to the union between Church and State, inasmuch as they were compounded of the Evening Hymn and God Save the Queen" (*OCS* lvi). The grotesque Quilp transforms music into a "dismal roar" and chooses as text for his song the sentence, "The worthy magistrate, after remarking that the prisoner would find some difficulty in persuading a jury to believe his tale, committed him to take his trial at the approaching sessions; and directly the customary recognizances to be entered into the pros-e-cu-tion" (*OCS*, lxii). By juxtaposing legalistic jargon and criminal machinations with the incongruous idea of music, Dickens exposes the ugliness of life without beauty, love, or spirituality.

In the earlier *Nicholas Nickleby* Madeline Bray escapes the evil Gride, but Little Nell dies of exhaustion, defeated by the corruption around her. Evil becomes increasingly powerful.

Dickens reflects his age's sentimentalism towards the poor in passages such as his description of Kit's simple, cheerful home in *The Old Curiosity Shop:*" . . . if ever household affections and loves are graceful things, they are graceful in the poor. The ties that bind the wealthy and the proud to home may be forged on earth, but those which link the poor man to his humble hearth are of the true metal and bear the stamp of Heaven" (*OCS*, xxxviii). Music often blesses these "humble Hearths" of Dickens' poor or oppressed characters. The Cratchett home in *A Christmas Carol* (1843) remains musical despite the family's hardships. Lame Tiny Tim provides entertainment by singing in his "plaintive little voice," and Scrooge's niece also turns family gatherings into occasions of warmth and fellowship through music. Musical imagery illustrates Scrooge's transformation. At the opening of the story, Scrooge dismisses a boy singing Christmas carols, but he later is moved by his niece's gentle playing:

> Scrooge's niece played well upon the harp; and played among other tunes a simple little air. . . When this strain of music sounded . . . he softened more and more; and thought that if he could have listened to it often, years ago he might have cultivated the kindnesses of life for his own happiness with his own hands.
>
> (*A Christmas Carol*, Stave 3)

Music here and elsewhere becomes a metaphor not only for rustic innocence and beauty but for humanity itself.

Tom Pinch's organ-playing in *Martin Chuzzlewit* (1834-44) brings him happiness and helps establish him as "one of the best fellows in the world. . . a harmless, gentle, well-intentioned, good fellow. . . made up of simplicity" (*Martin Chuzzlewit*, ii and xii). In *The Chimes* (1844) Meg's willingness to sing to the baby in her arms despite her life of starvation and drudgery illustrates her inner beauty and unselfishness. "The Cricket on the Hearth" (1845) describes two simple women whose music similarly enables them to bring beauty to themselves and those around them. In contrast to the wealthier Tackleton, a "sordid, grinding" man who "can't afford to sing," blind Bertha plays sweetly on a "rude kind of harp" made by her father, and Dot uses the same harp to brighten her husband's home, "for Nature had made her delicate little ear as choice a one for music as it would have been for jewels if she had had any to wear" ("Cricket on the Hearth," Chirp the Second). Life separated from the commercial sphere, Dickens implies, can remain more harmonious.

Dicken's depiction of the innately melodious lower class echoes descriptions found in Victorian musical treatises. Just two years before the publication of "The Cricket on the Hearth," for instance, the Reverend J.S. Curwen sketched a picture of a working home made beautiful by the sound of music (see Chapter II). Victorians loved to hear the charity children sing annually at St. Paul's, for this convinced them of their own benevolence.

As late as 1861, Dickens continued to imply in his novels that the lower "uncivilized" classes had a natural bent for music. The child-like, simple-minded Joe Gargery of *Great Expectations* sings "Old Clem" with Pip as they work at the forge (*GE*, xii, xiv). When Pip leaves this happy setting for grander surroundings, Herbert Pocket ironically gives him the name "Handel": "'We are so harmonious, and you have been a blacksmith--would you mind it?. . . There's a charming piece of music by Handel, called the Harmonious Blacksmith'"(*GE*, xxii). Once Pip has discarded the innocence of his happy though poor childhood, he can find very little harmony.

By portraying mistreated children and workers as naturally harmonious, Dickens did little to improve Victorian attitudes towards the poor. Fictional images of the melodious poor perhaps made reform seem less imperative and gave impetus to the movement advocating the spread of music to the masses in order to make them happy, productive, and politically harmless. As Reverend Haweis continued to notice in the 1870's, music's beauty could make workers forget their pain and thus "save the country millions in poor-rates" (see Chapter II).

Music in Dickens' early novels becomes not only a means of eulogizing the virtuous poor but of satirizing the greedy and pretentious middle class. *Sketches by Boz* (1833-36) includes unflattering sketches of English 'musicians' and their audiences. In "Public Dinners," out-of-tune singers perform a religious song "most dismally," and the audience, mistaking *Non nobis* for a comic song, claps and yells "Encore!" "The Mistaken Milliner: A Tale of Ambition" narrates the unsuccessful attempt of a milliner daughter to "come out" in the musical world and thus advance her social standing. Dickens' account to Amelia Martin's first performance satirizes English amateurs, the public's sentimental taste, and the fallibility of Victorian critical assessment:

> Miss Martin, after sundry hesitations and coughings, with a preparatory choke or two, and an introductory declaration that she was frightened to death to attempt it before such great judges of the art, commenced a species of treble chirruping containing frequent allusions to some young of the name of Hen-e-ry, with an occasional reference to madness and broken hearts. Mr. Jennings Rodolph frequently interrupted the progress of the song by ejaculating
> "Beautiful!"--"Charming!"--"Brilliant!"--"Oh! splendid," &c; and at its close the admiration of himself, and his lady, knew no bounds.

Dickens parodies the immensely popular ballads of his age which expressed maudlin sentiment or sensational horror, such as "The Maniac" (No! by heav'n, no! by heav'n, I am not mad!").[2] Amelia Martin's decision to "come out" has unfortunate consequences for her neighbors, who must listen to her practicing, and ends in failure, for Amelia, "as she couldn't sing out, never came out."

Many other Dickens females view music as a social vehicle. Unlike Madeline, Little Nell, Dot, Bertha, and other untutored musicians, most middle-class females use music not to bring joy and sweetness to themselves and others but for their own advancement. In "The Steamboat Excursion" Mrs Briggs and Mrs. Taunton fight each other for the chance to exhibit their daughters' musical talents at social gatherings. Dickens' battle imagery captures this rivalry: "If Miss Sophia Taunton learnt a new song, two of the Miss Briggses came out with a new duet. The

Tauntons had once gained a temporary triumph with the assistance of a harp, but the Briggses brought three guitars into the field, and effectually routed the enemy."

The Tauntons are accompanied for one performance by a captain who sings "in that grunting tone in which a man gets down, Heaven knows where, without the remotest chance of ever getting up again." The many unmusical male and female amateurs in Dickens' novels and sketches combine to create a picture of a country overrun by incompetent performers. "Private Theatricals" describes the lamentable performance of an operatic overture by performers who ignore the need for practice and discipline. A near-sighted, "self-taught deaf gentleman" who tries to play the flute part "at sight" epitomizes the unmusical and uneducated Englishman. *Pickwick Papers* (1836-37) includes descriptions of Mrs. Pott, who "was heard to chirp faintly forth something which courtesy interpreted into a song," a group of "something-ean singers. . . [whose] grand secret seemed to be that three of the something-ean singers should grunt while the fourth howled," a chairman of a musical gathering who only knows one song, and an Irish gentleman who "being asked if he could play the fiddle, replied he had no doubt he could, but he couldn't exactly say for certain, because he had never tried." In *Nicholas Nickleby*, the passengers of an overturned coach discover they cannot enliven their long wait with songs because none of them knows how to sing. Richard Swiveller's dismal flute-playing in *The Old Curiosity Shop* maddens his neighbors and leads to an eviction notice from his landlady, and Mr. Jinkins drunken, unrehearsed, and tone-deaf musical party in *Martin Chuzzlewit* is similarly a "complete failure," as the resulting performance consists of "a requiem, a dirge, a moan, a howl, a wail, a lament, an abstract of everything that is sorrowful and hideous in sound" (*MC*, xi).

Dickens' approach to the musical amateurs of his early novels seems good-humored. Swiveller's flute-playing, however dreadful, indicates he has redeeming qualities. John Browdie's thundering performance of a song in *Nicholas Nickelby* establishes him as robust and benevolent. The spirit of the performance concerns Dickens more than its quality.

In later novels, however, Dickens' tone changes from humor to irony. The musical amateur becomes a shirker of social responsibility or an evil schemer, and the amusical Englishman becomes a man whose narrowness restricts the beauty of those around him.

Dickens' portrayal of the Bowlers in *The Chimes* foreshadows his later cynicism and suggests Dickens' early independence from the patronizing sentimentalism of Hullah, Hogarth and others of his time. Sir Joseph Bowler, believing himself to be the "perpetual parent" of the poor, informs any starving visitor, "Now the design of your creation is--not that you should swill, and guzzle, and associate your enjoyments, brutally, with food . . . but that you should feel the Dignity of Labour." To aid the workers in this design, Lady Bowler turns the following words into a song:

> O let us love our occupations,
> Bless the Squire and his relations,
> Live upon our daily rations,
> And always know our proper stations.

Lady Bowler has the words "set to music on the new system, for them to sing," a direct reference to the Tonic-sol-fa system which Hullah promoted in England and which Dickens wanted taught at Shepherd's Bush house. The song's text echoes the sentiment of songs actually proposed for Victorian workers, such as Curwen's suggestion that songs like "Begone dull sloth" and "Try again" would teach workers diligence and persistence (see Chapter II).

The musical characters of *Dombey and Son* (1848) and *David Copperfield* (1849-50) illustrate Dickens' transition from sentimentalism to cynicism. Irony underlies Dickens' continuing portrayal of innocent musicians, and his attack on those who abuse or misuse music becomes increasingly bitter.

Music divides characters in *Dombey and Son*: the warm-hearted Florence, sensitive Paul, indulgent Mr. Chick, kindly Captain Cuttle, and sympathetic Mr. Morfin are all musical or affected by music's beauty; the capitalist Dombey and his scheming employee Carker dislike music and are depicted as discordant, and the haughty Edith Granger, her designing mother, and the socially aspiring Miss Tox regard music only as a means of display and entrapment.

Dickens presents Florence as a natural musician, singing old airs to her sensitive brother, Paul. He writes sentimentally of the two children's innocent singing: "She was toiling up the great, wide, vacant staircase, with him in her arms . . . So they went, toiling up; she singing all the way, and Paul sometimes crooning out a feeble accompaniment" (*Dombey and Son*, ch. viii). Like Madeline and Little

Nell, Florence sings to bring joy to others, not for personal gain, and is reluctant to perform in public:

> . . . though Florence was at first very much frightened at being asked to sing before so many people, and begged earnestly to be excused, yet, on Paul calling her to him, and saying, "Do, Floy! Please! For me, my dear!" she went straight to the piano, and began . . . when he saw her sitting there alone, so young, and good, and beautiful, and kind to him; and heard her thrilling voice, so natural and sweet, and such a golden link between him and all his life's love and happiness, rising out of the silence; he turned his face away, and hid his tears. Not, as he told them when they spoke to him, not that the music was too plaintive or too sorrowful, but it was so dear to him. (ch. xiv)

Though Paul and Florence are mistreated by their insensitive father, they create a beautiful, insulated world for themselves through music.

Dickens contrasts Florence's singing of Paul's favorite air, one she sings following his death in remembrance of him, with Edith Granger's rendition of the same piece. As in *The Woman in White*, natural musicians are saintly, but cultivated musicians are demonic. Paul listens to Florence's "natural and sweet" singing with love and joy; Dombey coldly regards Edith's "rich," skillful singing and dexterous playing as accomplishments which prove the value of the "merchandise":

> She came at last, and sat down to her harp, and Mr. Dombey rose and stood beside her, listening. He had little taste for music, and no knowledge of the strain she played, but he saw her bending over it, and perhaps he heard among the sounding strings some distant music of his own, that tamed the monster of the iron road, and made it less inexorable. . . .
>
> When the haughty beauty had concluded, she arose, and receiving Mr. Dombey's thanks and compliments in exactly the same manner as before, went with scarcely any pause to the piano, and began there.
>
> Edith Granger, any song but that! Edith Granger, you are very handsome, and your touch upon the keys is brilliant, and your voice is deep and rich; but not the air that his neglected daughter sang to his dead son!
>
> Alas he knows it not; and if he did, what air of hers would stir him, rigid man! (xxi)

Dickens suggests that perhaps Dombey, like Scrooge, may have some remaining humanity despite his obsession with money, but if so, such feelings are a "distant music." Edith's performance is "brilliant" but without warmth, for her mother has taught her to be "artful, designing, mercenary," displaying her arts to enhance her value. Edith's mother, Mrs. Skewton (also called "Cleopatra" because of her melodramatic pose), feigns a love of music because it seems fashionable:

> "You are fond of music, Mr. Dombey?"
> "Eminently so," was Mr. Dombey's answer.
> "Yes, It's very nice," said Cleopatra, looking at her cards.
> "So much heart in it--undeveloped recollections of a previous state of existence--and all that--which is so truly charming." (xxi)

Dickens mocks the affectation and sham of Mrs. Skewton's attempts to appear "natural" and artless, a la Rousseau, for she is hollow. Only the children of the novel (Paul, Florence) and the lower classes can experience music with the heart.

Like Edith Granger, Miss Tox aspires to be Mrs. Dombey, and so she begins practicing waltzes on her harpsichord, an instrument which is ostentatiously "illuminated round the maker's name with a painted garland of sweet peas" (vii). Miss Tox views her harpsichord as her "little post of display" (xxxviii). Unlike Florence, whose warm, tender singing soothed the infant Paul, Miss Tox "froze its young blood with airs upon the harpsichord" (vii).

The novel's gentle characters find themselves in a world in which music seems to have died: the church organ "rumbled and rolled as if the church had got the colic," and a discarded cabinet piano is "wasting away" in Mr. Bragley's second-hand furniture shop, sending forth melancholy, "shrill complainings" (lvi, ix). Music becomes a retreat: Florence retires to the solitude of her room to sing, and the musical amateur Mr. Morfin uses his cello playing to forget the ugliness of the business world. Dickens' portrayal of Morfin suggests his increasing ambivalence towards this use of art as a means of escape.

Mr. Morfin, employee of Dombey's firm, is genial and kind; his music, though hardly professional, indicates that he has a soul and human feelings despite his involvement in an atmosphere of competition and impersonal transactions:

> He was a great musical amateur in his way--after business; and had a paternal affection for his violoncello, which was once in every week transported from Islington, his place of abode, to a certain club-room hard by the Bank, where quartettes of the most tormenting and excruciating nature were executed every Wednesday evening by a private party. . .

> He worked early and late to unravel whatever was complicated or difficult in the records of the transactions of the House; . . . and then would go home to Islington, and calm his mind by producing the most dismal and forlorn sounds out of his violoncello before going to bed. (xiii, lviii)

Although Morfin's co-worker, Carker, wishes he would "make a bonfire of his violoncello, and burn his music books in it," Morfin finds great relief through his music (liii). The more oppressive the day, the more melancholy his music becomes that night. The conclusion to *Dombey and Son* finds Morfin and Florence happily performing the "Harmonious Blacksmith," a song which underlines the scene's sentimentality.

Morfin's music may provide him with pleasure, but it also enables him to escape from unpleasant situations. Rather than taking action, Morfin plays his cello. He tries to ignore the injustice Mr. Carker is perpetrating on his brother and sister: "My Wednesday nights came regularly round, our quartette parties came regularly off, my violoncello was in good tune, and there was nothing wrong in my world--or if anything not much--and little or much it was no affair of mine" (*DS*, liii). In his office Morfin's humming of Beethoven to drown out Carker's voice represents his attempt to cover reality's discord. While playing the cello, Morfin's expression is "monstrously pathetic and bland" (*DS*, lviii).

As in *Dombey and Son*, music in *David Copperfield* separates "good" and "bad" characters, but the division becomes even more equivocal. The saintly Agnes plays old airs on the piano "with great sweetness and expression" to soothe her aging father, mild-mannered Mr. Mell loves his flute, and the gentle, guileless Dr. Strong is "very fond of music" (*David Copperfield*, xxix, xix). Sinister Rosa Dartle, on the other hand, plays her harp with "fearful" power rather than tenderness, and affected Dora plays meaningless French ballads on "a glorified instrument resembling a guitar" in order to captivate David. David Copperfield "loves music from his soul," but this love reveals both his strengths and failings. His appreciation of Agnes' sweet playing indicates his own receptivity to beauty and feelings, yet David also falls into a trance when he listens to Rosa's music and is "lost in blissful delirium" at Dora's performances. David's susceptibility to music's sway over the emotions suggests not only his capacity for passion and goodness but also his lack of firmness and his romantic delusions.

Dickens regards the good musical characters of *Dombey and Son* and *David Copperfield* with sympathy but also a degree of condescension. Increasingly in Dickens' novels, innocent, old-fashioned characters who love music are weak, set apart from the world of competition and made its victims. Tom Pinch of *Martin Chuzzlewit* may be "high-souled," but he also is childlike, short-sighted, and easily manipulated, a man whose naivete blinds him to Pecksniff's abominable character. In *Dombey and Son*, Florence is bullied by her father, Mr. Chick is hen-pecked by his wife, Mr. Morfin suffers abuse from Mr. Carker, and Paul dies because "his soul is too large for his frame" (*DS*, vii). Agnes Wickfield spends most of the chapters of *David Copperfield* waiting patiently and silently for David to recognize her value, ineffectual Mr. Mell loses his job, and the weakness of music-lover Dr. Strong belies his name. Joe Gargery in *Great Expectations* may sing while he works, but he endures hardship at the hands of his domineering wife and cannot function in the slick urban life of London. Innocence has its price.

In novels such as *Bleak House* (1852-53), *Our Mutual Friend* (1864) and *Edwin Drood* (1870), Dickens views musicians with greater scorn and implies that artists should seek to improve social conditions rather than escape them. Dickens' maturity as an artist seems to have brought with it a greater intolerence of artistic pretense and incompetence, a stronger belief in art's social function, and a growing detachment from Victorian sentimentalism. Perhaps Dickens' travels abroad made him more aware of England's faults, and his already assured success as a novelist made him more independent of his readers' taste.

Musical amateur Harold Skimpole of *Bleak House*, like Morfin, is an escapist, but Dickens depicts him with far less sympathy. "A musical man," Skimpole uses his artistic nature as an excuse not to work. Because Skimpole lacks discipline, his talents are superficial:

> He is a musical man; an Amateur, but might have been a Professional. He is an Artist, too; an Amateur, but might have been a Professional. He is a man of attainments and of captivating manners. . . Mr. Skimpole could play on the piano, and the violoncello: and he was a composer--had composed half an opera once, but got tired of it--and played what he composed with taste. (*Bleak House*, vi)

What Skimpole lacks in musical acumen he makes up for in "delicate sentiment," tender feeling, and taste.

Skimpole's musicianship forms part of his "romantic" nature, just as Leigh Hunt, the model of Dickens' Skimpole, prided himself on his musical taste. Hunt's taste was notoriously shallow and affected; his musical criticism a series of sentimental outbursts. Keats wrote of Hunt's approach to music, "Through him I am indifferent to Mozart. . . many a glorious thing when associated with him becomes a nothing."[3] In his unfinished, unpublished work *Musical Evenings*, Hunt exclaims of Gluck's *Alceste*, "How noble! How affecting! How simple, dignified, yet full of entreaty!"[4] Hunt's contrived, stilted poems on music represent no genuine or informed musical appreciation on his part; in "On Hearing a Little Musical Box," for example, Hunt gushes:

> HALLO! - what? - where, what can it be
> That strikes up so deliciously?
> I never in my life - what no!
> That little tin box playing so?
> It really seemed as if a sprite
> Had struck among us, swift and light,
> And come from some minute star
> To treat us with his pearl guitar.[5]

Dickens' mocks Hunt's affectation and shallowness by presenting Skimpole as a man who prides himself on his musicality even though he only sings, plays, and composes "a little."

Dickens portrayal of Hunt as Skimpole reveals his growing disenchantment with romanticism. Merely to be full of feeling and spontaneity no longer suffices. In a setting of social injustice, crying for reform, Skimpole's pursuit of music is "childish irresponsibility," an escape from reality which is selfish and unproductive.

Like Skimpole and Morfin, Mr. Podsnap in *Our Mutual Friend* chooses to ignore any disturbing news. Skimpole falls back on his innocent pose, Morfin retreats to his cello and Podsnap insists, "I don't want to know about it; I don't choose to discuss it; I don't admit it!" (*Our Mutual Friend*, I, xi). Dickens used Skimpole to attack artistic dabbling; in his late novel, he uses the Podsnap family's musical taste to attack the artistic conservatism and incompetence of the English public. Mr. Podsnap will tolerate only respectable, sedate music, his wife hammers on the piano with alarming force, his daughter lacks the nerve to play "M-m-m-m-music," and they hire as musician an "automaton" to play "blossomless tuneless" pieces (*OMF*, I, xi). Just as Podsnap's refusal to acknowledge poverty in England has dire consequences for the poor, so his rigid view of the arts stifles the creativity of English artists.

Although Dickens considers innate musicality to be a proof of inner beauty and satirizes those who lack musical ability and taste, he increasingly doubts the worth of those who pursue the art of music at the expense of other, more serious endeavors. Perhaps Dickens' growing belief in the moral function of art made him less tolerant of music, particularly the type of music popular in nineteenth century England, for it lacked substance and meaning. Amelia Martin is silly but harmless; later female musicians such as Edith Granger and Rosa Dartle acquire a sinister quality. In *David Copperfield* Agnes wickfield's musicianship demonstrates her virtue, but in *Bleak House* Esther Summerson is too busy working to have time for such amusement. The amateur instrumentalists in *Sketches by Boz* are unmusical but innocuous; Morfin and Skimpole use music to avoid redressing society's wrongs.

In Dickens' final, unfinished novel, *Edwin Drood*, music no longer functions as a reliable index to character. A musician can be genial and "boy-like," like Mr. Crisparkle, or terrifying and enigmatic, like Mr. Jasper. Wilkie Collins' Count Fosco (*The Woman in White*, 1860) could plot a murder and play glorious music at the same time; similarly, Jasper obtains extraordinary "melodious power" when apparently filled with thoughts of vengeance. Like other Victorians, Dickens observed music's troubling amorality.

Music also becomes a metaphor for sexual potency in *Edwin Drood*. Just as Marian Holcombe reacts to Count Fosco's thundering performances as if she were being raped, so Rosa in Edwin Drood views Jasper's music as a terrifying invasion:

> "He terrifies me. . . He haunts my thoughts like a dreadful ghost. I feel as if he could pass in through the wall when he is spoken of. . . He has made a slave of me with his looks. . . When he corrects me, and strikes a note, or a chord, or plays a passage, he himself is in the sounds, whispering that he pursues me as a lover, and commanding me to keep his secret. . .tonight when he watched my lips so closely as I was singing, besides feeling terrified I felt ashamed and passionately hurt. It was as if he kissed me, and I couldn't bear it, but cried out." (*ED*, vii)

Like sex, music's amorality and irrational power over the passions disturbed Victorians.

In *Edwin Drood* art not only has been severed from morality but has lost its ability to transcend the ugliness of corrupt urban life. "Oppressively respectable" Mr. Sapsea has banished any "un-English" music, the cathedral bell of Cloisterham is harsh, choir members dress in "sullied white robes," and the musical sounds of London's streets grate painfully on the ears of its inhabitants:

> There was music playing here and there, but it did not enliven the case. No barrel-organ mended the matter, and no big drum beat dull care away. Like the chapel bells that were also going here and there, they only seemed to evoke echoes from brick surfaces, and dust from everything. As to the flat wind-instruments, they seemed to have cracked their hearts and souls in pining for the country. (*ED*, xxi)

A portrait of Handel beams down from Mr. Crisparkle's wall in ironic oblivion to the surrounding discord of contemporary England.

Although references to music pervade Dickens' novels, not one professional musician emerges in a wholly favorable light. In some ways, Dickens was a product of "das Land ohne Musik." His works reflect his age's distrust of music as an amoral, frivolous, and socially useless art, suitable only for women, children, and foreigners. Yet Dickens' musical characters do far more than "reflect to a nicety the general condition of ordinary musical life in England," but provide Dickens with a brilliant vehicle for revealing character and exposing the strengths and failings of Victorian England.[6] The change in Dickens' musical imagery from his early to late novels reveals not only his growing departure from Victorian aesthetics but also his increasingly cynical vision of English society. Dickens' use of music to expose his age's artistic, moral, political, and social shortcomings greatly influenced later Victorian novelists.

Chapter IV: Notes

1   *Dickens' Correspondence with John Hullah* (Hitherto Unpublished From the Collection of Count de Suzannet), Private Printing by Walter Dexter, Sept. 1933, pp. 18-19.

2   Henry Russell, "The Maniac," quoted in John W. Dodds, *The Age of Paradox: A Biography of England* 1841-1851 (N.Y.: Rinehart, 1952), p. 272.

3   *The Letters of John Keats*, 1814-1821, ed. H.E. Rollins (Cambridge, Mass.: Harvard University Press, 1958), II, 11. For a discussion of Hunt and Skimpole see Luther Brewer, *Leigh Hunt and Charles Dickens: the Skimpole Caricature* (Iowa, 1930). Brewer claims Dickens did Hunt a great injustice.

4   Hunt, *Musical Evenings*, p. 43.

5   *The Poetical Works of Leigh Hunt and Thomas Hood*, ed. Harwood Panting (London: Scott, 1889), p. 123.

6   James T. Lightwood, *Charles Dickens and Music* (London: Charles Kelly, 1912), p. vii. Lightwood's book provides a useful catalogue of Dickens' musical references but offers little criticism of these passages.

Chapter V

Satire: The Musicians of William Thackeray

Like Dickens, William Thackeray (1811-63) shared Reverend Haweis' indignation against young ladies who "trundle through Beethoven's sonatas in the drawing room" in order to captivate a man, and also scorned avaricious foreign musicians and their ignorant English audiences. The contrast between the godlike musicians of Romantic literature and the actual performers of contemporary London offered Thackeray an irresistible opportunity for satire. Instead of passionate musical heroes and heroines with divine power, one finds in his novels calculating spinsters devoting hours of study to the piano so that they may attract a wealthy widower, lower middle-class families hoping to gain financially from their children's musical talent, unappealing foreign maestros profiting from the gullibility of their English pupils, and stolid British citizens dutifully attending concerts they know and care nothing about in order to become members of a 'cultured' elite. With greater originality than any preceding British novelist, Thackeray used musicians not to portray otherworldliness and supernatural power, but to expose the plight of the mortal artist in a society lacking education and vision. Together, Dickens and Thackeray dealt a devastating and well-deserved blow to the literary convention of the romantic musician.

Thackeray used music with greater frequency and subtlety than Dickens, perhaps because his knowledge of music was greater. Thackeray's references to twenty-eight different operas, his observations about the instruction of young women, and his masterful parodies of contemporary musical performances and reviews demonstrate his familiarity with music and its place in Victorian society. As J.A. Watson observes, Thackeray is a "conspicuous instance . . . of a great literary genius in whose works music holds a place of honour."[7]

Only by implication, however, does music hold "a place of honour" in Thackeray's novels. Thackeray treats the musician with merciless satire, and uses musical events to expose the failings of what he despairingly called "this stupid public." Thackeray's cynicism towards the musicians of his time reflects not his dislike of music but rather his attraction to this art and respect for its skilled practitioners.

The young woman who dutifully performs one or two light pieces on the piano as a mandatory social obligation appears in nearly all of Thackeray's novels. Thackeray ridicules the amount of labor involved in her acquisition of musical talent and suggests the result brings little genuine pleasure to either listener or performer. In his musical scenes Thackeray also perfects the delineation of England's phony middle-class, condescending aristocracy, and obtuse citizenry.

Thackeray's *Book of Snobs* (1847) draws on Dickens' satirical portraits in *Sketches by Boz* of accomplished females and their mothers, but Thackeray's emphasis differs. While both poke fun at the thinly-disguised ambition of middle-class 'artists', Thackeray adds the realistic observation that for young women to acquire the mediocre skill needed to perform tinkling, insipid music wastes time, labor, money, and intelligence.

In *Book of Snobs* Thackeray describes the musical performances of the Miss Pontos, prodded by their ambitious mother, and Miss Wirt, who can only play popular tunes:

> The jingling of a harp and piano soon announced that MRS. PONTO'S *ung pu de Musick* had commenced . . . we could command a fine view of the backs of the young ladies who were performing the musical entertainment . . . MISS EMILY PONTO at the piano, and her sister MARIA at that somewhat exploded instrument, the harp, were in light blue dresses that looked all flounce . . .
> "Brilliant touch EMILY has - what a fine arm MARIA's is" MRS. PONTO remarked goodnaturedly . . .
> When the performance was concluded, I had the felicity of a presentation and conversation with the two tall and scraggy MISS PONTOS, and MISS WIRT, the governess, sat down to entertain us with variations on "Sich a gettin' up stairs." For the performance of the "Gettin' up Stairs," I have no other name but that it was a stunner. (*Book of Snobs*, xxxii)

The Miss Pontos' dresses and arms rival the music for the audience's attention.

Later in *Book of Snobs* Thackeray discusses the amount of effort necessary for the Pontos to produce "*ung pu de Musick*" and mocks the assumption that such activity is a worthwhile employment of time:

> Piano strumming begins at six o'clock in the morning; it lasts till breakfast, with but a minute's intermission, when the instrument changes hands, and MISS EMILY practises in place of her sister, MISS MARIA.
>
> In fact, the confounded instrument never stops: when the young ladies are at their lessons, MISS WIRT hammers away at those stunning variations, and keeps her magnificent finger in exercise . . .
>
> "I hope you weren't disturbed by the music," PONTO says. "My girls, you know, practise four hours a-day, you know - must do it, you know - absolutely necessary." (xxxiii)

In "Club Snobs" Thackeray adds that such musical practice forms an inevitable and unfortunate part of any respectable English household: "Say the girls are beginning to practice their music, which in an honourable English family, ought to occupy every young gentlewoman three hours; it would be rather hard to call upon poor papa to sit in the drawing room all that time, and listen to interminable discords and shrieks which are elicited from the miserable piano during the above necessary operation. A man, with a good ear especially, would go mad, if compelled daily to submit to this horror" (xliv).

The picture of a young woman slaving away at her music recurs with astonishing frequency, indicating its importance to Thackeray as a symbol of the trivial state of female education in England. In *Ravenswing* (in *Men's Wives*, 1843) he labels musical practice one form of bondage and mocks Victorian sentimentalism towards music:

> Have you not remarked the immense works of art that women get through? The worsted-work sofas, the counterpanes patched or knitted . . . the bushels of pincushions, the albums they laboriously fill, the tremendous pieces of music they practise, the thousand other fiddle-faddles which occupy the attention of the dear souls . . . Women's fancy-work is of this sort often - only prison work, done because there was no other exercising-ground for their poor little thoughts and fingers; and hence these wonderful pincushions are executed,. . . these sonatas learned. By everything sentimental, when I see two kind, innocent, fresh-cheeked young women go to a piano, and . . . go through a set of double-barrelled variations upon this or that tune by Herz or Kalkenbrenner, - I say, far from receiving any satisfaction at the noise made by the performance, my too susceptible heart is given up entirely to bleeding for the performers. What hours, and weeks, nay, preparatory years of study, has that infernal jig cost them! What sums has papa paid, what scoldings has mamma administered ("Lady Bullblock does

not play herself," Sir Thomas says, "but she has naturally the finest ear for music ever known!"); what evidences of slavery, in a word, are there! It is the condition of the young lady's existence. (*Ravenswing*, ix)

The young ladies' choice of Herz and Kalkenbrenner, like Miss Wirt's choice of Thalberg, reveals their fondness for sentimental music designed to display the performer's technical showmanship: Grout notes that Thalberg and Kalkenbrenner were "successful display pianists but, as composers, decidedly of second rank."[8]

Barry Lyndon (1844) similarly includes a cynical look at the "accomplished" female: "We know very well that a lady who is skilled in dancing or singing never can perfect herself without a great deal of study in private, and that the song or the minuet which is performed with so much graceful ease in the assembly-room has not been acquired without vast labour and perseverance in private" (*Barry Lyndon*, i). And in *Vanity Fair* (1848) Thackeray notes that the intended result of such labor is matrimony: "What causes them to labour at pianoforte sonatas, and to learn four songs from a fashionable master at a guinea a lesson, and to play the harp if they have handsome arms and neat elbows . . . but that they may bring down some 'desirable' young man with those killing bows and arrows of theirs?" (*Vanity Fair*, iii). Although Thackeray describes female performers with contempt, his remarks suggest that he believed that the nature of Victorian society, not the sex of the performers, kept them from realizing their intellectual and artistic potential.

Ravenswing contains Thackeray's most extensive treatment of the female musician, her instruction and training, reception in society, and commercial exploitation. Thackeray shows a cynical awareness of the artist's fate in Victorian England and portrays Morgiana Walker with a greater realism than was accorded the musicians of previous Victorian novelists.

Miss Morgiana, who "believed herself to be the most fascinating creature that the world ever produced," considers her music to be one of her fascinations. Her choice of music, like Amelia Martin's ballad about Hen-e-ry, relects the maudlin and ornate taste of the time:

> . . . you might often hear Miss Morgiana employed at the little red-silk cottage piano, singing, "Come where the haspens quiver," or "Bonny lad, march over hill and furrow," or "My 'art and lute," or any other popular piece of the day. And the dear girl sang with

> very considerable skill too, for she had a fine loud voice, which, if not always in tune, made up for that defect by its great energy and activity; and Morgiana was not content with singing the mere tune, but gave every one of the roulades, flourishes, and ornaments as she heard them at the theatres by Mrs. Humby, Mrs. Waylett, or Madame Vestris. (*Ravenswing*, i)

Following her marriage to the capitalistic Captain Walker, Morgiana continues her music but primarily as a way to pass the time during her husband's absence:

> Among the other articles of luxury with which the Captain furnished his house, we must not omit to mention an extremely grand piano, which occupied four-fifths of Mrs. Walker's little back drawing-room, and at which she was in the habit of practising continually. All day and all night during Walker's absences (and these occurred all night and all day) you might hear - the whole street might hear - the voice of the lady at No. 23 gurgling, and shaking, and quavering, as ladies do when they practice. The street did not approve of the continuance of the noise, but what would Morgiana have had to do if she had ceased to sing? (iv)

Captain Walker's "extremely grand" piano, like the pianos of many Victorians, provides a tangible symbol of his wealth and status.

Like Dickens' Amelia Martin, Morgiana Walker decides to "come out" musically, and she goes through a series of musical instructors. While Captain Walker is no appreciator of music, he willingly finances his wife's musical instruction in order to make her capable of earning money. Podmore, a fat English chorus-master, is inexpensive but lacks the prestige of a foreign maestro; therefore, Walker engages Signor Baroski "at a vast expense."

Thackeray describes Baroski as an unappealing, inmoral, and greedy man; his allusion to Baroski's Jewishness reflects the almost universal antisemitism of his age: "Little Baroski is the author of the opera of 'Eliogabala', of the oratorio of 'Purgatorio', which made such an inmense sensation, of songs and ballet-musics innumerable. He is a German by birth, and shows such an outrageous partiality for pork sausages, and attends at church so constantly, that I am sure there cannot be any foundation in the story that he is a member of the ancient religion. He is a fat little man, with a hooked nose and jetty whiskers, and coal-black shining eyes" (iv). Thackeray implies that Baroski is a bad Jew who hides his Jewishness (by attending church and eating pork) in order to be accepted in English society. Baroski accepts Morgiana as a pupil because of his greed and lust. Elsewhere in

Thackeray the same link between Jews and music appears, as in his description of a musical ensemble in *The Newcomes*; "The Jew with the beard . . . is Herr von Lungen, the eminent hautboy player. The three next gentlemen are Mr. Smee, of the Royal Academy (who is shaved as you perceive), and Mr. Moyes and Mr. Crooper, who are both very hairy about the chin. At the piano, singing, accompanied by Mademoiselle Leburn, is Signor Mezzocaldo, the great barytone from Rome" (*Newcomes*, I, viii). Once again, Jews and Italians seem to thrive on music.

In noting Captain Walker's dismissal of Podmore in favor of the foreign Baroski, Thackeray mocks Englishmen's tacit assumption that foreigners are more cultured. In *Book of Snobs* he similarly ridicules misplaced English reverence for foreign maestros by showing the ignorance of the "Party-giving Snobs" (*Book of Snobs*, ch. xxv). He writes:

> All this while, amidst the crowd and the scuffle, and a perpetual buzz and chatter, and an intolerable smell of musk . . . a scrubby-looking yellow-faced foreigner, with cleaned gloves, is warbling inaudibly in a corner, to the accompaniment of another. "The Great CACAFOGO," Mrs. Botibol whispers, as she passes you by - "A great creature, THUMPENSTRUMPFF, is at the instrument - the HETMAN PLATOFF's pianist, you know."
>
> To hear this CACAFOGO and THUMPEN-STRUMPFF, a hundred people are gathered together - a bevy of dowagers, stout, or scraggy; a faint sprinkling of misses, six moody-looking lords, perfectly meek and solemn; wonderful foreign Counts, with bushy whiskers and yellow waists and open necks, and self-satisfied simpers, and flowers in their buttons . . .
>
> . . . Poor CACAFOGO is quavering away in the music room, under the impression that he will be *lance*, in the world by singing inaudibly here. And what a blessing it is to squeeze out of the door, and into the street.

Like Cacafogo, Baroski hopes for advancement in London's musical world and profits from the gullibility of the public. His foreignness helps assure him a wide following of students:

> Benjamin Baroski was one of the chief ornaments of the musical profession in London; he charged a guinea for a lesson of three-quarters of an hour abroad, and he had, furthermore, a school at his own residence, where pupils assembled in considerable numbers, and of that curious mixed kind which those may see who frequent these places of instruction. There were very innocent

> young ladies with their mammas, who would hurry them off trembling to the further corner of the room when certain doubtful professional characters made their appearance. There was Miss Grigg, who sang at the "Foundling," . . . and Madame Fioravanti (a very doubtful character), who sang nowhere but was always coming out at the Italian Opera. There was. . . Mr. Bulger, the dentist of Sackville Street, who neglectd his ivory and cold plates for his voice, as every unfortunate individual will do who is bitten by the music mania. Then among the ladies there were a half score of dubious pale governesses and professionals . . . who were parting with their poor little store of half-guineas to be enabled to say they were pupils of Signor Baroski, and so get pupils of their own . . .
>
> The prima donna of the little company was Amelia Larkins, Baroski's own articled pupil, on whose fortune and reputation the eminent master staked his own, whose profits he was to share, and whom he had formed, to this end, from her father, a most respectable sheriff's officer's assistant, and now, by his daughter's exertions, a considerable capitalist. (iv)

The collection of pupils Baroski assembles illustrates the range of people desirous of acquiring musical prowess: young ladies seeking a social accomplishment, governesses eager to learn a marketable skill, male amateurs wanting an innocent amusement, dubious "professional characters," and women like Morgiana or Amelia Larkins who hope to make their fortunes on the stage.

Amelia Larkins' father becomes a "considerable capitalist" from his daughter's musical performances, and Captain Walker also finds Morgiana's new musical ability to be a social and financial boon: "Hearing so much of his wife's skill as a singer, the astute Captain Walker determined to take advantage of it for the purpose of increasing his 'connections'." "Great personages" appear at Morgiana's parties and invite her to perform, but her profession excludes her from genuine acceptance. Thackeray writes: "After a short time, Mrs. Howard Walker's musical parties began to be considerably *suivies*. Her husband had the great satisfaction to see his rooms filled by many great personages; and once or twice in return (indeed, whenever she was wanted, or when people could not afford to hire the first singers) she was asked to parties elsewhere, and treated with that killing civility which our English aristocracy knows how to bestow on artists. Clever and wise aristocracy! It is sweet to mark your ways, and study your commerce with inferior men" (iv). Like Meredith's Purcell Barrett, Morgiana faces aristocratic contempt because of her career as professional musician.

Morgiana dismisses Baroski because of his declaration of love and ruthless pursuit of the 220 guineas Walker owes him. Her new music mentor is Sir George Thrum, eminently English and eminently respectable. Thrum is Thackeray's brilliant caricature of the Victorian musician: musically conservative, concerned with appearance and propriety, and motivated primarily by the promise of financial gain.

Like most nineteenth-century English composers, Thrum composes works which reflect the taste of his age and are thus quite forgettable: "He was the author of several operas ("The Camel Driver," "Britons Alarmed; or the Siege of Bergen-op-Zoom," &c. &c.) and, of course, of songs which had considerable success in their day, but are forgotten now, and are as much faded and out-of-fashion as those old carpets which we have described in the professor's house, and which were, doubtless, very brilliant once."

Thrum's "indomitable respectability," however, assures his success:

> But, though his hey-day of fashion was gone, Sir George still held his place among the musicians of the old school, conducted occasionally at the Ancient Concerts and the "Philharmonic" . . .
>
> Respectability has been his great card through life; ladies can trust their daughters at Sir George Thrum's academy. "A good musician, Madam," says he to the mother of a new pupil, "should not only have a fine ear, a good voice, and an indomitable industry, but, above all, a faultless character - faultless, that is, as far as our poor nature will permit. And you will remark that those young persons with whom your lovely daughter, Miss Smith, will pursue her musical studies, are all, in a moral point of view, as spotless as that charming young lady." (vii)

Lady Thrum, "dragon of virtue and propriety, kept watch over the master and pupils, and was the sternest guardian of female virtue on or off any stage" (vi). She insists that their music academy be conducted on the highest of moral principles and helps Thrum turn each young woman into "a siren . . . without the dangerous qualities of one." Thrum and his wife deliberately avoid the atmosphere of scandal connected with foreign musicians in order to attract respectable customers. Lady Thrum deplores "the sad condition of other musical professors" (vii).

Thackeray contrasts Thrum and Baroski with his satire directed at both:

> The two famous professors conduct their academies on very opposite principles. Baroski writes ballet music; Thrum, on the contrary, says "he cannot but deplore the dangerous fascinations of the dance," and writes more for Exeter Hall and Birmingham. While Baroski drives a cab in the park with a very suspicious Mademoiselle Leocadie, or Amenaide, by his side, you may see Thrum walking to evening church with his lady, and hymns are sung there of his own composition. He belongs to the "Athenaeum Club," and he goes to the levee once a year, he does everything that a respectable man should, and if, by the means of this respectability, he manages to make his little trade far more profitable than it otherwise would be, are we to quarrel with him for it?

Thackeray wryly observes that Thrum's morality has a shrewd financial basis, "for Sir George, respectable as he was, had the reputation of being extremely clever at a bargain." The pragmatic Englishman regards music as "his little trade" (vii).

Thrum helps prepare Morgiana for her debut, an event which receives a tremendous build-up in the London press. Thackeray includes fictitious excerpts from local newspaper articles in which he parodies the affected style of music critics and mocks Victorian provincialism. Before Morgiana's appearance, Thackeray writes, "The English press began to heave and throb in a convulsive manner, as if indicative of the near birth of some great thing." One article complains that "the *most illustrious audiences* in the realm prefer *foreign* melodies to *the native wood-notes wild* of the sweet song-bird of Avon," and *The Flowers of Fashion* observes:

> We have been accused of preferring the *produit of the etranger* to the talent of our native shores; but those who speak so, little know us. We are *fanatici per la musica* wherever it be, and welcome merit *dans chaque pays du monde* . . . Sir George Thrum . . . is a *maestro* whose fame *appartient a l' Europe.*
> . . . We have heard THE RAVENSWING [Morgiana] . . . and a creature more beautiful and gifted never bloomed before *dans nos climats.* She sang the delicious duet of the "Nabucodonosore," with Count Pizzicato, with a *bellezza,* a *grandezza,* a *raggio,* that excited in the bosom of the audience a corresponding *furore.* (viii)

Thackeray skillfully imitates the pretentious style of Victorian musical journalism and shows remarkable insight in his description of London's hysterical reception of "The Ravenswing." Four years after Thackeray's *Ravenswing* appeared in print, Jenny Lind took England by storm. As *The Times* reported of Lind, "the uproar which followed her entrance is something to be remembered, not described."9 John W. Dodds observes that Jenny Lind portraits, statuettes, cigars, and silks appeared in London shops, and Englishmen flocked to her concerts from miles around.10 Thackeray's *Ravenswing* foreshadows this response, suggesting his awareness of England's musical climate; in Morgiana's case, however, success is hardly deserved.

Thackeray also uses newspaper accounts to reveal England's musical chauvinism. The *Tomahawk* heralds Thrum's music as infinitely preferable to Italian compositions: "Old Thrum, the composer, is bringing out an opera and a pupil. The opera is good, the pupil first-rate. The opera will do much more than compete with the infernal twaddle and disgusting slip-slop of Donizetti, and the milk-and-water fools who imitate him; it will (and we ask the readers of the *Tomahawk*, were we EVER mistaken?) surpass all these; it is good, of downright English stuff" (viii). Like Meredith's Mr. Pole, who likes good manly English music, the *Tomahawk* critic insists on "downright English stuff" and considers foreign music effeminate.

Morgiana's performances bring wealth to her instructor and husband: Sir Thrum earns so many guineas he can afford to have his portrait engraved, and Captain Walker shrewdly makes sure that he "received every shilling before he would permit her to sing a note." Morgiana's personal fate, however, is less successful. Steeped in the immoral atmosphere of the stage, she falls into bad company and loses her good reputation: "Lady Thrum would die sooner than to speak to that unhappy young woman . . . People are very shy about receiving her in society; and when she goes to sing at a concert, Miss Prim starts up and skurries off in a state of the greatest alarm, lest 'that person' should speak to her" (viii). Artists like Morgiana not only are patronized and exploited but feared and condemned as well.

The end of *The Ravenswing* (Morgiana retires from the stage and marries a loyal, devoted tailor) provides a snug, sentimental, and thus incongruous conclusion for a story containing much serious satire. The Victorian musician, Thackeray demonstrates, has been turned into a croaking, predatory raven, a far cry from the nightingales and larks of romanticism.

Fitz-Boodle, narrator of *The Ravenswing*, insists that he himself is tone-deaf: "for, between ourselves, none of the male Fitz-Boodles ever could sing a note, and the jargon of scales and solfeggios is quite unknown to me." Yet Fitz-Boodle seems to have greater common sense and artistic judgment that the affected critics, for he notes of Morgiana's concert, "as far as I can understand matters, (and I believe to this day that Mrs. Walker was only an ordinary singer) - the songs lasted a great deal longer than I liked" (vii). In *Cox's Diary* (1840; rpt. 1855) Thackeray similarly adopts the persona of an Englishman whose refusal to pretend musical appreciation seems refreshing:

> No lady is a lady without having a box at the Opera; so my Jemmy, who knew as much about music, - bless her! - as I do about Sanscrit, algebra, or any other foreign language, took a prime box on the second tier.
>
> . . . What a place that Opera is, to be sure! and what enjoyments us aristocracy used to have! Just as you have swallowed down your three courses . . . in bursts my Jemmy, as fine as a duchess, and scented like our shop. "Come, my dear," says she, "it's 'Normy' to-night" (or 'Annybalony', or the 'Nosey di Figaro', or the 'Gazzylarder', as the case may be). "Mr. Forster strikes off punctually at eight, and you know it's the fashion to be always present at the very first bar of the aperture." And so off we are obliged to budge, to be miserable for five hours, and to have a headache for the next twelve, and all because it's the fashion!
>
> After the aperture, as they call it, comes the opera, which, as I am given to understand, is the Italian for singing. Why they should sing in Italian, I can't conceive; or why they should do nothing *but* sing. Bless us! . . . Not that I don't admire Lablash, and Rubini, and his brother, Tomrubini: him who had that fine bass voice, I mean, and acts the Corporal in the first piece, and Don June in the second; but three hours is a *little* too much, for you can't sleep on those little rickety seats in the boxes.

Thackeray admires the honesty of such men, particularly when contrasted with middle-class pretense, but he did not share their dislike of classical music. Letters from Thackeray to G. H. Lewes reveal Thackeray's love of opera, and in the autobiographical *Pendennis* he writes that Pen loved listening to Mozart's *Don Giovanni*, "which he admired of all things in the world" (*Pendennis*, I, xix).[11]

Vanity Fair (1848) includes satirical portraits both of accomplished musicians who misuse their art and musical amateurs whose sentiment surpasses their skill. Thackeray's description of Amelia's and Becky's musical abilities suggest he was torn between his two heroines.

Amelia, product of Miss Pinkerton's academy, has only a "little store of songs" which she sings in a "sweet fresh little voice" (*Vanity Fair*, iv-v). She plays waltzes to try to capture George's attention and spends hours in his absence practising melancholy airs on her little cabinet piano, weeping as she plays. Thackeray mocks the sentimentalism of this picture, though, by showing that Amelia's love is not for the music but for George: she only plays because she thinks the piano was his gift, and finds it "valueless" and "out of tune" when this belief is destroyed (lix). Furthermore, her "feeble," "simple" art makes her incapable of earning an income following George's death, so that she is dependent on the patronage of the wealthy Osbornes and the generous Dobbin. Thackeray praises the guileless Amelia's susceptibility to the beauty of Mozart's *Don Juan*, but he ridicules Amelia's priggish concern that the music is immoral and wicked: "This lady had the keenest and finest sensibility, and how could she be indifferent when she heard Mozart? The tender parts of *Don Juan* awakened in her raptures so exquisite that she would ask herself when she went to say her prayers of a night, whether it was not wicked to feel so much delight as that with which *Vedrai Carino* and *Batti, Batti* filled her gentle little bosom?" (lxii).

Like Amelia, Dobbin is moved by music's beauty but not musically gifted himself. "He could sing no better than an owl," and plays his flute with questionable talent (vi). Dobbin's love of music reflects his compassionate, sensitive nature but also shows him to be somewhat weak and emasculated. Just as Amelia likes her piano because she thinks it is from George, so Dobbin enjoys concerts primarily because Amelia is with him: his "chief pleasure . . . in these operas was in watching Emmy's rapture while listening to them" (lxii). Amelia and Dobbin, though virtuous, lack potency in the world of Vanity Fair and are victims, deluded by their own sentimentalism.

Becky Sharp's musicianship is far superior to Amelia's, and Thackeray treats this proficiency equivocally. On the one hand, Becky's talent makes her into a scheming, immoral siren (*with* all the dangerous qualities of one), but on the other hand, her musicianship reveals an intelligence and independence lacking in the helpless Amelia. Becky's musical ability sets her above the silly young ladies of Miss Pinkerton's academy, women like Miss Swartz, who "can play two pieces on the piano" and sing three songs (xx). Becky "speedily went through the little course of study which was considered necessary for ladies in those days" and practises "incessantly" (ii). She becomes so good that Miss Pinkerton shrewdly realizes that she can use Becky to teach the other girls, thus saving herself the expense of a music-master. This is Becky's first lesson in the exploitation of the artist but not her last.

Throughout *Vanity Fair* Becky skillfully changes her music to suit the needs of her situation, and she successfully uses her talent to rise in society. At the Sedley's she plays the sentimental ballads of her day:

> Rebecca sang far better than her friend . . . and exerted herself to the utmost . . . She sang a French song . . . and then a number of those simple ballads which were the fashion forty years ago, and in which British tars, our King, poor Susan, blue-eyed Mary, and the like, were the principal themes. They are not, it is said, very brilliant, in a musical point of view, but contain numberless good-natured, simple appeals to the affections, which people understand better than the milk-and-water *lagrima, sospiri,* and *felicita* of the eternal Donizettian music with which we are favoured nowadays. (iv)

This passage echoes a scene in Fielding's *Tom Jones* where Sophia Western reluctantly pleases her father by playing tunes such as "Old Sir Simon the King, Saint George he was for England, Bobbing Joan, and some others" (*Tom Jones*, IV, v). Becky, however, performs willingly, as she is aware of her own power. She captivates the glittery, immoral Lord Steyne by singing "little French songs in such a charming, thrilling voice" (xxxvii), but for Steyne's wife, who grew up in a convent, she sings "religious songs of Mozart, which had been early favourites of Lady Steyne . . . with such sweetness and tenderness that the lady lingering round the piano, sat down by its side, and listened until the tears rolled down her eyes" (lxix). Becky sings Handel and Haydn to the respectable Pitt Grawleys, quadrilles to the dissolute baronet, and hymns for the aging Lady Crawley. As Thackeray later wrote, musical talent and appreciation provide no reliable index to character, as "the very greatest scamps like pretty songs, and are welted by them; so are honest people" (*The Newcomes*, I, i).

In *Men, Women and Pianos* Loesser oversimplifies Thackeray by claiming that he "connects Becky's pianistic talent with her green eyes, her half-French descent, and her disreputable artist parents . . . her guile and her 'immorality' are thereby all the more plausible . . . Amelia too plays the piano, but she could not be permitted to compromise her position as heroine by playing it really well."[12] For Thackeray, though perhaps not for his Victorian readers, *both* Amelia and Becky compromise their "position as heroines" by misusing music. Becky's skillful use of music is only the successful version of Amelia's attempts to woo George with waltzes, Glorvina O'Dowd's efforts to catch Dobbin by singing "Irish melodies at him unceasingly" (xliii), Miss Swartz's and the Misses Osbornes' pitiable attempts to interest men by performing "some of the loudest and most brilliant new pieces of their repertoire" (xxi), and the Misses Bute Crawleys' "power of rattling sonatas in the Herz manner" for the edification of any eligible men (xii). None are admirable.

Becky learns quickly, beginning with Miss Pinkerton's attempt to use her as cheap labor, that the artist in Victorian society must fight back. Mrs. Pinkerton discriminates against Becky because her father was a painter and her mother a French opera-girl. Becky's letter to Amelia after her appointment as governess to the Crawleys indicates an awareness of her own position: "Mrs. Bute has all of a sudden taken a great fancy to me. 'My dear Miss Sharp,' she says, 'why not bring your girls to the Rectory? - their cousins will be so happy to see them.' 'I know what she means. Signor Clementi did not teach us the piano for nothing; at which price Mrs. Bute hopes to get a professor for her children" (xi).

The wealthy, vulgar Mr. Osborne, whose house contains a "great carved-legged leather-cased grand piano," contemptuously ridicules a man for speaking to a "damn fiddler - a fellar I despise" at a party, a sign of poor breeding (xlii). Becky counters this contempt of artists by treating the artists at her own parties with cordiality and respect, but Thackeray cynically implies that one of her motives is to ensure she has good entertainers for her parties and cheap musical instruction for herself:

> "Hush! silence! there is Pasta beginning to sing." Becky always made a point of being conspicuously polite to the professional ladies and gentlemen who attended at these aristocratic parties - of following them into the corners where they sat in silence, and shaking hands with them, and smiling in the view of all persons. She was an artist herself, as she said very truly: there was a frankness and humility in the manner in which she acknowledged her origin, which provoked, or disarmed, or amused lookers on, as the case might be . . . Becky went her own way, and so fascinated the professional personages, that they would leave their sore-throats in order to sing at her parties, and give her lessons for nothing. (li)

Like Mrs. Bute's sudden friendship for Becky, Becky's politeness to the professional musicians is hypocritical and affected. Even artists become exploiters of other artists in the money-grubbing world of Vanity Fair.

Thackeray continues his expose of England's amusicality in *The Newcomes* (1853-5), subtitled "Memoirs of a Most Respectable Family." Although the narrator of *The Newcomes* claims to be a cynic (*The Newcomes*, I, v), Thackeray's tone in this late novel becomes increasingly nostalgic, his defense of art more direct and impassioned.

The Newcomes narrates the fortunes and misfortunes of Clive Newcome, a Colonel's son who pursues a career as a painter despite strong opposition. Thackeray reintroduces the varying types of musicians he created in his earlier works and uses discussions of both music and painting to protest Victorian attitudes towards art.

Young women seek to ensnare Clive and his simple-minded father through their musical charms. Miss Billing tries to woo the colonel, but "she played her most brilliant sonatas and variations in vain" (I, v). Rosey Mackenzie, however, triumphantly secures Clive as husband by displaying her musical talent. Scheming Mrs. Mackenzie makes Rosey practice her piano by subjecting her to "prodigious vehemence of language" and hard slaps every time she plays incorrectly. Like Amelia Sedley, Rosey sings ballads in a "sweet fresh artless voice" and has a little store of songs - five to be exact (I, xxiii). Her singing charms Clive but not the more cynical narrator:

> Most persons . . . were pleased with the pretty little Rosey. She sang charmingly now, and looked so while singing. If her mother would but have omitted that chorus, which she cackled perseveringly behind her daughter's pretty back: about Rosey's angelic temper; about the compliments Signor Folonini paid her . . . but for these constant remarks of Mrs. Mack's, I am sure no one would have been better pleased with Miss Rosey's singing and behaviour than myself. (II, xviii)

Thackeray treats the sweet, weak Rosey with less ambiguity that he did Amelia Sedley. Just as Lady Middleton in Austen's *Sense and Sensibility* gives up her piano-playing following her marriage, so Rosey's five songs cease to be heard after her marriage to Clive, the end of her music having been attained. Rosey's lack of talent, vision, and intelligence brings Clive no joy: "They were not made to mate with one another" (II, xxv). Clive soon learns the folly of his belief that "To be beautiful is enough. If a woman can do that: who shall demand more from her?" (I, xxv).

In contrast to Rosey, Ethel Newcome has intelligence and independence; Thackeray implies that she and Clive are happily united following Rosey's convenient demise at the close of the novel. Ethel lacks musical accomplishment but, after her rejection of worldly ambition and social snobbery, teaches herself to play "so as to be able to soothe herself and to charm and delight" her brother's orphaned children (II, xxiv). Ethel's concept of the arts, however, goes no further because she considers professional artists beneath her. She writes to Colonel Newcome, "your son might look higher than to be an artist. It is . . . a fall for him. An artist, an organist, a pianist, all these are very good people, but you know not *de notre monde*" (I, xxvii).

Ethel observes that "there never were, since the world began, people so unblushingly sorkid! . . . Will there be no day when this mammon-worship will cease among us?" (I, xxxii); Clive adds that the world seems "so false, and base, and hollow" (II, xi). Their pessimistic vision of Victorian society is borne out by the many characters in *The Newcomes* who treat the arts, and life itself, with crass materialism and hypocrisy. Wine-merchant Mr. Sherrick, for instance, notes of his wife's musical performances, "you can calculate how the music draws" (II,v).

Snobbish Ann Newcome and her sister-in-law use musical parties to advance in society. The Newcome ladies perhaps provided Meredith with the models for the Pole sisters of *Sandra Belloni*, published a decade later than *The Newcomes*. Like the Pole sisters, *Mrs. Newcome* is a merchant's daughter who unconvincingly claims she will "seek to be *no more*" (I, viii). Lady Ann Newcome professes to "reverence genius and talent" because she knows that musicians at her parties will help attract members of London's cultured elite. Ann Newcome hires foreign musicians while her sister-in-law chauvinistically sticks with English music: "Once or twice in a year Lady Ann Newcome opened her salons for a concert and a ball, at both of which the whole street was crowded with carriages, and all the great world, and some of the small, were present. Mrs. Newcome had her ball too, and her concert of English music in opposition to the Italian singers of her sister-in-law. The music of her country, Mrs. Newcome said, was good enough for *her*" (I, v). Both are "uncommonly sentimental" (I, x).

Ethel Newcome's attempt to discourage Clive from becoming a painter or any other type of artist reflects the attitudes of many. Clergyman Mr. Honeyman, though a musical amateur, exclaims to Clive, "You surely cannot think of being a professional artist" (I, xi), and Lady Kew observes of a musician, "when he had given up singing and had made his fortune, no doubt he can go back into the world again" (I, xxxii). Colonel Newcome defends his son's artistic profession by claiming not to share the views of Lord Chesterfield and Dr. Johnson: "If he were to take a fancy on the fiddle - actually on the fiddle - I shouldn't object" (I, xi). But even the Colonel hopes his son's artistic interests soon give way to more serious employment (I, xxvii).

Clive's dissolute bohemian life and mediocrity as a painter seem to support the others' objections. He is, Thackeray notes, no Beethoven, and "his genius is not gloomy, solitary, gigantic, shining alone" (II, i). Not only is Clive no romantic artist, but his surroundings are hardly the sort to inspire artistic inspiration: Thackeray parodies Keats (see Chapter I) by noting, "At the end of the lime-tree avenue is a broken-nosed damp Faun, with a marble panpipe, who pipes to the spirit ditties which I believe never had any tune" (II, ix).

Thackeray departs from his cynical stance when he describes the old pianist Miss Cann and the gifted, musically sensitive painter J.J. Ridley. Accompanied by two canaries, Miss Cann plays Handel and Haydn with sincerity and skill, providing the sickly Ridley with visions of transcendent beauty:

> Old and weazened as that piano is, feeble and cracked as is her voice, it is wonderful what a pleasant concert she can give in that parlour of a Saturday evening . . . to a lad, who listens with all his soul, with tears sometimes in his great eyes, with crowding fancies filling his brain and throbbing at his heart, as the artist plies her humble instrument. She plays old music of Handel and Haydn, and the little chamber anon swells into a cathedral, and he who listens beholds altars lighted, priests ministering, fair children swinging censers, great oval windows gleaming in sunset. . . the heart beats with happiness, and kindness, and pleasure. Piano, piannissimo! the city is hushed.
> All these delights and sights, and joys and glories, these thrills of sympathy, movements of unknown longing, and visions of beauty, a young sickly lad of eighteen enjoys in a little dark room where. . . a little old woman is playing under a gas lamp on the jingling keys of an old piano. (I, xi)

Music stimulates Ridley's visual imagination and provides inspiration for his painting. Ridley's artistic temperament sets him apart from the others: "0 enchanting boon of Nature, which reveals to the possessor the hidden spirits of beauty round about him! spirits which the strongest and most gifted masters compel into painting or song. To others it is granted but to have fleeting glimpses of that fair Art-world; and tempted by ambition, or barred by faint-heartedness, or driven by necessity, to turn away thence to the vulgar life-track, and the light of common day" (I, xi). Later Thackeray adds, "Art is truth: and truth is religion; and its study and practice a daily work of pious duty. What are the world's struggles, brawls, successes, to that calm recluse pursuing his calling?" (II, xxvi).

Colonel Newcome, as well as Miss Cann and Ridley, genuinely appreciates beautiful music, particularly the songs and singers of the past. Rejecting Mrs. Newcome's concerts "with all the Squallinis," Colonel Newcome prefers "quaint and charming old songs." He sings the ballad "Wapping Old Stairs" (a ballad also sung by Amelia Sedley in *Vanity Fair*) with "heart and soul" and with all the "flourishes and roulades in the old Incledon manner, which has pretty nearly passed away" (I, i). Newcome sings with sweetness and sincerity. Dickens could write with unabashed sentimentalism of Florence singing to her infant brother or Agnes playing sweet old melodies on the piano; Meredith could write glowingly of the vibrant romantic artist. Thackeray shares their attraction to such scenes but remains more detached. Even Thackeray's pictures of the harmonious old Colonel or of Ridley's glorious artistic life are laden with irony. The Colonel's sentimentalism and nostalgic admiration for things of the past make him weak and easily deluded, Miss Cann is aging and ineffectual, and Ridley is sickly and "almost deformed" (I, xi). Retreat from "this vulgar life-track, and the light of common day" has its dangers. Although other Victorian novelists, particularly those later in the century, would find great consolation in the vision of an earlier, more musical age, Thackeray senses that nostalgia is just another form of sentimentalism.

If Thackeray is using the musician as metaphor for the artist, then the conclusion one must reach in *Book of Snobs*, *Ravenswing*, *Vanity Fair*, and *The Newcomes* is that art in Victorian England is at its nadir. Those who have skill quickly become wise to the ways of a snobbish, scheming public and lose their artistic integrity and spontaneity; those without skill subject their listeners to amateurish renditions of the noisy "Battle of Prague," maudlin popular ballads, and tedious pieces designed for technical display. Thackeray demonstrates in *Vanity Fair* that only by leaving England can one hear music of quality - the beautiful performance of *Don Juan* in Germany and of *Fidelio* in Belgium - for in England truly exquisite music, or art, had been silenced by the public's ignorance, snobbery, misplaced morality, xenophobia, and worldliness. In *The Newcomes* Thackeray suggests that inspired music and musicians are rapidly becoming things of the past.

Chapter V: Notes

1   J. A. Watson, "Thackeray and Music," *The Monthly Musical Record*, 82 (March-April, 1952), 60.

2   Grout, p. 566.

3   *The Times*, May 4, 1847, in Dodds, p. 305.

4   Dodds, p. 306.

5   Thackeray, Letter to G. H. Lewes (in 'Reminiscences of Weimar and Goethe'), cited in Watson, p. 60.

6   Arthur Loesser, *Men, Women and Pianos* (N.Y.: Simon and Schuster, 1954), p. 276.

Chapter VI

Nostalgia: The Old-fashioned Musician

from Peacock to Hardy

In 1899 at the first meeting of the English Folk-song Society, Sir Hubert Parry remarked, "In these days of high-pressure and commercialism . . . the tendency is to become cynical; and the best remedy is to revive a belief in one's fellow creatures. And nothing has such a curious way of doing this as folk-music."[1] W.R. Greg complained in his essay on "Life at High Pressure," 1875, that "the most salient characteristic of life in the latter portion of the nineteenth century is its SPEED."[2] Victorian novelists similarly were appalled by the tawdriness of English life and staggered by the rapidity of growth and change. As I discussed in Chapters III, IV, and V, some found escape by embracing exotic cultures or by adopting a cynical mask, but for others the answer was a nostalgic return to the values and tastes of the past.

While recognizing the extraordinary advances made in science and technology, novelists such as Thomas Love Peacock (1785-1866), Anthony Trollope (1815-82), Samuel Butler (1835-1902), and Thomas Hardy (1840-1928) feared there had been a corresponding decline in the quality of art and morality. Nowhere is this feeling of artistic inferiority more evident than in their nostalgic portrayal of the musician. Beset by money-grubbing businessmen, artistic hypocrites, and the noise of clanking steam-engines, the guileless musician symbolized a vanishing age of harmony and peace. While admiring their fictional musicians, Victorian novelists recognized that they would be incongruous and ineffectual in modern British society; nostalgia turns to irony as novelists towards the end of the century narrate the unhappy fate of the musician.

Thackeray writes in *The Newcomes*, "There was once a time when the sun used to shine brighter than it appears to do in this latter half of the nineteenth century; when the zest of life was certainly keener . . . when one could go to the play and see Braham in 'Fra Diavolo', and end the frolic evening by partaking of supper and a song at the 'Cave of Harmony'" (*Newcomes*, I, i). Thackeray's devastating vision of a society so greedy, pretentious, and worldly that music cannot survive - Becky's voice cracks, Colonel Newcome quits singing - left novelists with a nostalgia for an age of greater beauty, simplicity, and harmony. Nostalgic elements in the novels I discussed in earlier chapters suggest the close relationship between sentimentalism, cynicism, and nostalgia: Rochester's singing makes him part of a "Gothic" primeval world of passion; Chevalier Seraphael's Jewishness, like that of the many other Jewish musicians in Victorian novels, connects him with the purity and mystery of a Pre-Christian religion; Emilia's heroism stems from her devotion to "classical" and "Gregorian" music (*Vittoria*, I, xxi), and Count Fosco's modern Italian music threatens to undermine the heavenly tenderness of the older Mozart. Dickens and Thackeray countered their cynical portraits of scheming musicians with nostalgic descriptions of innocent musicians: Florence and Paul Dombey are "old-fashioned" singers and Morfin plays sentimental ballads and baroque counterpoint; Thackeray's kindly Amelia, Dobbin, Mr. Sedley, Miss Cann, and Colonel Newcome all prefer older music played on old instruments. Music filled many Victorian writers with a "nostalgic ache" like that experienced by the Englishmen listening to Trilby's inspired refrains.

The novels of Thomas Love Peacock bridge the Romantic and Victorian periods and illustrate the transition from sentimentalism to nostalgia. Throughout his novels Peacock uses music metaphorically to describe the artistic and moral superiority of cultures and eras uncorrupted by modern civilization and the sordidness of industrialism. Peacock's later novels acquire an increasing tone of nostalgia as he contrasts passionate musicians with their modern replacements.

Peacock's musical criticism reveals his distaste for many modern compositions, his abhorrence of contemporary performance practices, and his nostalgic admiration for the music and composers of the past. As it later would for Wilkie Collins, Mozart's music symbolized for Peacock art of beauty and simplicity: Peacock writes, "There is nothing perfect in the world except Mozart's music."[3] Peacock admires Italian operatic works because of their "classical simplicity" reminiscent "of the Athenian stage," and also praises the passion of Beethoven's music. In contrast, he finds modern English music little more than "egregious rigamarol" containing excessive ornamentation and "musical trickery." Peacock complains of English musical ignorance: he mocks the *Times* critic who discussed the whole of Rossini's *Tancredi* even though just the first act was performed, and he censures the "Mohawk management" of King's Theatre for going to work on operas "as a cook does with a chicken; cuts off the head, plucks off its tail, takes out its interior, flattens its breast, and trusses it up into the smallest possible compass." Peacock laments that people have lost their taste for the harpsichord and other old instruments.

Peacock's novels illustrate many of the ideas contained in his music criticism. The musicians of Peacock's early novels are mythical figures of romance set apart from the mechanism of "civilized" society. In *Melincourt* (1817) Peacock introduces the natural musician, Sir Oran Haut-ton, a savage caught in the woods of Angola. Peacock writes sentimentally of Oran Haut-ton who, as his name suggests, is "a specimen of the natural and original man" and can play "wild and singular" melodies on the flute despite his lack of technical training or understanding (*Melincourt*, vi). *The Misfortunes of Elphin* (1829) takes place in a time when "They had no steam-engines, with fires as eternal as those of the nether world, wherein the squalid many, from infancy to age, might be turned into component portions of machinery for the benefit of the purple-faced few" (*Misfortunes*, v). In this pre-industrial age, one finds apocalyptic bards such as the harp-player Taliesin, an Orpheus figure whose music strikes his hearers like magic

Peacock's heroines are naturally musical, play with feeling as well as skill, and are uncorrupted by the modern style and theory of music. As Mr. Forester notes of the ideal woman, "She should be musical, but she should have music in her soul as well as her fingers: her voice and her touch should have no one point in common with that mechanical squalling and jingling which are commonly dignified with the insulted name of music: they should be modes of the harmony of her mind" (*Melincourt*, xi). Peacock uses Miss Marionetta in *Nightmare Abbey* (1818) to illustrate that England turns its women into "mere musical dolls" (*Nightmare Abbey*, i).

The modern musician fares poorly in Peacock's novels. In *Gryll Grange* (1860), the spokesman for the new music has the appropriately unprepossessing name of Mr. Minim. As Mr. Forester noted in *Melincourt* (ch. xvi), "man under the influence of civilization has fearfully diminished in size and deteriorated in strength. "Minim, an amateur composer of music for the comedy, likes light Italian operatic music and brilliant technical showpieces. In contrast, the more likable Mr. Falconer and Dr. Opimian argue for the beauty of older music: simple ballads, Greek monody, and the music of Romantic composers. The heated musical debate in *Gryll Grange* reveals Peacock's sympathy with the nostalgic sentiments of Falconer and Opimian:

Mr. Falconer: I will say, that to my taste a simple accompaniment, in strict subordination to the melody, is far more agreeable than that Niagara of sound under which it is now the fashion to bury it . . .
Mr. Minim: In that case, you would prefer a song sung with a simple pianoforte accompaniment to the same song on the Italian stage.
Mr. Falconer: A song sung with feeling and expression is good, however accompanied. Otherwise, the pianoforte is not much to my mind. . .
Dr. Opimian: I like the old organ-music such as it was, when there were no keys but C and F, and every note responded to a syllable . . . Who cares to hear sacred music on the piano?
Mr. Minim: Yet I must say that there is a great charm in that brilliancy of execution which is an exclusively modern and very modern accomplishment.
Mr. Falconer: . . .To me music has no charm without expression. (*Gryll Grange*, xiv)

For Opimian and Falconer, as for Peacock, the piano with its iron frame and technological advancements symbolizes the newer taste in music.

To counter modern music, Mr. Falconer employs seven nymphs to sing Beethoven and Mozart and to play on harps. Falconer praises the great delicacy of Greek music: "Their scales were in true intervals; they had really major and minor tones; we have neither, but a confusion of both. They had both sharps and flats: we have neither, but a mere set of semitones which serve for both. In their enharmonic scale the fineness of their ear perceived distinctions, which are lost in the coarseness of ours" (*Gryll Grange*, xiv). Pauline Salz in "Peacock's Use of Music in His Novels" notes that Peacock shared this dislike of the rigidity and mechanism of the eighteenth century tempered scale and favored the improvisatory vocal melodies of ancient Greece.[4]

A musical performance by "one of the young visitors" in *Gryll Grange* further illustrates the distasteful modern style, for it is "a brilliant symphony . . . in which runs and crossings of demisemiquavers in *tempo prestissimo* occupied the principal share . . . a splendid piece of legerdemain; but it expresses nothing" (xv). The speed of the piece and its lack of expression echo the bustle and pragmatism of the modern age. Spokesmen of this new age, such as Minim and the utilitarian Mr.

Macborrowdale, use prosaic language and regard music as nothing more than a technical craft capable of providing amusement. Macborrowdale notes dispassionately, "If devotion is good, if cheerfulness is good, and if music promotes each of them in proper turn and place, music is useful" (xiv).

Mr. Falconer remarks, "there is a beauty and an appeal to the heart in ballads which will never lose its effect except on those with whom the pretence of fashion overpowers the feeling of Nature" (*Gryll Grange*, xv). For Peacock, musicians who play the passionate music of Beethoven's *Fidelio*, pure intervals and modes of ancient Greek melodies, and tuneful old ballads symbolize an art and age of greater power, directness, and beauty. Like the Victorian businessman George Edmund Street, who insisted that his employees speak to each other in Gregorian chants, Peacock clings to ancient music as an escape from modern culture; Peacock's descriptions of musicians from the romantic past seem affected.

While sharing Peacock's attraction to older music, Anthony Trollope recognized that attempts to ward off the invasion of modern sounds were futile. Trollope's novels treat the musician with a mixture of nostalgic admiration and ironic contempt.

The Warden (1855) and *Barchester Towers* (1857) describe the declining fortunes of the musical clergyman, Mr. Harding. Harding represents a passing age pushed aside by the spirit of reform.

The Warden introduces Mr. Harding as a mild-mannered cellist with "delicately white" hands who lacks industriousness and verve:

> Mr. Harding's warmest admirers cannot say that he was ever an industrious man; the circumstances of his life have not called on him to be so; and yet he can hardly be called an idler. Since his appointment to his precentorship, he has published with all possible additions of vellum, typography, and gilding, a collection of our ancient church music with some correct dissertations on Purcell, Crohe, and Nares. He has greatly improved the choir of Barchester, which, under his dominion, now rivals that of any cathedral in England. He has taken something more than his fair share in the cathedral services, and has played the violoncello daily to such audiences as he could collect or, *faute de mieux*, to no audience at all. (*Warden*, i)

Trollope regards Harding's love of old music ambivalently: it stems from his kindly spirit and appreciation of beauty but also reveals his weakness and fondness for leisure. Chapter III of *The Wardenn* shows the eager reformer John Bold impatiently waiting for Harding to conclude his musical performance:

> As he raised the latch he heard the notes of Mr. Harding's violoncello from the far end of the gardens and, advancing before the house and across the lawn, he found him playing: and not without an audience. The musician was seated in a garden-chair just within the summer-house so as to allow the violoncello which he held between his knees to rest upon the dry stone flooring: before him stood a rough music desk, on which was open a page of that dear sacred book, that much-loved volume of church music, which had cost so many guineas; and around sat, and lay, and stood, and leaned, ten of the twelve old men who dwelt with him beneath old John Hiram's roof. The two reformers were not there-- I will not say that in their hearts they were conscious of any wrong done or to be done to their mild Warden, but latterly they had kept aloof from him, and his music was no longer to their taste.
>
> It was amusing to see the positions, and eager listening faces of these well-to-do old men. I will not say that they all appreciated the music which they heard, but they were intent in appearing to do so . . . It gladdened the precentor's heart to think that the old bedesmen whom he loved so well, admired the strains which were to him so full of almost ecstatic joy; and he used to boast that such was the air of the hospital, as to make it a precinct specially fit for the worship of St. Cecilia.

Bold's impatience and the absence of the two reformers have symbolic overtones, as Trollope shows that in a society devoted to social change and rapid progress, there is little time to savor the beauty of art. Harding's recourse to his music is indeed self-indulgent, for many of his audience do not appreciate his selections. His ornate edition of ancient church music places him in debt to his son-in-law, and he uses his music as an excuse not to talk or work. Trollope adds in *Barchester Towers* (ch. ii), "If Mr. Harding was vain on any subject, it was on that of music."

Like Dickens' cellist Morfin, who retreats to his music to escape the pressures of the business world, Trollope's Harding finds music a way of keeping his life "so free from strife" (*Warden*, v). Throughout *The Warden* and *Barchester Towers* Harding plays on an imaginary cello whenever he faces pressures, decisions, or arguments he would like to avoid. When his impetuous son-in-law Grantley said in his "brazen trumpet" of a voice, "We must be doing something, you know," and urges Harding to fight those attacking his right to a salary, Harding's only response is to finger his cello:

> The warden still looked mutely in his face, making the slightest possible passes with an imaginary fiddle bow, and stopping, as he did so, sundry imaginary strings with the fingers of his other hand. 'Twas his constant consolation in conversational troubles. While these vexed him sorely, the passes would be short and slow, and the upper hand would not be seen to work; nay the strings on which it operated would sometimes be concealed in the musician's pocket, and the instrument on which he played would be beneath his chair; but as his spirit warmed to the subject, --as his trusting heart, looking to the bottom of that which vexed him would see its clear way out, --he would rise to a higher melody, sweep the unseen strings with a bolder band, and swiftly fingering the chords from his neck down along his waistcoat, and up again to his very ear, create an ecstatic strain of perfect music, audible to himself and to St. Cecilia, and not without effect. (*Warden*, v)

Harding plays a dirge when he considers the prospect of a reduced income, plays melancholy music at his interview with Sir Abraham Haphazard, and in *Barchester Towers* plays a slow tune when convinced of his daughter's marriage to the odious Slope: in all cases, he uses the imaginary music to avoid action.

As Bold and the reformers force the reluctant Harding to evaluate his position, he looks back nostalgically at the quieter, trouble-free days when he could enjoy his sweet music:

> He, that shy retiring man, who had so comforted himself in the hidden obscurity of his lot, who had so enjoyed the unassuming warmth of his own little corner, he was now to be dragged forth into the glaring day, and gibbeted before ferocious multitudes . . . that friend of friends, that choice ally that had never deserted him, that violoncello of his--ah, how happy he had been! but it was over now; his easy days and absence of work had been the crime which brought on him his tribulation . . . He could never again lift up his voice boldly as he had hitherto done among his brethren, for he felt that he was disgraced; and he feared even to touch his bow, for he knew how grievous a sound of wailing, how piteous a lamentation, it would produce. (*Warden*, x)

Harding searches for a way to escape active conflict and again finds the answer in a life of music: "a gleam of joy shot across his brow as this idea of escape again presented itself . . . Ah, what happiness might be there in the distance, with Eleanor and him in some small cottage; and nothing left of their former grandeur but their music! Yes, they would walk forth with their music books, and their instruments, and shaking the dust from off their feet as they went, leave the ungrateful place" (*Warden*, x). As in the picture of Harding playing in the garden, the image here is of an Edenic world untouched by modern strife and troublesome questionings.

Mr. Slope in *Barchester Towers* fights against Harding's musicianship and, like the reformers in *The Warden*, represents an age of change. Before Slope's arrival, services at Barchester were noted for quality of the music:

> The service was certainly very well performed. Such was always the case at Barchester, as the musical education of the choir had been good and the voices had been carefully selected. The psalms were beautifully chanted; the *Te Deum* was magnificently sung; and the litany was given in a manner which is still to be found at Barchester, but, if my taste is correct, is to be found nowhere else. The litany in Barchester cathedral has long been the special task to which Mr. Harding's skill and voice have been devoted. (*Barchester Towers*, vi)

The beauty of Barchester's music contrasts with the matter-of-fact service conducted at London's Westminster Abbey where, in keeping with modern efficiency, "there was no music, and time was not unnecessarily lost in the chanting" (*Warden*, xv). After hearing the Barchester service, the puritanical Mr. Slope denounces the practice of chanting and calls for innovation:

> . . . from thence he came round to the undue preponderance which, he asserted, music had over meaning in the beautiful service they had just heard. He was aware, he said, that the practices of our ancestors could not be abandoned at a moment's notice; the feelings of the aged would be outraged and the minds of respectable men would be shocked. There were many, he was aware, of not sufficient calibre of thought to perceive, of not sufficient education to know, that a mode of service which was effective when outward ceremonies were of more moment than inward feelings had become all but barbarous at a time when inward conviction was everything, when each word of the minister's lips should fall intelligibly into the listener's heart. Formerly the religion of the multitude had been an affair of the imagination: now, in these latter days, it had become necessary that a Christian should have a reason for his faith--should not only believe but digest--not only hear, but understand. The words of our morning service, how beautiful, how apposite, how intelligible they were, when read with simple and distinct decorum! But how much of the meaning of the words was lost when they were produced with all the meretricious charms of melody! &c. &c. (*Barchester Towers*, vi)

Harding meekly concedes, "That chanting of his! Perhaps, in truth, the time for it was gone by" (*Barchester Towers*, xii). Trollope notes that there is truth in Slope's remark, for "it certainly was the fact that people went to the cathedral to hear the music, &c. &c.," but he further adds, "I myself do not like Mr. Slope" (*Barchester Towers*, vii, viii). Slope's "reformed" religion is without poetry and grace; his approach, that of "casting away the useless rubbish of past centuries" (*Barchester Towers*, xii), threatens to destroy any lasting works of beauty.

Trollope refuses to make his musician Harding into a hero: he observes, "Mr. Harding was by no means a perfect character. In his indecision, his weakness, his proneness to be led by others, his want of self-confidence, he was very far from being perfect" (*Barchester Towers*, xviii). Yet there is a great sense of loss at the end of *Barchester Towers* when a "newfashioned" instrument replaces Harding's old cello, and one senses Trollope's nostalgia for the age Harding represents. Archdeacon Grantley's gifts at the close of the novel typify the musical taste of the Victorian era. To the Arabins, he presents "a magnificent piano by Erard"; Erard pianos were the first to employ the complicated "double escapement" mechanism which is the basis of all modern piano actions allowing pianists to play more rapidly and with a louder tone. Like the gaudy grand piano owned by Thackeray's Mr. Osborne, Grantley's ostentatious Erard reflects a society interested in display and technology. Grantley's gift to Harding similarly suggests his materialism: "On Mr. Harding he bestowed a magnificent violoncello with all the newfashioned arrangements and expensive additions, which on account of these novelties that gentleman could never use with satisfaction to his audience or pleasure to himself" (*Barchester Towers*, liii).

During the course of *The Warden* and *Barchester Towers* Harding's music thus fades into the past. Attacked as an idler by those crying for reform and viewed by Mr. Slope as an impediment to worship, Mr. Harding retreats to enjoy his cello in solitude, but Grantley's "magnificent" gift deprives him of the sweeter sounds of his older instrument. For Trollope the musician is no longer a glorious romantic hero but rather an impotent, child-like old man who symbolizes both the beauty and the shortcomings of the past.

Samuel Butler observes in his *Notebooks* (ch. viii), "Unless a man writes in the exotic style of Brahms, Wagner, Dvorak, and I know not what other Slav, Czech, Teuton, or Hebrew the critics are sure to accuse him of being an anachronism. The

Teuton, or Hebrew the critics are sure to accuse him of being an anachronism. The only man in England who is permitted to write in a style which is in the main of home growth is the Irish Jew, Sir Arthur Sullivan. If we may go to a foreign style why may we not go to one of an earlier period?" Rather than celebrating the music of Judaism or of foreign cultures, as Disraeli, Meredith, and others did, Butler champions the compositions of "an earlier period." Like Trollope, Butler treats the musician with a mixture of nostalgia and irony.

What Mozart was to Peacock, Handel was to Butler. "As a boy," Butler writes, "I always worshipped Handel" (*Notebooks*, viii). In his *Notebooks* Butler also expresses his dislike of much foreign music: "If Bach wriggles, Wagner writhes," he complains, and he finds works by Beethoven and Mozart boring and tedious (*Notebooks*, viii). Butler's admiration of Handel perhaps reflects the growth of English nationalism. Although not born in England, Handel lived there long enough for many Englishmen to claim him as their own. Victorian novelists who wished to praise the art of their own country rather than the works of foreigners found the only answer was to turn to England's glorious past: the immortal works of Shakespeare, the mighty oratorios of Handel.

Although Butler admits that his acquaintance with music is "very limited and superficial" (*Notebooks*, viii), he uses music extensively in his novels as a source of metaphor. Butler's nostalgia finds its fullest expression in *The Way of All Flesh*, written 1872-84.

Butler's descriptions of unmusical English men and women show his indebtedness to Thackeray and Austen. Butler employs music to illustrate Theobald and Christina Pontifex's pretentiousness and shallowness. Christina wins Theobald by displaying her musical "talent":

> What her voice wanted in range and power was made up in the feeling with which she sang. She had transposed "Angels ever bright and fair" into a lower key, so as to make it suit her voice, thus proving, as her mamma said, that she had a thorough knowledge of the laws of harmony; not only did she do this, but at every pause she added an embellishment of arpeggios from one end to the other of the keyboard, on a principle which her governess had taught her; she thus added life and interest to an air which everyone--so she said--must feel to be rather heavy in the form in which Handel left it. (*Way of All Flesh*, xi)

Unmusical Theobald regards fondness for music as a dangerous tendency and whistles out of tune (xxiii, lxxxiii).

In contrast to his parents, Ernest Pontifex has an instinctive love and understanding of music. Like his grandfather, old Mr. Pontifex, Ernest cherishes Handel's organ music. Ernest defends his musical taste in a conversation with Miss Skinner:

> "And are you still as fond of music as ever, Mr. Pontifex?" said Miss Skinner to Ernest during the course of lunch.
> "Of some kinds of music yes, Miss Skinner, but you know I never did like modern music."
> "Isn't that rather dreadful? --Don't you think you rather" --she was going to have added, "ought to?" but she left it unsaid, feeling doubtless that she had sufficiently conveyed her meaning.
> "I would like modern music, if I could; I have been trying all my life to like it, but I succeed less and less the older I grow."
> "And pray, where do you consider modern music to begin?"
> "With Sebastian Bach."
> "And don't you like Beethoven?"
> "No; I used to think I did, when I was younger, but I know now that I never really liked him." (ch. lxxxvi)

For Butler, Ernest's rejection of modern music distinguishes him from others and reflects his greater sensitivity and purity.

Butler's vision in *The Way of All Flesh* of older musicians doomed to obsolescence reveals his longing for a simpler time:

> Gone now are the clarinet, the violoncello and the trombone, wild minstrelsy as of the doleful creatures in Ezekiel, discordant, but infinitely pathetic. Gone is that scarebabe stentor, that bellowing bull of Bashan, the village blacksmith, gone is the melodious carpenter, gone the brawny shepherd with the red hair, who roared more lustily than all, until they came to the words, "Shepherds, with your flocks abiding," when modesty covered him with confusion, and compelled him to be silent, as though his own health were being drunk. They were doomed. . . When I was last in Batersby church there was a harmonium played by a sweet-looking girl with a choir of school children around her, and they chanted the canticles to the most correct of chants, and they sang Hymns

> Ancient and Modern; the high pews were gone, nay, the very gallery in which the old choir had sung was removed as an accursed thing ... (xiv)

The harmonium, invented in 1848, provides Butler with the ideal symbol of modern "progress." Cheap, portable, out of tune, and mechanical, the harmonium reflected an age which valued efficiency and economy more than beauty and permanence. In *The Reign of Queen Victoria: A Survey of Fifty Years of Progress* (1887), Walter Parratt writes of the harmonium, "After the piano no instrument is so extensively used as the harmonium. It is of French invention, and may be said to be new during this reign. In spite of its fatiguing and even harsh tone, the harmonium ... has a value of its own. It is inexpensive, portable ... and supplies the place of an organ in many churches and schools which could not afford money or space for a larger instrument."[5]

Butler recognizes his own nostalgia and admits his harmonious blacksmith, carpenter, and shepherd are sentimental figments of his imagination. Further, he adds irony to his description of the musically sensitive Ernest Pontifex by noting his weakness (Ernest is "unusually devoid of physical strength") and his mediocrity as a musician (xxxiv). Despite Ernest's attempts to escape contemporary English life, his remarks on music suggest his entrenchment in this culture:

> Ernest is as fond of music as ever, perhaps more so, and of late years has added musical composition to the other irons in his fire. He finds it still a little difficult, and is in constant trouble through getting into the key of C sharp after beginning in the key of C and being unable to get back again.
>
> "Getting into the key of C sharp," he said, "is like an unprotected female travelling on the Metropolitan Railway, and finding herself at Shepherd's Bush, without quite knowing where she wants to go to. How is she ever to get safe back to Clapham Junction? And Clapham Junction won't quite do either, for Clapham Junction is like the diminished seventh--susceptible of such unharmonic change, that you can resolve it into all the possible termini of music." (lxxxvi)

Butler mocks Ernest's use of railroad terminology to describe music, but he also celebrates the humor of this incongruity.

Although Butler does little more than imitate earlier novelists' satirical portraits of unmusical English men and women, his musical imagery shows originality. The parts of Mr. Badcock's back are "like the two extreme notes in the chord of the augmented sixth" (xlix); "life," Butler observes, "is like a fugue" (xlvi). Butler suggests that only by finding music in the admittedly unmusical Victorian society can sensitive Englishmen keep their sanity.

The Musicians of Thomas Hardy

To a greater extent than Peacock, Trollope, and Butler, Thomas Hardy brought musical imagery and characters into his works as metaphor for the past. Hardy shares the other authors' nostalgia, but his irony becomes far more bitter. The change in Hardy's depiction of the musician from *Under the Greenwood Tree* (1872) through *Jude the Obscure* (1895) reveals his growing pessimism and despair.

For Hardy, music provided a direct link to the past because of its connection with his own childhood. Hardy's father and grandfather, both builders, played string instruments in the gallery of their church at Stinsford, but while Hardy was an infant this orchestral group was forced to disband and give way to newer organ music. For Hardy, the good-natured group of musicians meeting to practice simple hymn tunes and carols on their old instruments stood for the past, and their extinction became a fitting metaphor for destructive change.

In addition to his veneration of old-fashioned musicians and their instruments, Hardy favored the folk ballads of pre-Industrial England to the stilted music fashionable in Victorian England. Richard Curle writes of Hardy's musical preferences, "his taste was of limited range, which apparently excluded classical and modern music, and his devotion to old-time Dorset airs was, likely enough, only one facet of his harmonious conception of the past, which embraced the scenes and events and characters of his youth and struck those nostalgic chords which were the source and inspiration of his creative powers."[6] Hardy's acquaintance J. Vera Mardon tells of Hardy's own ability to play the violin, which he preferred to call a fiddle, and his obsession with the music of England's rural past.[7] In 1871, a year before *Under the Greenwood Tree* was published, Hardy visited old people and wrote down snatches of the ballads they sang.[8]

Hardy's poems clearly reveal that he envisioned music as a symbol of the past. In "The Dead Quire," "To My Father's Violin," "A Duettist to her Pianoforte,"

"Haunting Fingers," and "Music in a Snowy Street," musicians have died and instruments lie dusty and worm-eaten in the "voiceless, crippled, corspelike state."9 Hardy writes nostalgically:

> Where once we danced, where once we sang,
>   Gentlemen,
> The floors are sunken, cobwebs hang,
> And cracks creep; worms have fed upon
> The doors, Yea, sprightlier times were then
> Than now, with harps and tabrets gone . . .
>   ("An Ancient to Ancients")

A choirmaster's request for a musical funeral service is ignored because such a service would take too much time:

> Hence, that afternoon,
> Though never knew he
> That his wish could not be
> To get through it faster
> They buried the master
> Without any tune.
>   ("The Choirmaster's Burial")

Shelly's skylark has become merely a "tiny pinch of priceless dust," a "little ball of feather and bone" ("Shelley's Skylark"). The death of music and musicians represents the passing of a romantic age and the coming of a time of streamlined, unimaginative efficiency.

In his novels Hardy also uses music as a metaphor for the past. Hardy's portrayal of the musician as a weak, anachronistic figure reflects his growing awareness that Victorian pragmatism and commercialism had extinguished the spirit of romanticism.

An older Hardy dismissed *Under the Greenwood Tree* (1872) as a work of his youth which reflected his age's sentimental taste, but he remained firm in his praise of the Mellstock Quire. In the Preface to the 1896 edition of *Under the Greenood Tree* Hardy comments:

> This story of the Mellstock Quire and its old established west-gallery musicians is intended to be a fairly true picture, at first

> hand, of the personages, ways, and customs which were common among such orchestral bodies in the villages of fifty or sixty years ago.
>
> One is inclined to regret the displacement of these ecclesiastical bandsman by an isolated organist (often at first a barrel-organist) or harmonium player; and despite certain advantages in point of control and accomplishment which were, no doubt, secured by installing the single artist, the change has tended to stultify the professed aims of the clergy, its direct result being to curtail and extinguish the interest of parishioners in church doings. Under the old plan, from half a dozen to ten full-grown players, in addition to the numerous more or less grown-up singers, were officially occupied with the Sunday routine, and concerned in trying their best to make it an artistic outcome of the combined musical taste of the congregation. . .
>
> The zest of these bygone instrumentalists must have been keen and staying, to take them, as it did, on foot every Sunday after a toilsome week through all weathers to the church, which often lay at a distance from their homes. They usually received so little in payment for their performances that their efforts were really a labour of love. In the parish I had in my mind when writing the present tale, the gratuities received yearly by the musician at Christmas were . . . just enough, as an old executant told me, to pay for their fiddle-strings, repairs, rosin, and music-paper (which they mostly ruled themselves). Their music in those days was all in their own manuscript, copied in the evenings after work, and their music-books were home-bound.

The rustic musicians with their home-bound books, sincere love of art, and camaraderie represent the "bygone" days of faith, fellowship, and individualism. As in *The Way of All Flesh*, the portable harmonium symbolizes the new age of machines and conformity.

Old William Dewy, chief musician of *Under the Greenwood Tree*, embodies the tastes and values of the past; his exclusion from the church service and subsequent death, alluded to in *Tess of the d'Urbervilles*, marks the passage of time. Old Dewy has "an ardent vitality" and "a warm and roughened bloom upon his face." Hardy continues, "His was a humorous and kindly nature, not unmixed with a frequent melancholy; and he had a firm religious faith" (*Under the Greenwood Tree*, I, iv). Dewy's instrument, the cello, reflects his spirituality and warm-hearted soul. As he notes himself, "nothing will spak to your heart wi' the sweetness o' the man of strings!" Dewy loves music with a rare passion: "Never such a mortal man as he for tunes. They do move his soul . . . he'd starve to death for music's sake now" (I, viii). Son Reuben Dewy adds: "Father there is a perfect figure o' wonder, in the way of being fond of music! . . . if you or I, or any man or woman of the present generation, at the time music is a-playing, was to shake your fist in father's face . . . and say, 'William, your life or your music!', he'd say, 'My life!' Now that's father's nature all over" (II, iv).

Dewy's hearty band of musicians practices diligently and strives to bring beauty to the community, but their task becomes increasingly unrewarding as they are cast aside by a utilitarian, pragmatic age which labels them "useless." On Christmas Eve the choir members go caroling with their "old brown music-books" and instruments "in faded green-baise bags" (I, vi). Their music is sincere and moving: "Then into the quiet night an ancient and time-worn hymn, embodying a quaint Christianity in words orally transmitted from father and son through several generations down to the present characters, who sang them out right earnestly" (I, iv). Despite their effort and good intentions, the choir members receive little praise from those of the newer age who regard them as mere noise-makers. Dewy's neighbors dismiss him as a child-like simpleton (I, iv), and abrasive Farmer Shiner responds to the caroling with, "Shut up, woll 'ee! Don't make your blaring row here! A feller wi' a headache enough to split his skull likes a quiet night!" (I, v).

The musicians' contributions to the church service are similarly unappreciated, and Dewy's group is pushed out in favor of the organist, Fancy Day. Tenor Micheal Mail laments, "Times have changed from the times they used to be . . . People don't care much about us now! I've been thinking we must be almost the last left in the country of the old string players? Barrel-organs, and the things next door to 'em that you blow with your foot, have come in terribly of late years." Another choir member nostalgically remembers, "Time was--long and merry ago now! --when not one of the varmits was to be heard of" (I, iv). When the group performs poorly, musician Mr. Spinks remarks with a bitterness felt only by his comrades, "Really, I think we useless ones had better march out of church, fiddles and all!" Hardy adds, "Only the initiated body of men he addressed could understand the horrible bitterness of irony that lurked under the quiet word 'useless ones', and the ghastliness of the laughter apparently so natural" (I, iv).

The new vicar Maybold, who has "no more ear than that chair," disbands the choir with the remark, "I myself, I must own, prefer organ-music to any other. I consider it most proper, and feel justified in endeavouring to introduce it" (II, iv).

Maybold's sense of propriety is sham, for he is far more interested in the looks of his female organist than in her "proper" music. The Mellstock Quire members plead for a chance to have a final performance and "not just have 'us old ancient singers to be choked off quiet at no time in particular" (II, iv). Reuben Dewy urges Maybold not to injure his father's pride by casting him aside without any ceremony; although Maybold agrees to the choir members' demand, he cannot fathom their love of music.

The new organ-player who supercedes Dewy's band has a musical exterior (her eyebrows are like "two slurs in music"), has received fine musical training in the city, and can play correctly, but her performance lacks soul (I, viii). Her name - Fancy - suggests her want of simplicity; Fancy cares more about her appearance than her music. Part IV of *Under the Greenwood Tree*, "Autumn," describes Fancy's first performance in church while the discarded musicians listen in impotent sorrow:

> The old choir, with humbled hearts, no longer took their seats in the gallery as heretofore . . . but were scattered about with their wives in different parts of the church. Having nothing to do with conducting the service for almost the first time in their lives they all felt awkward, out of place, abashed, and inconvenienced by their hands.
>
> So they stood and watched the curls of hair trailing down the back of the successful rival, and the waving of her feather as she swayed her head. After a few timid notes and uncertain touches her playing became markedly correct, and towards the end full and free. But, whether from prejudice or unbiassed judgment, the venerable body of musicians could not help thinking that the simpler notes they had been wont to bring forth were more in keeping with the simplicity of their old church than the crowded chords and interludes it was her pleasure to produce. (IV, v)

Fancy's "crowded chords" on the mechanical harmonium fit the Victorian age; Dewy and his choir are doomed to obsolescence.

Under the Greenwood Tree ends with an image wrought with irony - Hardy describes Fancy listening to the music of the nightingale, emblem of romantic love and heavenly music, but destroys this picture by noting that Fancy does not hear the bird because she is busy thinking of a secret she hopes to hide from her husband. Fancy's oblivion to the nightingale, like Maybold's indifference to the Mellstock Quire, signals the end of an age of greater romance and poetry.

Like Fancy, the vain Bathsheba in *Far from the Madding Crowd* (1894) plays skillfully and insists on new instruments. In contrast, shepherd Gabriel Oak plays an old flute with an "Arcadian sweetness" which brings joy to himself and his listeners. Like the rural musicians of *Under the Greenwood Tree*, Gabriel stands for a pastoral age of innocence; like them, too, he lacks aggressiveness and power. The final salute to Gabriel and Bathsheba comes from a group of musicians whose "hideous" music cannot equal that of their venerable forefathers:

> The rays fell upon a group of male figures gathered upon the gravel in front, who, when they saw the newly-married couple in the porch, set up a loud 'Hurrah!' and at the same moment bang again went the cannon in the background, followed by a hideous clang of music from a drum, tambourine, clarionet, serpent, hautboy, tenor-viol, and double-bass--the only remaining relics of the true and original Weatherbury band--venerable worm-eaten instruments, which had celebrated in their own persons the victories of Marlborough, under the fingers of the forefathers of those who played them now.
> (*Far from the Madding Crowd*, lvii).

As in Hardy's poem "The Dead Quire," the absence of the original choir members and their Christmas caroling symbolizes the decline of religious faith:

> The singers had followed one by one,
> Treble, and tenor, and thorough bass:
> And the worm that wasteth had begun
>   To mine their mouldering place.
>
> For two-score years, ere Christ-day light,
> Mellstock had throbbed to strains from these;
> But now there echoed on the night
>   No Christmas harmonies.

The old group of musicians, so integral to Hardy's symbolism, reappears in *Return of the Native* (1878) to celebrate the sham marriage of Damon Wildeve and Thomasin Yeobright. Old Granfer Cantle, who is "as full of notes as a bird," simple-minded Timothy Fairway, and other villagers serenade the couple, but the restless, impatient Damon dismisses them as "blundering fools" and feels "intolerably bored" by Sam's account of the late Mr. Yeobright's ability to play clarinet and bass-viol (*Return of the Native*, I, v). Hardy contrasts Damon's contempt of the musicians with Diggory's warm response to them at the end of the novel. When Diggory asks Cantle to sing the wedding song, it suggests a return to old-fashioned customs and mores.

Hardy's three early novels, *Under the Greenwood Tree*, *Far from the Madding Crowd*, and *Return of the Native*, use music straightforwardly as an index to a character's spiritual state: the Mellstock Quire, Gabriel Oak, and Grandfer Cantle and his band possess an inner goodness lacking in the vain, hurried younger generation. In the novels of the 1880's and 1890's, however, Hardy's use of music becomes more complex. Hardy treats the musicians of *The Mayor of Casterbridge* (1886), *Tess of the d'Urbervilles* (1891), and *Jude the Obscure* (1895) with greater ambiguity, and the metaphorical function of music becomes highly ironic.

At first glance, musician Donald Farfrae in *The Mayor of Casterbridge* seems a Scottish Gabriel Oak, for he sings sentimental ballads ("O Nannie") and songs of neighborly love ("Auld Lang Syne"). Farfrae's rare gift of singing entrances the citizens of Casterbridge. Elizabeth-Jane "had never heard any singing like this; and it was evident that the majority had not heard such frequently"; a glazier sadly notes, "Folks don't lift up their hearts like that in this part of the world . . . Danged if our country down here is worth singing about like that!" (*Mayor of Casterbridge*, viii). Dewy's band was out of the innocent past; Donald Farfrae comes from the virgin North. Hardy's symbolic use of music as a foil to mechanism and civilization becomes apparent during Farfrae's performance: "the singer himself grew emotional . . . Then the ventilator in the window-pane spasmodically started off for a new spin, and the pathos of Donald's song was temporarily effaced" (viii).

Unlike Gabriel Oak, however, Farfrae shrewdly uses music to gain power: his singing bewitches the susceptible Elizabeth-Jane; his "fascinating melodies" convince the townspeople that he is "cordial and impassioned" and they become his political supporters; the deposed Henchard admits of Farfrae, "it was partly by his songs that he got over me, and heaved me out," and he refrains from killing Farfrae because he is humming (xxxiii). Farfrae shows as much interest in the horse-drill as he does in his old-fashioned singing. Although Farfrae's music, like Oak's, reflects his honesty, charity, and goodness, Hardy also presents Farfrae as a dandy and ladies' man, incapable of strong emotion and love.

Farfrae's opposite, Michael Henchard, lacks the ability to sing but has greater emotional depth. Henchard feels sincere grief for Lucetta's death, whereas Farfrae quickly recovers and remarries; similarly, Henchard responds to music more intensely. Although Henchard has no musical talent, "nothing moved Henchard like an old melody"' (xxxiii). Henchard's lack of musical ability is an ironic twist of fate, since with it he would have found comfort and grace:

> He had no interest, hobby, or desire. If he could have summoned music to his aid, his existence might even now have been borne; for with Henchard music was of regal power. The merest trumpet or organ tone was enough to move him. But hard fate had ordained that he would be unable to call up this Divine spirit in his need. (xli)

Although Hardy quotes Novalis's "Character is Fate" (xvii), he implies conversely that "Fate is Character." "Hard fate" deprives Henchard of a talent which could have brought him greater humanity and peace; instead, musical gift has been given to the light-hearted Farfrae, who views it as a superfluity.

Throughout *The Mayor of Casterbridge* Hardy uses musical imagery to augment the novel's irony and sense of human tragedy. In the opening the narrator cynically describes the "trite old song" of a "weak bird" (i): Wordsworth's celebration of nature's melodies has given way to jaded "realism." Just as the narrator's outlook corrupts the bird's singing, so Henchard's evil actions are a perversion of harmony: "the man . . . recurred to the old strain, as in a musical fantasy the instrument fetches up the original theme. 'Here--I am waiting to know about this offer of mine. The woman is no good to me. Who'll have her?'" (i). What greater incongruity than to compare the notion of wife-selling to a musical theme? Unmusical Henchard resembles "a well-braced musical instrument" and plays "second fiddle" to Farfrae (xxiii, xvi). In Chapter IV the narrator describes the river as a musical symphony:

> The wanderer in this direction, who should stand still for a few moments on a quiet night, might hear singular symphonies from these waters, as from a lampless orchestra, all playing in their sundry tones, from near and far parts of the moor. At a hole in a rotten weir they executed a recitative; under an arch they performed a metallic cymballing; and at Durnover Hold they hissed. The spot at which their instrumentation rose loudest was a place called Ten Hatches, whence during high springs there proceeded a very fugue of sounds.

Joan Grundy notes in her study of Hardy and the arts that Hardy uses musical imagery to reflect his character: "the music of Nature harmonises with or is appropriate to the feelings of the characters: that is, it is a *fitting* accompaniment. The music within the character finds its echo in, or is articulated by, the music without. This is one of the principal means by which character and environment are brought into a living, dynamic relationship."[10] This interpretation overlooks the extent of Hardy's irony, because the harmony of nature often clashes markedly with fate and thoughts of the characters. After giving us his romantic description of Ten Hatches, where the sound of the waters resembles a symphony, Hardy adds that Henchard has been looking at the melodious river as a possible death-bed.

Hardy's ironic symbolism becomes blatant when he describes Farfrae's horse-drill: "It was the new-fashioned agricultural implement called a horse-drill . . . It might have been likened to an upright musical instrument with the front gone. That was how it struck Lucetta. 'Why, it is a sort of agricultural piano,' she said" (xxiv). As Elizabeth-Jane observes, "romance . . . is done for good . . . How things change!" (xxiv). Machines are the music of the new age; musicians must become businessmen if they are to survive.

The theme of music as a business recurs in *Tess of the d'Urbervilles* and *Jude the Obscure*. Tess's mother, a remnant of an older time, sings "The Spotted Cow" and other folk ballads because of sheer enjoyment, and Tess begins her life with an innate, uncorrupted appreciation of music:

> . . . She liked to hear the chanting--such as it was--and the old Psalms, and to join in the Morning Hymn. That innate love of melody, which she had inherited from her ballad-singing mother, gave the simplest music a power over her which could well-nigh drag her heart out of her bosom at times . . . When the chants came and one of her favourites happened to be chosen among the rest-- the old double chant 'Langdon' --but she did not know what it was called, though she would much have liked to know. She thought, without exactly wording the thought, how strange and godlike was a composer's power, who from the grave could lead through sequences of emotion, which he alone had felt at first, a girl like her who had never heard of his name, and never would have a clue to his personality.
>
> (*Tess of the d'Urbervilles*, xiii)

Tess sings ballads and psalms as she walks along, but after her fall from innocence learns that music can be used not just to bring pleasure to herself: she practices her music hoping to please Angel Clare (xlix).

The dairymen in *Tess* who sing as they work are a far cry from the musical artisans of *Under the Greenwood Tree*, for they sing only because it is profitable to their business: "Songs were often resorted to in dairies hereabout as an enticement to the cows when they show signs of withholding their usual yield; and the band of milkers at this request burst into melody in purely business-like tones, it is true, and with no great spontaneity, the result, according to their own belief, was a decided improvement during the song's continuance" (xvii). To these prosaic workmen, the musicians of Mellstock are legendary figures from the past. One dairyman tells the others about the late William Dewy, "an old aged man over at Mellstock" who appeased a bull with his fiddle-playing. As Angel notes, "It's a curious story; it carries us back to medieval times, when faith was a living thing!" (xvii).

Angel Clare plays an old harp, an instrument appropriate to an "angel," and his playing sends Tess into a synaesthetic rapture in which she loses consciousness of time and space. Tess "undulated upon the thin notes of the second-hand harp, and their harmonies passed like the breezes through her, bringing tears into her eyes. The floating pollen seemed to be his notes made visible, and the dampness of the garden the weeping of the garden's sensibility. Though near nightfall, the rank-smelling weed-flowers glowed as if they would not close for intentness, and the waves of colour mixed with the waves of sound" (viii). Yet just as Hardy exposes Angel as a weak man whose moral standards are higher for others than for himself, so he belittles Angel's harp-playing as the exertions of an amateur. "Both instrument and execution were poor," Hardy writes, as Clare produces only "a very simple performance, demanding no great skill" (viii).

Jude shares Tess's susceptibility to music but, like Tess, must lose his innocence and romanticism to "the grind of stern reality" (*Jude the Obscure*, VI, ix). The image of music destroyed by change appears in the very first paragraph of *Jude the Obscure*, as school-master Phillotson moves away from the rural village and leaves his piano behind in a fuel-house. Hardy's description of Marygreen concentrates on the modern loss of poetry and music:

> The fresh harrow-lines seemed to stretch like the channellings in a piece of new corduroy, lending a meanly utilitarian air to the expanse, taking away its gradations, and depriving it of all history beyond that of the few recent months, though to every clod and stone there really attached associations enough to spare--echoes of songs from ancient harvest-days, of spoken words, and of sturdy deeds . . . All around you there seemed to be something glaring, garish, rattling, and the noises and glares hit upon the little cell called your life and shook it, and warped it. (I, ii)

Jude's first job is to scare birds away with a clacker, the first stage in the destruction of his soul's romantic music. Jude, like many Victorians, finds refuge from the noise of machines in the music of the past: he practices Gregorian chants in his room and "developed his slight skill in church-music and thorough-bass" (III, x).

Hardy skillfully uses music to illustrate Jude's disillusionment. One Easter, Jude hears the choir sing a new hymn by a Wessex composer, "a strangely emotional composition" which "moved him exceedingly." Because Jude has a surge of hope that the composer of such inspired strains will be a romantic hero, a kindred soul, he makes inquiries about him:

> "Yes," said the organist. "He is a local man. He is a professional musician at Kennetbridge--between here and Christminster. The vicar knows him. He was brought up and educated in Christminster traditions, which accounts for the quality of the piece" . . .
> As he walked humming the air on his way home, Jude fell to musing on its composer and the reasons why he composed it. What a man of sympathies he must be . . . how he would like to know that man! "He of all men would understand my difficulties," said the impulsive Jude. If there were any person in the world to choose as a confidante, this composer would be the one, for he must have suffered, and throbbed, and yearned . . . "I must speak to that man!"

Viewing himself as "a hungry soul in pursuit of a full soul," Jude arrives at the composer's house in great anticipation, but he finds the composer is hardly a Beethoven:

> "I have been singing in the choir of a little church near Melchester," he said. "And we have this week practised 'The Foot of the Cross,' which I understand, sir, that you composed?"
> "I did--a year or so ago."
> "I--like it. I think it supremely beautiful!"

> "Ah well - other people have said so too. Yes, there's money in it, if I could only see about getting it published. I have other compositions to go with it, too; I wish I could bring them out; for I haven't made a five-pound note out of any of them yet. These publishing people--they want the copyright of an obscure composer's work, such as mine is, for almost less than I would have to pay a person for making a fair manuscript copy of the score. The one you speak of I have lent to various friends about here and Melchester, and so it has got to be sung a little. But music is a poor staff to lean on--I am giving it up entirely. You must go into trade if you want to make money nowadays. The wine business is what I am thinking of. This is my forthcoming list--it is not issued yet-- but you can take one."
>
> He handed Jude an advertisement list of several pages in booklet shape, ornamentally margined with a red line, in which were set forth the various clarets, champagnes, ports, sherries, and other wines with which he purposed to initiate his new venture. It took Jude more than by surprise that that man with the soul was thus and thus, and he felt that he could not open his confidences.
>
> They talked a little longer, but constrainedly for when the musician found that Jude was a poor man his manner changed from what it had been while Jude's appearance and address deceived him as to his position and pursuits. Jude stammered out something about his feelings in wishing to congratulate the author on such an exalted composition, and took an embarrassed leave. (III, x)

Just as Thackeray's English composer Sir George Thrum regarded music as "his little trade," so Hardy's Wessex composer views music only in terms of profit: Victorian commercialism has corrupted the romantic artist. Like Count Fosco in *The Woman in White*, Hardy's composer remains separate from his composition, thus demonstrating the amorality of artistic form.

Jude and Sue share a passion for music, but this supersensitivity makes them easy victims of an unromantic age. Sue resembles "a harp which the least wind of emotion from another's heart could make to vibrate as readily as a radical stir in her own" and views the world as "a stanza or melody composed in a dream" (VI, iii; VII, iii). Jude and Sue are a Shelleyan couple linked with a time of Aeolian harps, romantic composers, and inspired melodies, but they cannot survive in modern society. Ironically, Jude catches a chill when he does the stone-work of a music-hall (V, vii). Throughout *Jude the Obscure* Hardy reiterates the theme that the music of "merry England" is no more.

Nostalgia pervades Hardy's novels, from *Under the Greenwood Tree* to *Jude the Obscure*, and music consistently functions as an emblem of the past. Hardy's sentimental attraction to the old musicians he describes in *Under the Greenwood Tree* turns to anger in his later novels, as he writes with acerbic irony of a harsh, petty, and unmusical age.

Victorian novelists' nostalgic portrayal of the musician demonstrates their strong sense of dissatisfaction with the ideals of their own time. Just as J.S. Mill had worried that the musical scale had been exhausted and that there never again could be composers as great as Beethoven or Mozart, so many Victorian novelists feared that all great art lay in the past. Victorian society had no *time* for music and poetry, no appreciation for their value. Beethoven, symbol of the romantic artist, seemed a mythical legend bearing no resemblance to actual musicians. Jude's disillusionment with the Wessex composer parallels Victorian novelists' own loss of consolation in the figure of the musician.

While writing nostalgically of England's musical past, Trollope, Butler, and Hardy occasionally sensed that such absorption in the past was stagnating, self-indulgent, and unproductive. Mr. Harding and Ernest Pontifex lack potency and discipline. Hardy's Mellstock Quire members similarly are weak: one is "bowed and bent," another is "little . . . round-shouldered," a third has "a weak lath-like form," and a fourth has "no distinctive appearance" (*Under the Greenwood Tree*, i). Henchard, Tess, and Jude are all deeply moved by the music of the past, but all three suffer dreadfuppnl fates: Henchard dies a social outcast, Tess is hanged, and Jude dies a drunken pauper. Victorian novelists suggest that one cannot cling to the beauty of the past or experience life too intensely or one will be lost in a society of rapid change, sordid practicality, and impersonal relationships.

Chapter VI: Notes

1   Reginald Nettel, *The Englishman Makes Music* (London: Dennis Dobson, 1952), p. 179.

2   W.R. Greg, "Life at High Pressure," *Literary and Social Judgments* (1875), II, 263.

3   *The Works of Thomas Love Peacock* (London: Constable, 1926), IX, 430. Subsequent quotations from Peacock's musical criticism are from this volume.

4   Pauline Salz, "Peacock's Use of Music in his Novels," *Journal of English and German Philology*, LIV (1955), p. 371.

5   Walter Parratt, "Music," in *The Reign of Queen Victoria: A Survey of Fifty Years of Progress*, ed. Thomas Humphrey Ward (London: Smith, Elder, 1887), p. 603.

6   Richard Curle, Introduction to J. Vera Mardon, "Thomas Hardy as a Musician," *Monographs on the Life of Thomas Hardy*, No. 15, ed. J. Stevens Cox (Beaminster, Dorset: Toucan Press, 1964), p. 5.

7   J. Vera Mardon, "Thomas Hardy as a Musician," pp. 9, 20.

8   F.E. Hardy, *The Life of Thomas Hardy* (London: 1963), p. 84.

9   Thomas Hardy, "Haunting Fingers: A Fantasy in a Museum of Musical Instruments," *The Collected Poems of Thomas Hardy* (N.Y.: Macmillan, 1953), p. 559. Quotations from other Hardy poems are from this collection.

10   Joan Grundy, *Hardy and the Sister Arts* (London: Macmillan, 1979), p. 162.

Chapter VII

Towards Realism: The Musicians of George Eliot

George Eliot (1819-1880) read and admired Carlyle, Mill, Austen, Thackeray, and Dickens, translated works by the German Romantics, experienced both the excitement of the Evangelical movement and the doubts of rationalism and atheism, encountered feminism and the rising spirit of reform, and felt the lure of other cultures and ages. Because of the extraordinary range of her influences and experiences, George Eliot seems to embody Victorian England, its social theories, moral questionings, and artistic debates. In addition, Eliot was a keen observer of her age's music: she met Liszt and Rubinstein, saw Wagner conduct, attended concerts with Herbert Spencer, knew the Reverend H.R. Haweis,[1] heard the Pop Concerts at the Crystal Palace, and observed the state of musical education in England and abroad. The numerous musical maestros, dilettantes, and philistines in her novels, from *Scenes of Clerical Life* (1858) to *Daniel Deronda* (1876), reveal the complex Victorian attitude towards music and thus provide a fitting conclusion to this study. Like her contemporaries Eliot viewed the musician with sentimentalism, cynicism, and nostalgia, but her late novels acquire a new note of realism.

Music filled George Eliot's life. The extensive commentary on pieces and composers she provides in her letters, journal entries, and essays helps elucidate her changing attitude towards music and the musicians of her novels.

Of all the arts, music affected George Eliot the most deeply. Her husband J.W. Cross writes that even at age thirteen Eliot's "enthusiasm for music was already very strongly marked." Although she disliked playing in public, Eliot was "the best performer in the school" at Coventry and a delight to her instructor: "Her music-master, a much-tried man, suffering from the irritability incident to his profession, reckoned on his hour with her as a refreshment to his wearied nerves, and soon had to confess that he had no more to teach her."[2]

Just five years later, however, Eliot adopted a life of Evangelical asceticism which included a renunciation of music. In 1838 she wrote to Maria Lewis of her feelings after hearing an oratorio:

> We have had an oratorio at Coventry lately, Braham, Phillips, Mrs. Knyvett, and Mrs. Shaw--the last, I think, I shall attend. I am not fitted to decide on the question of the propriety or lawfulness of such exhibitions of talent and so forth, because I have no soul for music. "Happy is he that condemneth not himself in that thing which he alloweth." I am a tasteless person, but it would not cost me any regrets if the only music heard in our land were that of strict worship, nor can I think a pleasure that involves the devotion of all the time and powers of an immortal being to the acquirement of an expertness in so useless (at least in ninety-nine cases out of a hundred) an accomplishment, can be quite pure or elevating in its tendency.[3]

Yet two years later at an oratorio "the attention of people sitting near was attracted by her hysterical sobbing. And in all her later life music was one of the chiefest delights to her, and especially oratorio" (Cross, I, 32).

Eliot felt a tension between her enthusiasm for music and her belief that it was a frivolous, self-indulgent art. Although she rejected the asceticism of her youth, Eliot never lost the feeling that enjoying music was somehow hedonistic. In 1859 she wrote to George Henry Lewes' son Charles Lee, an accomplished musician:

> I look forward to playing duets with you as one of my future pleasures, and if I am able to go on working, I hope we shall afford to have a fine grand piano. I have none of Mozart's Symphonies, so that you can be guided in your choice of them entirely by your own tastes. I know Beethoven's Sonata in E flat well. It is a very charming one, and I shall like to hear you play it. That is one of my luxuries--to sit still and hear someone playing my favourite music; so that you may be sure you will find willing ears to listen to the fruits of your industrious practising. (*Letters*, III, 125-26)

Here music is a "luxury"; elsewhere, she refers to it as an indulgence. In 1863 she writes, "I am rather ashamed to hear of anyone trying to be useful just now, for I am doing nothing but indulge myself--enjoying being petted very much . . . enjoying our new pretty quiet home and the study of Beethoven's Sonatas for piano and violin" (*Letters*, IV, 118-19). Music's lack of utility made it hard for Eliot to justify. When she does admit to practicing, she frequently feels compelled to rationalize her action in terms of other benefits, as in her remark to Charles Lee that "I think it will be good for me hygienically as well as on other grounds, to be roused into practicing" (*Letters*, IV, 478). In a similar vein she writes to Mrs. Richard Congreve: "I have been playing energetically on the piano lately . . . It has given me a fresh kind of muscular exercise, as well as nervous stimulus, and I think, has done its part towards making my health better" (*Letters*, IV, 127). These remarks echo the claims of Herbert Spencer and other Victorians that music had physiological benefits.

Like John Stuart Mill, Eliot also found music to be a relief from the pressures and ugliness of urban life, a soothing balm. From 1860-62, while living in London, Eliot's letters repeatedly place music in opposition to the rest of city life. In 1860 she writes: "The opportunity of hearing some inspiring music is one of the chief benefits we hope for, to counterbalance our loss of the wide common and the fields" (*Letters*, III, 346). Eliot and Lewes attended *Faust* in 1863 as a "compensation for the necessity of living among bricks in this sweet summer-time" (*Letters*, IV, 92). Music becomes a substitute for simple rural pleasures and the beauty of nature.

Although Eliot preserved the Evangelical association between music and an underlying spiritual order, she also appropriated the romantic link between music and emotion. In her early letters, Eliot uses music as a metaphor for God and religious love; for instance, she writes in 1841, "we . . . have our place of usefulness and fitness, and cannot fail if we are true to the indications of His will who has originated and sustains our existence to be harmonizing notes in the great chorus of praise ever ascending from every part of the universe" (*Letters*, I, 123). Several years later, after reading the German Romantics, she writes John Sibree in a different tone: "I agree with you as to the inherent superiority of music--as that questionable woman the Countess Huhn-Huhn says, painting and sculpture are but an idealizing of our actual existence. Music arches over this existence with another and a diviner" (*Letters*, I, 247).

In 1854 Eliot translated Feuerbach's *Essence of Christianity*; this work contains extensive commentary on music which is central to an understanding of Eliot's aesthetics. Eliot wrote Sara Hennell, "with the ideas of Feuerbach I everywhere agree" (*Letters*, II, 153). Feuerbach's ideas on music are those of the German Romantics, who saw music as the medium through which the soul could best express its yearnings and hidden mysteries. Above all, music is *feeling*:

> How can the feeling man resist feeling, the loving one love, the rational one reason? Who has not experienced the overwhelming power of melody? And what else is the power of melody but the power of feeling? Music is the language of feeling; melody is audible feeling--feeling communicating itself . . .
>
> The man who is affected by musical sounds is governed by feelings; by the feeling, that is, which finds its corresponding element in musical sounds. But it is not melody as such, it is only melody pregnant with meaning and emotion, which has power over feeling. Feeling is only acted on by that which conveys feeling, i.e., by itself, its own nature.4

Later in the same chapter, Eliot's translation of *Essence of Christianity* continues:

> If thou hast no sensibility, no feeling for music, thou perceivest in the finest music nothing more than in the wind that whistles by thy ear, or than in the brook which rushes past thy feet. What, then, is it which acts on thee when thou art affected by melody? What dost thou perceive in it? What else than the voice of thy own heart? Feeling speaks only to feeling; feeling is comprehensible only by feeling, that is, by itself--for this reason, that is the object of feeling is nothing else than feeling. Music is the monologue of emotion.

One finds many passages in Eliot which adopt this Feuerbachian parallel between music and feeling. In her essay on the poet Young, written just three years after her translation of Feuerbach, she writes: "In proportion as a man would care less for the rights and the welfare of his fellow, if he did not believe in a future life, in that proportion is he wanting in the genuine feelings of justice and benevolence; as the musician who would care less to play a sonata of Beethoven's finely in solitude than in public, where he was to be paid for it, is wanting in genuine enthusiasm for music."5 As William Sullivan notes in his study of George Eliot and the fine arts, "In the mature George Eliot, these two strains - the Evangelical habit of considering music as a metaphor for spiritual existence and progress, and the Feuerbachian premise that music is a metaphor for the divinity of feeling - merge and synthesize with multiple implications in Eliot's work."6

Eliot's visit to Europe stimulated her interest in music and provided the background material for her article entitled "Liszt, Wagner, and Weimar," 1855. The flamboyant Liszt captivated her imagination, and her article staunchly defends him against the charge that he is "merely an erratic, flighty, artistic genius, who has swept through Europe, the Napoleon of the *salon*, carrying devastation into the hearts of countesses."7 She admires Liszt as a romantic artist - an "archimagus of pianists" with a "preternatural grey light in his eyes" and "floating hair'" - but seems equally concerned that he possess perfect manners and a moral character: "you will discern in him a man of various thought, of serious purpose, and of a moral nature which, in its mingled strength and gentleness, has the benignest influence on those about him."

For Eliot, Liszt's compositions insured that he would not be a "mere" performer of ephemeral fame: "the memory of the *prima donna* scarcely out-lives the flowers that are flung at her feet on her farewell night . . . It is possible, however, that Liszt will turn out to be something more than one of those coruscating meteors, who come, are seen, and are extinguished in darkness; he is now devoting himself principally to composition, and may perhaps produce something perennial." She repeats the same notion in her descriptions of performances, and one senses that it was her romantic concept of the composer rather than the actual rendition of his works which affected her most deeply. In 1855, after hearing a Beethoven performance, she writes to Miss Sara Hennell: "We have been to hear 'Fidelio' this evening--not well executed, except so far as the orchestra was concerned; but the divine music positively triumphs over the defects of execution. One is entirely wrapped in the *idea* of the composer" (Cross, I, 262).

Wagner and opera in general seemed foreign to Eliot; she preferred instead Schubert's intimate *Lied*, Beethoven's quartets and sonatas, and Handel's oratorios. As her companion George Henry Lewes observed after visiting Germany, "We came to the conclusion that Wagner' s music is not for us" (*Letters*, V, 85, n. 4). Eliot notes in her letters and journals that *Lohengrin* is "monotonous," Meyerbeer's and Weber' s operas "absurd," and concludes: "The opera is a great, great product--pity we can't always have fine Weltgeschich[t]liche dramatic motives wedded with fine music, instead of trivialities or hideousnesses. Perhaps this last is too strong a word for anything except the Traviata. Rigoletto is unpleasant, but it is a superlatively fine tragedy in Nemesis" (*Letters*, IV, 92). She also objected to Mozart's music as akin "to the Italian 'sugared' view," but admits, "I find him, Haydn, and the Italians a welcome rest from more searching music" (*Letters*, VII, 344). Although she reserves her highest praise for Beethoven and Schubert, she admits enjoying Rossini's *William Tell*, Haydn's *Creation*, and even the Monday Pop Concerts conducted by the flashy Joachim (*Letters*, II, 16, IV, 67).

After returning to England, Eliot grew increasingly aware that her country was indeed "das Land ohne Musik," and she became irate at the poverty of musical education and the shallowness of English taste. In 1859 she complains to Sara Hennell:

> We are going on Wednesday evening to hear Acis and Galatea--our first attempt at a musical treat since we came back to England. It is a cruel thing, the difficulty and dearness of getting any music in England--concerted music, which is the only music I care for much now. At Dresden we could hear thoroughly enjoyable instrumental music every evening for two-pence, and I owed so many thoughts and inspirations of feelings to that stimulus. (*Letters*, III, 71)

Nearly twenty years later she still bemoans the dearth of good music in England and looks back to her time in Europe with great nostalgia:

> . . . the changes you describe are such as we have to witness in all prosperous towns . . . Dresden, for us--which used to have a clear heaven about it and quiet amusements within the streets and beyond them where one could sit and hear the best music without being overcrowded. The last time we were there the times had changed all that. Everywhere there is a prosperous crowd to be amused, and the tastes of the crowd are not yet refined, so that Art must condescend to please the low average. This condescension is painfully marked in our huge rich London; but of late we have been a little cheered by a revived interest in the Shakespearean drama to counterbalance Offenbach. (*Letters*, VI, 174)

Eliot uses Offenbach's *opera bouffe* to epitomize the public's taste for facile music.

As well as lamenting her country's musical taste, Eliot became convinced that her own playing was amateurish, and confesses, "I was a very idle practiser, and I often regret now that when I had abundant time and opportunity for hours of piano-playing, I used them so little" (*Letters*, III, 177). In "Silly Novels by Lady Novelists" Eliot attacks the sketchy instruction which comprised female education in England and notes that females expose their want of talent more readily in music than in any other art form:

> Ladies are not wont to be very grossly deceived as to their power of playing on the piano; here certain positive difficulties of execution have to be conquered, and incompetence inevitably breaks down. Every art which has its absolute technique is, to a certain extent, guarded from the intrusion of mere left handed imbecility. But in novel-writing there are no barriers for incapacity to stumble against,

no external criteria to prevent a writer from mistaking foolish facility for mastery. (*Essays*, 324)

Eliot reiterates this comparison between music and her own art, literature, in her comment to Charles Bray: "Literature is Fine Art, and the man who writes mere literature with insolent slovenliness is as inexcusable as a man who gets up in a full drawing-room to sing Rossini's music in a cracked voice and out of tune" (*Letters*, II, 210).

Because of Eliot's continual use of music as a metaphor for the divine, for human emotion, and for art, the musicians in her novels serve a highly symbolic function. Eliot devotes many pages of her novels to discussion of pieces and performances and descriptions of maestros, musical amateurs, and anti-musical Englishmen; she uses music subtly to reveal character and to illustrate the state of art in Victorian England. With an understanding of Eliot's diverse views on music, one can analyze the musician figures in her novels as an index to her changing aesthetics.

Scenes of Clerical Life

Scenes of Clerical Life appeared in 1857, only three years after Eliot published her translation of Feuerbach. In this early work, Eliot sentimentally depicts the musician as either a simple soul from a bygone era or an impassioned artist of another race.

Like Dickens, whom she read thoroughly, Eliot uses music in her early novels as a foil to mechanism. *The Sad Fortune of Reverend Amos Barton* opens with a description of Shepperton Church which contrasts the sincere musical efforts of the town's musicians with the newer style of church music:

> And the singing was no mechanical affair of official routine; it had a drama . . . in company with a bassoon, two key-bugles, a carpenter understood to have an amazing power of singing "counter," and two lesser musical stars, [the clerk] formed the complement of a choir regarded in Shepperton as one of distinguished attraction, occasionally known to draw hearers from the next parish . . . the greatest triumphs of the Shepperton choir were reserved for Sundays when the slate announced an ANTHEM, with a dignified abstinence from particularisation, both words and music lying far beyond the reach of the most ambitious amateur in the congregation: --an anthem in which the key-bugles always ran away at a great pace, while the bassoon every now and then boomed a flying shot at them. (*Amos Barton*, ch. i)

The closing description of the bassoon and bugles racing along owes much to Dickens's descriptions of amateur orchestral performances in *Sketches of Boz*.

Mr. Barton brings the new music into Shepperton, music which the congregation "can't join in at all." Old Mrs. Patten complains, "It's well for me as I can't go to church any longer, for, if th' old singers are to be done away with, there'll be nothing left, as it was in Mr. Patten's time" (i). Barton persists in disbanding the singers and introducing proper music; as he notes, " . . . we have got a new choir together, which will go on very well with a little practice. I was quite determined that the old set of singers should be dismissed. I had given orders that they should not sing the wedding psalm, as they call it, again, to make a newly-married couple look ridiculous, and they sang it in defiance of me" (iii). Eliot uses music metaphorically to contrast Barton's mundane approach to religion with sincere religious passion: "We read, indeed, that the walls of Jericho fell down before the sound of trumpets; but we nowhere hear that those trumpets were hoarse and feeble. Doubtless they were trumpets that gave forth clear ringing tones, and sent a mighty vibration through brick and mortar. But the oratory of the Reverend Amos resembled rather a Belgian railway horn" (ii). Barton's "railway horn" of a voice, like the dismissal of the old singers, suggests his firm grounding in an age of progress and mechanism.

Eliot's highly dramatic conclusion to *Amos Barton* describes the death of Barton's saintly, long suffering wife Milly. Although she does not die singing, like Scott's Zilia, she dies like a Shakespearean heroine with an allusion to the harmony of the spheres:

> About half-past twelve she seemed to be trying to speak, and they leaned to catch her words.
> "Music--music--didn't you hear it?" (viii)

Milly's ability to hear music indicates her spiritual purity: this use of music as a metaphor for one's religious state reappears throughout *Scenes of Clerical Life*. In *Janet's Repentance* Eliot directly describes Evangelicalism in musical terms: "The movement, like all other religious 'revivals', had a mixed effect. Religious ideas have the fate of melodies, which, once set afloat in the world, are taken up by all sorts of instruments, some of them woefully coarse, feeble, or out of tune, until people are in danger of crying out that the melody itself is detestable" (*Janet's Repentance*, x).

The melodramatic tone Eliot adopts in describing Mrs. Barton's death becomes more pronounced in *Mr. Gilfil's Love Story*, the tale of an emotional singer with a thrilling contralto voice. Like Collins and Meredith, Eliot links music with the character of Italy: Caterina's Italian heritage seems to account for her musicality.

The beautiful Caterina looks like a "furriner, wi' such eyes, you can't think, an' a voice as went through you when she sung in church." Mrs. Patten observes, "It's them Italians as has such fine voices, an' Mrs. Gilfil sung, you never heard the like ... her voice seemed sometimes to fill the room; an' then it went low an' soft as if it was whisperin' close to your heart like" (*Mr. Gilfil's Love Story*, i). Caterina's "sweet mellow voice" seems to come effortlessly to her, and she sings like a dove (iv).

Although Eliot mocks ignorant remarks such as Mrs. Assher's "All Italians sing so beautifully" (v), she does make all her Italian characters musical: Caterina, her father, and Maestro Albani are "natural" Italian musicians. Caterina's father is a faded opera singer who is:

> ... a small meagre man, sallow and dingy, with a restless wandering look in his dull eyes, and an excessive timidity about his deep reverences, which gave him the air of a man who had been long a solitary prisoner ... The time was far off in which he had trod the stage in satin and feathers, the *primo tenore* of one short season. He had completely lost his voice in the following winter, and had ever since been little better than a cracked fiddle, which is good for nothing but firewood. For, like many Italian singers, he was too ignorant to teach, and if it had not been for his one talent of penmanship, he and his young helpless wife might have starved. (iii)

This description parallels Eliot's comment in "Liszt, Wagner, and Weimar" that a *prima donna's* fame fades with the flowers cast upon the stage. Eliot's remarks suggest that she had difficulty accepting performing musicians as artists of equal rank to authors, painters, or composers because of the ephemeral nature of their art. The theme of fleeting music reappears in her poem *Armgart*, 1870, in which she describes a *prima donna's* tragic loss of voice.

As in Feuerbach, music is for Caterina Gilfil a vehicle for the emotions. Rejected by her lover Anthony Wybrow for the wealthy Miss Assher, Caterina vents her jealousy and anger in song:

> . . . her emotion, instead of being a hindrance to her singing, gave her additional power. Her singing was what she could do best; it was her one point of superiority, in which it was probable she would excel the highborn beauty whom Anthony was to woo; and her love, her jealousy, her pride, her rebellion against destiny, made one stream of passion which welled forth in the deep rich tones of her voice. She had a rare contralto, which Lady Cheverel, who had high musical taste, had been careful to preserve her from straining. (ii)

Caterina's passions are unrestrained and so strong that she considers murder; the intensity of her emotions, when translated into music, gives rise to exquisite melody. Music provides her with a welcome outlet for her misery:

> And her singing--the one thing in which she ceased to be passive, and became prominent--lost none of its energy. She herself sometimes wondered how it was that, whether she felt sad or angry, crushed with the sense of Anthony's indifference, or burning with impatience under Miss Assher's attentions, it was always a relief to sing. Those full deep notes she sent forth seemed to be lifting the pain from her heart--seemed to be carying away the madness from her brain . . .
>
> Handel's "Messiah" stood open on the desk, at the chorus, "all we like sheep," and Caterina threw herself at once into the impetuous intricacies of that magnificent fugue. In her happiest moments she could never have played it so well; for now all the passion that made her misery was hurled by a convulsive effort into her music, just as pain gives new force to the clutch of the sinking wrestler, and as terror gives far-sounding intensity to the shriek of the feeble. (x)

The danger of music as an art form is clear: Fosco can play *Moses in Egypt* and plot an abduction and murder; Caterina can play Handel's glorious oratorio while wishing for revenge.

Like Bronte's Blanche Ingram, Miss Assher is proud, cool and unfeeling. Just as Bronte illustrated Miss Ingram's coldness through her lack of genuine feeling for music, so Eliot reveals Miss Assher's insensibility and false pride through her indifference to music and her contempt of "those musical people." The conversation between Caterina and Miss Assher exposes the latter's arrogance and affectation. Miss Assher says to Caterina:

> "I envy you such a charming talent. Do you know, I have no ear; I cannot hum the smallest tunes and I delight in music so. Is it not unfortunate? . . ."

> "I should have thought you wouldn't care about music, if you have no ear," said Caterina...
> "Oh, I assure you, I dote on it; and Anthony is so fond of it; it would be so delightful if I could play and sing to him; though he says he likes me best not to sing, because it doesn't belong to his idea of me. What style of music do you like best?"
> "I don't know. I like all beautiful music." . . .
> Miss Assher was thinking at the same time, "This Miss Sarti seems a stupid little thing. Those musical people often are. . . ." (v)

Like Edith Granger's mother ("Cleopatra") in Dickens' *Dombey and Son*, who professes to be charmed by music, Miss Assher and her ignorant mother pretend to understand an art they know and care nothing about. As Caterina plays the harpsichord, Miss Assher listens "with that air of ostentatious admiration which belongs to the absence of real enjoyment" (v).

Although she admires Catherina's musical talent, Eliot does not sanction her moral abandon and impulsiveness. Caterina must learn to sing not as a means of personal triumph, as a chance to exhibit her demonic power, but as a way of calming her soul and filling it with peace. She leaves the Cheverels' house, where she sang arias of Gluck and Paisiello, for the quiet home of Mr. Gilfil and his sister. A simple chord on the harpsichord shakes her out of her dejection and reminds her of life's beauty:

> The vibration rushed through Caterina like an electric shock: it seemed as if that instant a new soul were entering into her, and filling her with a deeper, more significant life. She looked round, rose from the sofa, and walked to the harpsichord. In a moment her fingers were wandering with their old sweet method among the keys, and her soul was floating in its true familiar element of delicious sound, as the water-plant that lies withered and shrunken on the ground expands into freedom and beauty when once more bathed in its native flood.

But, in good melodramatic fashion, Caterina soon dies, for "the delicate plant had been too deeply bruised, and in the struggle to put forth a blossom it died" (xx).

Eliot's sympathies seem to lie as much with the humble English servants who sing ballads together for fellowship as with her glittery Italian heroine performing the arias of eighteenth century operas. The good-natured servant Mr. Bellamy urges his companion to perform:

> "Come, Mr. Bates, let us hear 'Roy's Wife.' I'd rather hear a good old song like that, nor all the fine Italian toodlin."
> Mr. Bates, urged thus flatteringly, . . . struck up a remarkably *staccato* rendering of "Roy's Wife of Aldivalloch." This melody may certainly be taxed with excessive iteration, but that was precisely its highest recommendation to the present audience, who found it all the easier to swell the chorus . . . Mr. Bates's song formed the climax of the evening's good fellowship. (ix)

Eliot uses inappropriate language ("excessive iteration") to describe the simple song not because of her pedantry but because she deliberately mocks the inability of words to convey the effect of such singing. In Adam Bede, discussed in more detail later, she similarly writes of the joyous harvest song in language designed to ridicule recondite musical criticism:

> As to the origin of this song--whether it came in its actual state from the brain of a single rhapsodist, or was gradually perfected by a school or succession of rhapsodists, I am ignorant. There is a stamp of unity, or individual genius, upon it, which inclines me to the former hypotheses, though I am not blind to the consideration that this unity may rather have arisen from that consensus of many minds which was a condition of primitive thought, foreign to our modern indication of a lost line, which later rhapsodists, failing in imaginative vigour, have supplied by the feeble device of iteration: others, however, may rather maintain that this very iteration is an original felicity, to which none but the most prosaic minds can be insensible. (*Adam Bede*, VI, liii)

Eliot shows the incongruity of this verbose passage and its subject matter.

Although Eliot's sentimentalism detracts from the success of *Mr. Gilfil's Love Story*, there simultaneously is a note of cynicism in the story which she develops more fully in her later novels. Like Thackeray's heroines, the artist Caterina suffers exploitation at the hands of the aristocrats. The Cheverels cultivate her talent so she can become their own personal "minstrel." Lady Cheverel cares about Caterina only when she realizes her voice has promise, and Sir Cheverel patronizingly views her as a little pet: Sir Cheverel says to her, "Now, little monkey, you must be in your best voice; you're the minstrel of the Manor, you know; and be sure you have a pretty gown and a new ribbon" (v). Caterina also must endure the condescension of the arrogant and chauvinistic Asshers.

There are striking similarities between Eliot's *Mr. Gilfil's Love Story*, 1858, and Meredith's *Vittoria*, 1860: both narrate the life of an Italian *prima donna* with a disreputable musical father; the heroine is adopted by an affected, aristocratic

English family, and falls in love with an Englishman who regards her only as a wild plaything and underestimates the intensity of her emotions. These likenesses suggest not only Meredith's possible familiarity with Eliot's early work but the fact that both writers created musicians who were stock characters, well-established literary conventions.

Adam Bede

Eliot dedicated her next novel, *Adam Bede*, (1860), to Thomas Carlyle, whose attitude towards music was discussed in Chapter II; like Carlyle, Eliot regards the musical workman as an ideal figure, and she also echoes Wordsworth and other Romantic writers in her repeated use of music as an emblem for beauty and love.

Carlyle had written, "Give me the man who sings at his work. He will do more in the same time--he will do it better--he will persevere longer"[8]; Eliot gives us such a man in the figure of Adam Bede. The opening scene shows the carpenter Adam Bede singing Anglican hymns while he works. Eliot praises "the concert of the tools and Adam's voice," and concludes, "Men's muscles move better when their souls are making merrry music" (Adam Bede, I, i; II, xix). The workmen find beauty in the music of their implements: "The sound of tools to a clever workman who loves his work is like the tentative sounds of the orchestra to the violinist who has to bear his part in the overture: the strong fibres begin their accustomed thrill, and what was a moment before joy, vexation, or ambition, begins its change into energy" (ii, xix). Eliot stressses Adam's strength (his "strong barytone voice . . . could only come from a broad chest"), his lack of self-consciousness, and the piety of his musical selections. A typical scene shows Adam walking home singing about "God's all-seeing eye" while "unconscious of the admiration he was exciting" (I, i). Adam always works or moves while singing, for he has no time to indulge in music simply for its own sake.

Similarly, the evangelical Dinah Morris sings psalms to move her hearers, sings gentle music to soothe the oppressed widow Bede, and sings hymns while she mops and cleans. Her music, like Adam's, seems an outgrowth of her soul's purity. Dinah's "mellow treble tones" as she speaks are "like that of a fine instrument touched with the unconscious skill of musical instinct" (I, ii). Her words affect her listeners like music: "The simple things she said seemed like novelties, as a melody strikes us with a new feeling when we hear it sung by the pure voice of a boyish chorister"; Adam listens for Dinah's voice "as for a recurrent music" (I, ii; VI, 1). Dinah, like Adam, has a "total absence of self-consciousness" which allows her to speak "directly from her own emotions, and under the inspiration of her own simple faith" (I, ii). Eliot uses music to show Dinah's purity and directness: her singing is as natural as "the swallows as was under the thack last 'ear, when they fust begun to sing low an' soft-like i' the mornin'" and resembles "a sweet summer murmur" (I, x; VI, 1).

Eliot also uses musical terms to express Adam's and Dinah's ability to love. Their musicality is but one indication of their souls' capacity to feel God's love, human passion, and the beauty of nature. Music leads both to contemplate the benevolence and power of the Creator:

> Our caresses, our tender words, our still rapture under the influence of autumn sunsets, or pillared vistas, or calm majestic statues, or Beethoven symphonies, all bring with them the consciousness that they are mere waves and ripples in an unfathomable ocean of love and beauty; our emotion at its keenest moment passes from expression into silence, our love at its highest flood rushes beyond its object, and loses itself in the sense of divine mystery. (I, iii)

In an eloquent passage Eliot defends the susceptibility to music and compares it to the appreciation of human beauty:

> Is it any weakness, pray, to be wrought on by exquisite music? --to feel its wondrous harmonies searching the subtlest windings of your soul, the delicate fibres of life where no memory can penetrate, and binding together your whole being past and present in one unspeakable vibration: melting you in one moment with all the tenderness, all the love that has been scattered through the toilsome years, concentrating in one emotion of heroic courage or resignation all the hard-learnt lessons of self-renouncing sympathy, blending your present joy with past sorrow, or your present sorrow with all your past joy? If not, then neither is it a weakness to be so wrought upon by the exquisite curves of a woman's cheek and neck and arms. . . For the beauty of a lovely woman is like music. (IV, xxxiii)

Yet this passage has an undertone of irony, too, and Eliot seems to imply that it *is* sometimes a weakness to be carried away by music. Adam's attraction to "the exquisite curves" of Hetty Sorrel is a blindness on his part, an instance where he is guided by superficialities. Eliot's mixture of sympathy and disdain for her own musical passion seems evident here. It is not a weakness to be moved by music if it is the right sort of music - music capable of stimulating "heroic courage" and "self-renouncing sympathy" --, just as it is not a weakness to be moved by human love if it stimulates inner happiness and devotion.

Eliot illustrates the notion that music, like love, can be either ennobling or enervating by contrasting the musicianship of Adam and Dinah with that of Arthur and Hetty. Arthur, to whom applause is "pleasanter than a strain of sublimest music," is a dandy who trifles with Hetty's affection and ruins her character (III, xxiv). Rather than singing hymns while he works, Arthur whistles and sings operatic airs while he goes fishing: "The low whistle, which had assisted him in arriving at this resolution, here broke out into his loudest ringing tenor, and the corridor, as he hurried along it, echoed to his favourite song from the 'Beggar's Opera,' 'When the heart of a man is oppressed with cares'" (I, xii). The song he sings, which Eliot does not finish, continues:

If the heart of man is depressed with cares,
The mist is dispelled when a woman appears;
Like the notes of a fiddle, she sweetly,
    sweetly,
Raises the spirits, and charms our ears.

Again, women and music are compared, but here the emphasis is on the charming quality of each, not on the ability of music and love to fill man with gratitude and inspiration.

Hetty Sorrel's vanity contrasts with Dinah's want of self-consciousness, and she lacks the latter's inner harmony. Her encounter with the handsome Arthur Donnithorne makes her heart vibrate and play "its little foolish tunes over and over again"; Eliot wryly observes, "we must learn to accommodate ourselves to the discovery that some of those cunningly fashioned instruments called human souls have only a limited range of music, and will not vibrate in the least under a touch that fills others with tremulous rapture or quivering agony" (I, ix). In describing Dinah's effect on Hetty, Eliot employs an ironic musical simile: "'I knew you were not in bed, my dear,' she said, in her sweet clear voice, which was irritating to Hetty, mingling with her own peevish vexation like music with jangling chains" (I, xv). Dinah's presence is like music, but to Hetty, who is busy trying on earrings and admiring herself in the mirror, such sounds are nettlesome. Adam intrudes on her vanity with the same disapproval, and again music illustrates character: "I'd have you just as you are now," he says to Hetty, "without anything t'interfere with your own looks. It's like when a man's singing a good tune, you don't want t'hear bells tinkling and interfering wi' the sound' (II, xx).

To be unmusical, like Hetty, is to be narrow and worldly. The pompous Mr. Craig, who works with soil and compost, says, "I've never cared about singing myself. I've had something better to do" (III, xxiii). Eliot also attacks those who view music only in a technical, learned way. Schoolmaster Bartel Massey regards Scotch tunes as "fit for nothing but to frighten the birds with," contemptuously listens to the workmen's songs, and, like Amos Barton, introduces music into the church service which is inaccessible to the congregation. Old-fashioned musician Joshua Rann complains, "I've . . . sung i' the quire long 'afore Bartle Massey come from nobody knows where, wi' his counter-singin' and fine anthems, as puts everybody out but himself - one takin' it up after another like sheep a-bleatin' i' th' fold" (I, v). Eliot writes nostalgically of the rural church services: ". . . good Biship Ken's evening hymn was being sung to one of those lively psalm-tumes which died out with the last generation of rectors and choral parish-clerks. Melodies dies out, like the Pipe of Pan, with the ears that love them and listen for them" (II, xviii).

The simple Joshua Rann has more innate musicianship than the learned Bartle Massey, for "Nature . . . had poured some of her music into this honest conceited soul." He delivers the reading with a "rich chant . . . like the lingering vibrations of a violon-cello," and plays tunes on his fiddle "which his good ear really taught him to execute with some skill" (II, xviii; III, xxv). Eliot concludes in Wordsworthian fashion that rustics frequently have greater musical ability than their "betters": ". . . that is Nature's way: she will allow a gentleman of splendid physiognomy and poetic aspirations to sing woefully out of tune, and not give him the slightest hint of it; and takes care that some narrow-browed fellow, trolling a ballad in the corner of a pothouse, shall be as true as his intervals as a bird" (II, xviii). She further emphasizes the villagers' melodiousness by praising their harvest songs, the voices of the Methodist singers, and the musical "concert of noises and animals" at Poyser's farm (I, iii, vi).

In *Adam Bede* more than any other Eliot novel, music is replete with romantic connotations. Passages such as the following abound: "How is it that the poets have said so many things about our first love, so few about our late love? . . . The boy's flute-like voice has its own spring charm; but the man should yield a richer, deeper music" (VI, li). Music here and elsewhere in the novel serves as a metaphor for love and for the soul.

Eliot exhibits sentimentality in describing the melodious workmen and musical villagers, but there are several passages on music in the novel which foreshadow a later realism. She admits that although Adam has an "inborn inherited faculty," he also must work hard "to learn his musical notes and part singing" (II, xix). The drinking songs of the workmen are painfully out of tune, and the haymakers' voices seem less melodious when heard up close: "The jocose talk of haymakers is best at a distance; like those clumsy bells round the cows' necks, it has rather a coarse sound when it comes close, and may even grate on your ears painfully; but heard from far off, it mingles very prettily with the other joyous sounds of nature" (II, xix). Pastoral scenes, it appears, cannot bear close scrutiny.

Silas Marner

The nostalgia with which Eliot praises the beautiful Shepperton church service, with "key-bugle" and "bassoon," in *Scenes from Clerical Life* and the old-fashioned church service in *Adam Bede* continues in *Silas Marner*, 1861; Eliot's nostalgic description of the Raveloe musicians draws on many of the same tunes, images, and themes of the two earlier works.

The Raveloe musicians consist of the jocose choir leader, Mr. Winthrop, other villagers, such as two "who were known officially as the 'bassoon' and the 'key bugle'," and the fervently musical Solomon Macey (*Silas Marner*, I, vi). Like Joshua Rann, who impatiently waits for his chance to play violin at public gatherings, old Solomon Macey eagerly welcomes the chance to perform. At a New Year's Party, "Solomon Macey, a small, hale old man with an abundant crop of long white hair reaching nearly to his shoulders, advanced to the indicated spot, bowing reverently while he fiddled, as much as to say that he respected the company, though he respected the keynote more" (I, xi). The tunes he chooses, such as "The Flaxen-headed Ploughboy" and "Over the Hills and Far Away," are some of the same ones requested by the farmers in *Adam Bede*, and they link him with a time of pastoral innocence. Eliot, however, also stresses Macey's demonic power and the wizardry of his art: "Old Solomon, in his seedy clothes and long white locks, seems to be luring that decent company by the magic scream of his fiddle" (I, xi).

Solomon's age is significant, because it suggests that the time for such music has passed. As his son notes, ". . . our family's been known for musicianers as far back as anybody can tell. But them things are dying out, as I tell Solomon everytime he comes round; there's no voices like what there used to be, and there's nobody remembers what we remember, if it isn't the old crows" (I, vi).

The good-hearted Dolly Winthrop shares Solomon's love of old-fashioned music, and believes "there's no other music equil to the Christmas music." She praises her son Aaron's natural musicality: ". . . he's got a voice like a bird--you wouldn't think . . . he can sing a Christmas carril as his father's taught him; and I take it for a token as he'll come to good, as he can learn the good tunes so quick" (I, x). As in *Adam Bede*, Eliot stresses the link between the rural people's simple faith and their love of music; Aaron's choice of "a melody that had the rhythm of an industrious hammer" suggests that good music must not inspire indolence but be intimately linked to a world of work. Aaron's caroling and Eppie's love of bird songs signal their Edenic innocence.

The Mill on the Floss

Eliot delineates the musician more extensively in *The Mill on the Floss*, 1860, by presenting all four major characters - Maggie, Philip, Stephen, and Lucy - as differing types of musical performers and by contrasting them with their prosaic environment. Music retains its metaphorical link with passion, but Eliot's attitude towards the musician, and, by implication, romanticism, is far more ambivalent than in the fairy-tale story of *Silas Marner*.

Maggie Tulliver's response to music parallels Eliot's own. Like Eliot, Maggie is deeply affected by melody, views it as a sinful luxury, venerates musicians, prefers older music to the modern Italian style, regrets her lack of competence as a pianist, and finds in music a way of assuaging her troubles and transcending the dullness of her surroundings.

Maggie's practical brother Tom regards music as a bunch of "la la" and prefers percussion-caps to melody; Maggie, on the other hand, lives in a world of imagination and beautiful music. Eliot shows the difference in their attitudes as they listen to Christmas carollers:

> . . . There had been singing under the window after midnight-- supernatural singing, Maggie always felt, in spite of Tom's contemptuous insistence that the singers were old Patch, the parish clerk, and the rest of the church choir; she trembled with awe when their caroling broke in upon her dreams and the image of men in fustian clothes was always thrust away by the vision of angels

resting on the parted cloud. The midnight chant had helped as usual to lift the morning above the level of common days. (*Mill on the Floss*, II, ii)

Maggie has "an ear straining after dreamy music that died away and would not come near to her," and wants music intensely: "I was never satisfied with a little of anything . . . I never felt that I had enough music. I wanted more instruments playing together, I wanted voices to be fuller and deeper" (III, vi; V, iii). Maggie's desire for music is her romantic yearning.

Like Eliot, Maggie passes through an ascetic phase in which she denies herself the pleasure of music: "There was no music for her any more--no piano, no harmonized voices, no delicious stringed instruments with their passionate cries of imprisoned spirits, sending a strange vibration through her frame" (IV, iii). She limits herself to organ music at church but this self-imposed repression cannot last, just as she cannot stop herself from loving Philip. Maggie concedes, "I am too eager in my enjoyment of music and all luxuries," and admits that she cannot live without music's healing power: "I think I should have no other mortal wants if I could always have plenty of music. It seems to infuse strength into my limbs and ideas into my brain. Life seems to go on without effort when I am filled with music. At other times one is conscious of carrying a weight" (VI, vii, iii). Maggie's comments echo Eliot's remarks in her letters that music restores her health and provides her with inspiration.

Eliot does not sentimentalize her heroine: she shows that Maggie's susceptibility to music makes her dangerously vulnerable, and she stresses Maggie's lack of musical education. Maggie, like Eliot, is a pianist:

> It was pleasant . . . to sit down at the piano alone and find that the old fitness between her fingers and the keys remained, and revived, like a sympathetic kinship not to be worn out by separation--to get the tunes she had heard the evening before and repeat them again and again until she had found out a way of producing them so as to make them a more pregnant, passionate language to her. The mere concord of octaves was a delight to Maggie, and she would often take up a book of studies rather than any melody that she might taste more keenly by abstraction the more primitive sensation of intervals. Not that her enjoyment of music was of the kind that indicates a great specific talent; it was rather that her sensibility to the supreme excitement of music was only one form of that passionate sensibility which belonged to her whole nature. (VI, vi)

Maggie's attraction to primitive intervals, like her dreamy enchantment with the old Christmas carollers, stems from her romanticism. Because girls are denied a thorough education, Maggie has no "great specific talent"; her abstract interest in musical studies suggests her undeveloped potential. Symbolically, the impetuous Maggie's weak point as a pianist is "hurrying the tempo" (VI, vi).

Philip Wakem, like Maggie, has a greater musical appreciation than musical skill. Wakem's love of music has two interpretations: it reveals his sympathetic, sensitive nature, but also shows his weakness. The unmusical Tom Tulliver is a "well-made, active-looking boy," while the musical Philip is "a pale, puny fellow" with hair which "waved and curled at the ends like a girl's," "small, delicate hands," and a "nature half feminine in sensitiveness" (II, iii, vi). Eliot contrasts Philip and Tom at school as Tom discordantly intrudes on Philip's romantic reverie:

> Tom ran in to Philip, who was enjoying his afternoon's holiday at the piano in the drawing room, picking out tunes for himself and singing them. He was supremely happy, perched like an amorphous bundle on the high stool, with his head thrown back, his eyes fixed on the opposite cornice, and his lips wide open, sending forth with all his might impromptu syllables to a tune of Arne's which had hit his fancy.
> "Come, Philip," said Tom, bursting in; "don't stay roaring 'la la' there; come and see old Poulter do his sword-exercise in the carriage-house!"
> The jar of this interruption, the discord of Tom's tones coming across the notes to which Philip was vibrating in soul and body, would have been enough to unhinge his temper even if there had been no question of Poulter the drilling-master.
> Philip shuddered visibly as he paused from his music. Then turning red, he said with violent passion, "Get away, you lumbering idiot! Don't come bellowing at me; you're not fit to speak to anything but a cart-horse!" (II, iv)

Philip's pose - head thrown back, eyes dilated - is that of an inspired romantic genius, but he lacks the talent to accompany this stance. He is St. Ogg's "only apology for a tenor"; Philip's "pleading tenor had no very fine qualities as a voice" (VI, i, vii). Philip painfully recognizes his own mediocrity: "I'm cursed with susceptibility in every direction and effective faculty in none. I care for painting and music . . . I flutter all ways and fly in none . . . my voice is only middling, like everything else in me" (V, iii). Although he shares Maggie' s love of music as a transcendent power, he receives only transitory inspiration from it: "Certain strains of music affect me so strangely; I can never hear them without their changing my whole attitude of mind for a time, and if the effect would last, I might be capable of heroisms" (V, i).

Philip and Maggie experience music deeply because they feel deeply, but without a corresponding skill their fervor seems pitiable. Stephen Guest's sarcastic comment about Philip's "feeling" for music has a ring of truth: Stephen chooses to sing a piece which "exactly suits my feeling, which, Philip will have it, is the grand element of good singing. I notice men with indifferent voices are usually of that opinion" (VI, i). Philip shares Eliot's view of Haydn's *Creation* as a work marred by its "sugared complacency and flattering make-believe," yet he also admires Bellini's romantic and dreamy opera *Somnambula*, music which Eliot found distasteful and enervating (VI, i, vii).

Although Stephen Guest is not as swayed by music's emotional power as Philip and Maggie, he ironically is a more accomplished musician. Eliot attacks Maggie's and Philip's sentiment without action, desire without skill, but she also shows in her portrait of Stephen Guest that artistry does not insure morality. Stephen has "a full-toned bass" which surpasses Philip's middling tenor, and he uses music to gain power over Maggie. Stephen's musicianship is rare in St. Ogg's, which "is so miserably provided with musical gentlemen," and impresses Maggie as an extraordinary accomplishment. His singing, however, cannot rival the better-trained voices of London or Europe: "She had been hearing some fine music sung by a fine bass voice, but then it was sung in a provincial, amateur fashion such as would have left a critical ear much to desire" (VI, iii).

Stephen does display a sophisticated knowledge of musical repertoire and shrewdly chooses music to manipulate the vulnerable Maggie. Lucy, whose musical accomplishment is inferior even to Maggie's, correctly notes, "There is one pleasure, I know, Maggie, that your deepest dismalness will never resist . . . That is music" (VI, ii). Stephen's performance of Purcell vibrates through Maggie "with its wild passion and fancy," and Stephen and Philip's duet entrances her: "Poor Maggie! She looked very beautiful when her soul was being played on in this way by the inexorable power of sound" (VI, vii). As Barbara Hardy notes in *The Novels of George Eliot*, both Stephen and Philip tempt Maggie through her weakness for music: "Philip's voice, then Stephen's, in deeper tones, speak to her in the music which is one of the recurring images of the novel."[9] As in *Adam

Bede, it can be a strength to be moved by music but a weakness if one is blindly governed by the emotions and distracted from moral obligations.

Maggie Tulliver, like Caterina in *Scenes of Clerical Life*, has an impetuosity and sensitivity, symbolized by her love of music, which Eliot both praises and censures. But *The Mill on the Floss* treats music with greater realism than Eliot's first novel did, for Eliot concedes the necessity of education and practice. Maggie is *not* innately gifted in music; like Lucy, she has received only a smattering of education. Eliot does not depict life in St. Ogg's as full of pastoral beauty and natural melody, but rather shows a province "where music was so scarce" (VI, ii). *The Mill on the Floss* reveals Eliot's growing concern for the importance of education, in part stimulated by her travels abroad, and her increasing detachment from the romantic view of music. In *Adam Bede* Eliot used music as a symbol for love and for the divine mysteries of the universe; in *Silas Marner* musicians symbolized a time of simplicity and faith; but in *The Mill on the Floss* the musician is a more complex figure. Eliot's detailed observations in *The Mill on the Floss* concerning individual compositions which are performed and her comments on characters' amateurish renditions suggest a more realistic approach to music as an art requiring technical skill and practice; she refuses to sentimentalize the musician as a glorious hero. Her musicians - the effeminate Philip, kittenish Lucy, frivolous Stephen, and impulsive Maggie - lack the common sense and industriousness of the unmusical Tom Tulliver. Without imagination and beauty, Tom's life is too narrow, but without social purpose and moral restraint, Maggie's life of music is self-indulgent. Eliot implies that both artistic sensitivity and practical sense are vital.

Middlemarch

Middlemarch, 1872, was published in the same year as Hardy's *Under the Greenwood Tree*, but Eliot treats the musician with little of Hardy's sentimentalism. To be unmusical is to be narrow, Eliot again implies, but to give one's self to music is to be idle and frivolous. Although Eliot ridicules the unmusical philistines of Middlemarch society, she seems in this novel more than any other to have little sympathy with the musician.

A conversation about music occurring early in *Middlemarch* shows Eliot's skillful use of music to delineate character. At a dinner party Mr. Brooke begins:

". . . there is a lightness about the feminine mind--a touch and go--music, the fine arts, that kind of thing; they should study those up to a certain point, women should, but in a light way, you know. A woman should be able to sit down and play you or sing you a good old English tune. That is what I like; though I have heard most things--been at the opera in Vienna: Gluck, Mozart, everything of that sort. But I'm a conservative in music--it's not like ideas, you know. I stick to the good old tunes."

"Mr. Casaubon is not fond of the piano, and I am very glad he is not," said Dorothea, whose slight regard for domestic music and feminine fine art must be forgiven her, considering the small tinkling and smearing in which they chiefly consisted at that dark period. She smiled and looked up at her betrothed with grateful eyes. If he had always been asking her to play the "Last Rose of Summer," she would have required much resignation. "He says there is only an old harpsichord at Lowick, and it is covered with books."

"Ah, there you are behind Celia, my dear. Celia, now, plays very prettily, and is always ready to play. However, since Casaubon does not like it, you are all right. But it's a pity you should not have little recreations of that sort, Casaubon: the bow always strung--that kind of thing, you know--will not do."

"I never could look on it in the light of recreation to have my ears teased with measured noises," said Mr. Casaubon. "A tune much iterated has the ridiculous effect of making the words in my mind perform a sort of minuet to keep time--an effect hardly tolerable, I imagine, after boyhood. As to the grander forms of music, worthy to accompany solemn celebrations and even to serve as an educating influence according to the ancient conception, I say nothing, for with these we are not immediately concerned."

"No, but music of that sort I should enjoy," said Dorothea. "When we were coming home from Lausanne my uncle took us to hear the great organ at Freiberg, and it made me sob."

"That kind of thing is not healthy, my dear," said Mr. Brooke. (*Middlemarch*, I, vii)

Brooke, Celia, Casaubon, and Dorothea present contrasting views of music. Brooke, like many Victorians, views music as an innocent but unimportant amusement; music thus is a pastime suitable for females. By preferring "good old tunes" and by ignorantly assuming he has "heard most things," Brooke typifies the English philistine who justly deserves the scorn of the Europeans.

Celia, for Mr. Brooke, represents an ideal musician because she "plays very prettily, and is always ready to play." Earlier in the novel Eliot describes Celia's performance: "Celia was playing an 'air, with variations,' a small kind of tinkling which symbolized the aesthetic part of the young ladies' education" (I, v). The 'air, with variations' was undoubtedly one of the many "brilliant but not difficult" pieces so popular in the Victorian era which were designed merely to demonstrate the performer's technical ability. Celia performs as a social duty and without any genuine feeling for the art; in fact, she finds music rather contemptible and "she never could understand how well-bred persons consented to sing and open their mouths in the ridiculous manner requisite for that vocal exercise" (I, iii).

Dorothea rejects "the small tinkling and smearing" which her uncle and sister believe constitutes music and painting, and she is glad her husband does not require her to play sentimental tunes ("Last Rose of Summer") which do not affect her. At Lowich she ceases "practising silly rhythms on the hated piano" because this is part of the trivial life she hopes to transcend (III, xxvii). As in Austen, it is far better to dislike music than to affect understanding; like Elinor in *Sense and Sensibility*, Dorothea's rejection of her musical "accomplishment" suggests an independence of mind.

Dorothea's attitude towards music, however, is complex and changing. Like Eliot, Dorothea sobs at an oratorio because, despite her ascetic renunciation of music, she is too sensitive and vulnerable to be oblivious to music's great emotional power. Furthermore, Eliot emphasizes Dorothea's inner musicality. Although not an accomplished pianist or vocalist, Dorothea strikes others as a musician. Ladislaw admires "the melodious fragments in which her heart and soul came forth so directly and ingenuously" and compares her twice to an Aeolian harp: when he first hears her he exclaims, "What a voice! It was like the voice of a soul that had once lived in an Aeolian harp" (II, xxi; I, ix). Elsewhere Eliot notes that Dorothea's voice is like "a young chorister chanting a credo" and praises "the musical intonation which in moments of deep but quiet feeling made her speech like a fine bit of recitative" (IV, xxxix; I, v). Likewise, Caleb Garth links Dorothea's voice with religious music and observes that her "voice like music" reminds him "of bits in the *Messiah*" (VI, lvi). For Lydgate, Dorothea's musicality symbolizes his own potential and inspiration: "That voice of deep-souled womanhood had remained within him as the enkindling conceptions of dead and sceptred genius had remained within him . . . the tones were a music from which he was falling away" (VI, lviii). Dorothea's musical voice, like Dinah Morris' melodious talking and singing, is the outward manifestation of her soul's goodness.

The neoclassical scholar Casaubon, whose head reminds Dorothea of Locke, not surprisingly adheres to the eighteenth century conception of music as unimportant. Just as Dr. Johnson seemed to pride himself on his tin ear, so Casaubon believes his distaste for music signals his superiority and maturity: the effect of music, he notes, is "hardly tolerable . . . after boyhood." Casaubon's old harpsichord has become merely a piece of furniture covered with books. Yet Casaubon's amusicality differs sharply from Dorothea's: Dorothea's distaste for music stems from her dissatisfaction with the poor quality of music she hears, and her voice and response to religious music reveal her innate but undeveloped musicality; Casaubon's dislike of music, consistent with his monotonous "sing-song" voice, reveals his want of imagination and his incapacity for love. As Eliot notes, Casaubon's impotent attempts to speak of love are like "thin music" (I, iv).

In direct opposition to Casaubon, who approves of Dorothea's lack of musical talent, Lydgate finds Rosamond Vincy's musical acumen captivating and believes singing to be an essential accomplishment of the ideal woman. Rosamond's musical skill far surpasses Dorothea's but, interestingly, Eliot presents Rosamond as a far less admirable character. Just as Stephen Guest's musical superiority over Philip was not accompanied by greater moral goodness or emotional depth, so Rosamond's talent by itself can not make her a heroine in Eliot's moral scheme. She willingly presents herself as an "accomplished female," a hollow and degrading role which Dorothea strenuously avoids.

Rosamond, as a product of Mrs. Lemon's school, has "exceptional musical execution" and a repertoire versatile enough to accommodate the requests of her Middlemarch audiences (I, xi). For the uneducated Mr. Featherstone, who "approved of the sentimental song as the suitable garnish for girls," Rosamond sings "Flow on, Thou Shining River" and "Home, Sweet Home," and he pronounces her the best musician in Middlemarch (I, xii). With Lydgate in the audience, Rosamond adds classical music to her performance, but her mimetic style indicates that music for her is an acquired craft, not a pregnant language for her emotions:

> Rosamond played admirably. Her master at Mrs. Lemon's school . . . was one of those excellent musicians here and there to be found in our provinces . . . Rosamond, with the executant's instinct, had seized his manner of playing and gave forth his large rendering of noble music with the precision of an echo. It was startling, heard for the first time. A hidden soul seemed to be

flowing forth from Rosamond's fingers; and so indeed was, since souls live on in perpetual echoes . . . Lydgate was taken possession of and began to believe in her as something exceptional . . .

Her singing was less remarkable, but also well trained and sweet to hear as a chime perfectly in tune. It is true she sang "Meet me by Moonlight," and "I've Been Roaming," for mortals must share the fashions of their time, and none but the ancients can be always classical. But Rosamond could also sing "Black-eyed Susan" with effect, or Haydn's canzonet, or "Vio, che sapete," or "Batti, Batti" --she only wanted to know what her audience liked. (II, xvi)

Rosamond plays "what her audience liked" because for her, music is a social tool. Indeed, she is not mistaken in her view of her musical accomplishment, since it produces the desired effect on the susceptible and marriageable Lydgate. Eliot views Lydgate's vulnerability to music's charm ironically, and emphasizes his lack of true musical appreciation. Lydgate is no musician: "I know the notes of many birds, and I know many melodies by ear, but the music that I don't know at all and have no notion about, delights me--affects me" (II, xvi). Although Rosamond begins practising her music more diligently when she learns of Lydgate's arrival in Middlemarch, she soon realizes he lacks discernment as a listener: she wishes "he had known his notes so that his enchantment under her music had been less like an emotional elephant's" (III, xxvii).

Eliot mocks Lydgate's romantic view of the female musician, just as she satirizes his puerile infatuation with the theatrical Laure. Lydgate links music and women together in his nebulous idea of beauty. About Rosamond he gushes, "She is grace itself; she is perfectly lovely and accomplished. That is what a woman ought to be: she ought to produce the effect of exquisite music" (I, xi). Lydgate demands that "if he ever married, his wife would have that feminine radiance, that distinctive womanhood which must be classed with flowers and music" (II, xvi). Lydgate marries Rosamond because she is "an exquisite bird," and he acquires a charming ornament but little more. He soon realizes the emptiness of Rosamond's mind, the narrowness of her vision, and her insufficiency as a mate. In Lydgate's "old dreamland," Rosamond was "an accomplished mermaid, using her comb and looking-glass and singing her song for the relaxation of his adored wisdom alone," but he learns the tragic consequences of his romantic delusion. Rosamond's musicianship is external and cold - she has "a voice that fell and trickled like cold water-drops" - and indicates not that she has a great soul but only that she is "a little too much the pattern-card of the finishing-school" (VI, lviii, lxiv, lxiii).

Lydgate's susceptibility to music is a weakness and a distraction from his work. Consistent with this is Eliot's portrayal of the male musicians of *Middlemarch* as effeminate and indolent. Will Ladislaw and Fred Vincy both "indulge" in music, and both are presented as men needing discipline and motivation.

Will Ladislaw looks the part of a romantic musician, or "Ariel," as he has bright curly hair and "a delicate but rather petulant profile" (IV, xxxvii). His Middlemarch neighbors view him with suspicion and account for his eccentricity by referring to his parentage (a "musical father" and theatrical mother) and his "foreign blood." As Mrs. Cadwallader contemptuously observes, "Oh, he's a dangerous young sprig, that Mr. Ladislaw . . . with his opera songs and his ready tongue. A sort of Byronic hero" (IV, xxxviii). Ladislaw lounges around Rosamond's piano singing roulades and "warbling" his improvisations: his languid pose, like his choice of French music, suggests his indolence but also his alluring sensuality. Eliot writes of Ladislaw: "Sometimes, when he took off his hat, shaking his head backward and showing his delicate throat as he sang, he looked like an incarnation of the spring whose spirit filled the air - a bright creature, abundant in uncertain promises" (V, xlvii).

But Ladislaw's musicality, like Philip Wakem's, is "dilettantish and amateurish," and Eliot mocks his affectation. To Dorothea, Will sententiously observes, "To be a poet is to have a soul so quick to discern that no shade of quality escapes it, and so quick to feel that discernment is but a hand playing with finely ordered variety on the chords of emotion--a soul in which knowledge passes instantaneously into feeling, and feeling flashes back a new organ of knowledge. One may have that condition by fits only" (II, xxii). Will's sensitivity includes a responsiveness to music: "the bow of a violin drawn near him cleverly would at one stroke change the aspect of the world for him, and his point of view shifted as easily as his mood" (IV, xxxix). As with Lydgate, such blind response to music is a sign of weakness and instability. Ladislaw must learn to look beyond his own enjoyment of beauty and learn to "think about the rest of the world," as Dorothea tells him (VI, liv). Eliot shows Ladislaw singing in the middle of the day with another man's wife while others work for the good of society, and implies that art enjoyed in this manner is selfish and frivolous. Ladislaw's music, though indicating his aesthetic potential and ability to love, becomes one manifestation of his "mode of taking all life as a holiday" (II, xxi). Ladislaw's selfish indulgence in music at the exclusion of work is as mistaken, Eliot suggests, as Casaubon's stultifying denial of music's beauty and power.

Like Ladislaw, Fred Vincy prefers a life of enjoyment to a life of labor. In Ladislaw's case, music helps complete his pose as a romantic **artiste**; in Vincy's case, a musical hobby helps to fill the days of a gentleman of leisure. Rosamond belittles her brother's flute-playing not only because of its poor quality but, more importantly for her, because it is unmasculine: "Really, Fred, I wish you would leave off playing the flute. A man looks very silly playing the flute. And you play so out of tune" (I, xi). Fred delivers on the flute "a wheezy performance, into which he threw much ambition and an irrepressible hopefulness," and bores the audience by playing "Cherry Ripe" on the piano with one hand (II, xvi). As the serious Mary Garth notes, such behavior shows Fred to be "an idle, frivolous creature" (III, xxv). Fred must abandon his life of ease and learn to use music to augment a life of work, not supplant it.

Fred Vincy's father-in-law, Caleb Garth, stands at the moral center of *Middlemarch* and exhibits what for Eliot seems the appropriate response to music. The industrious Caleb, like Adam Bede, finds music in his work: "The echoes of the great hammer . . . the signal shouts of the workmen, the roar of the furnace, the thunder and splash of the engine, were a sublime music to him" (III, xxiv). Rather than employing music as an escape from mechanism, Garth uses his imagination to blend the two. Furthermore, Garth appreciates the power of religious music: "Caleb was very fond of music, and when he could afford it went to hear an oratorio that came within his reach, returning from it with a profound reverence for this mighty structure of tones, which made him sit meditatively looking on the floor and throwing much unutterable language into his outstretched hands" (VI, lvi). Alone of the characters of *Middlemarch*, Caleb Garth admires music for its ability to inspire him but does not let his fondness for music interfere with his work. He does not renounce music with puritanical narrowness, as Dorothea and Casaubon do; he does not abandon himself to its allure, as Ladislaw and Lydgate do; nor does he indulge in music at the expense of serious work and thought, as Fred and Rosamond do. One senses Eliot's uncertainty towards the art of music: her heroes and heroines are musical but not full-fledged musicians.

Middlemarch also includes satirical portraits of the musical amateurs and philistines of rural English society. Eliot mocks this amusicality in a conversation between Rosamond and Lydgate. Rosamond remarks:

> "You will find Middlemarch very tuneless. There are hardly any good musicians. I only know two gentlemen who sing at all well."
> "I suppose it is the fashion to sing comic songs in a rhythmic way, leaving you to fancy the tune--very much as if it were tapped on a drum?"
> "Ah, you have heard Mr. Bowyer." (II, xv).

Eliot objects to Fred Vincy's and Will Ladislaw's musicianship not so much because it is effeminate as because their approach to the art is dilettantish. In contrast, Rosamond's music-master, like Eliot's own piano instructor, is "one of those excellent musicians here and there to be found in our provinces, worthy to compare with many a noted *kapellmeister* in a country which offers more plentiful conditions of musical celebrity" (II, xvi).

D.J. Smith writes of *Middlemarch*, "From the novel, there is little doubt that George Eliot considered it better to avoid playing whenever possible, as Dorothea did, then to appear too clever at the keyboard, as Rosamond did."[10] This perhaps misses Eliot's point. Rosamond's cleverness at the keyboard is contemptible not because her proficiency is unladylike but because she misuses her skill and lacks a corresponding fineness of character. Her regard for music as a mere social obligation is in part forgivable because she lacks an intelligent audience: her suitors request insipid sentimental songs, her husband cannot distinguish notes, her brother is out of tune, and she must perform before many who are "secretly impatient of the music" because "the card-tables stood ready" (II, xvi). Such an environment, Eliot maintains, cannot foster a serious musician, one who uses music to inspire others with faith, love, and motivation, but only "ill-inspired" artists who are "unable to go beyond Offenbach's music" (II, xv).

Daniel Deronda

Eliot's interest in music and the musician finds its fullest expression in her final novel, *Daniel Deronda*, 1876. Even more extensively than in *The Mill on the Floss* and *Middlemarch*, music in *Daniel Deronda* forms an integral part of the novel's symbolic and dramatic structure. Eliot analyzes the "accomplished" female, the romantic maestro, the frivolous dilettante, and the amusical philistine with increasing realism in *Daniel Deronda* and employs the musician as metaphor for the artist. The peculiar blend of sentimentalism, cynicism, nostalgia, and realism Eliot uses to describe the musicians of her final novel both reflects and comments on the contradictory Victorian response to music.

Although Albert Cirillo claims that *"Daniel Deronda* represents the most ambitious and inclusive expression of George Eliot's view of mankind," many critics have been less enthusiastic in their reception of Eliot's last novel and claim it lacks unity.[11] Articles such as Shirley Levenson's "The Use of Music in Daniel Deronda" and Percy M. Young's "George Eliot and Music" have helped to demonstrate the book's cohesiveness by showing the thematic importance of music in *Daniel Deronda*; however, critical analysis of Eliot's ambivalent attitude towards her musicians has been inadequate.[12] Music functions not only as an index "for revealing Gwendolen's essential character faults" and illustrating "Gwendolen's failure to participate in humanity," as Levenson and Cirillo suggest, but as a device for exposing the inexcusable state of education in England and the poverty of Victorian aesthetic standards.[13]

Consistent with the Victorian racial stereotyping described in Chapter III of this study, Eliot assumes in *Daniel Deronda* that Jews are naturally musical. One finds an astonishing number of Jewish musicians in the novel; as Levenson notes:

> . . . nearly all the truly natural musicians in the book are Jews: Mirah, whose "voice was considered wonderful for a child"; Daniel, who, as a child, "had not only one of those thrilling boy voices which seem to bring an idyllic heaven and earth before our eyes, but a fine musical instinct"; his mother, the Princess Halm-Eberstein, who was a "born singer" . . .; Mordecai, who, speaking of Jewish martyrs, says that the soul born within his "sang with the cadence of their strain"; and, of course, Herr Klesmer . . .[14]

Eliot uses her Jewish musicians as foils to their English counterparts: the magnificent Klesmer towers over the the multitude of English philistines who have no musical taste or skill; the gifted, spontaneous, and passionate Mirah opposes the affected and superficially "accomplished" Gwendolen Harleth; Daniel Deronda's enjoyment of music as an amateur and his appreciation of the art as a means of inspiration surpasses Mr. Lush's frivolous and indulgent view of music. But

Eliot's use of music is not this simplistic, nor is her hierarchy of musicians, musical amateurs, and anti-musicians a reliable mirror of her moral scheme.

Julius Klesmer, the German-Jewish composer and pianist of *Daniel Deronda* who delivers impassioned aesthetic statements, is Eliot's fullest characterization of the musician. Although Eliot does present Klesmer as a genius whose talent, benignity, and aritistic principles are superior to those around him, it is a mistake to view him as her ideal of the artist. Critics such as William Sullivan, for instance, label Klesmer "Eliot's most complete representation of the artist . . . a fully rounded particularization of her concept of the true artist"; Sullivan adds, "In the creation of Klesmer, Eliot expresses her total conception of man as artist and in him she combined the highest development of human spiritual and aesthetic being . . . Eliot did not go beyond Klesmer . . . In her attempt to portray the true artist, there was no place to go."[15] Such an interpretation mistakes Eliot's irony and her complex treatment of the musician. While Eliot celebrates Klesmer's artistry and benevolence and satirizes his hostile reception in Victorian society, she also mocks Klesmer's egotism and the incongruity of his romantic pose.

Gordon Haight, who writes that "the formidable musician Julius Klesmer stands out in memory among the two or three finest creations in *Daniel Deronda*," rejects the earlier assumption that Klesmer is modelled after Liszt and maintains that Eliot's portrait more closely resembles Anton Rubinstein, whom she met in 1854.[16] Rather than intending Klesmer to read as the fictional version of one person, Eliot seems to view Klesmer as a conglomeration of various inspired musician figures. Klesmer has Beethoven's wild "mane of hair" and gruffness, Mendelssohn's and Rubinstein's Jewish heritage, Liszt's commanding power over the piano keyboard, and the passion and martyred pose of Hoffmann's Kreisler and the fictional musicians of other German Romantics; Eliot invites the reader to see Klesmer as more than one musician by referring to him as "not yet a Liszt" but one who "may rank with Schubert and Mendelssohn" (*Daniel Deronda*, III, xxii).

Eliot's portrait of Klesmer as a genius with long, bushy hair, noble features, and passionate integrity imitates the standard Victorian vision of the romantic composer. Reverend Haweis, for instance, describes Beethoven: ". . . the rough hair brushed impatiently off the forehead, the boldly arched eyebrows, resolute nose, and firmly set mouth--truly a noble face, with a certain severe integrity, and passionate power, and lofty sadness about it, seeming, in its elevation and wideness of expression, to claim kindred with a world of ideas out of all proportion to our own."[17] Similarly, Eliot emphasizes Klesmer's integrity, massive size, wide-glancing eyes, and noble features.

Klesmer's looks, talent, and ideas set him apart from his English neighbors. He is a tall, thin figure with a dignified face who speaks with animation, pointing his long fingers and "folding his arms and tossing his mane"; he has "grand features" and "brown hair floating in artistic fashion" (I, v, x; II, xi). So far, Eliot's description is of a romantic artist, but she adds satiric notes to her portrait by continually commenting on Klesmer's clothing and the way others view him. Despite Klesmer's formidable appearance, he has "a certain softening air of silliness which will sometimes befall even Genius," and wears a hat "which had the look of having been put on for a joke" (I, v, x). Klesmer looks physically impressive "even in kid," although "his garments seemed a deplorable mockery of the human form" (V, xxxix). When people see Klesmer, "some were inclined to laugh, others felt a little disgust" (I, x). Eliot places her inspired musician in incongruous situations and asks, "Short of Apollo himself, what great musical *maestro* could make a good figure at an archery meeting?" (I, x). Eliot notes that a genius is an anachronism in an age demanding social conformity:

> Draped in a loose garment with a Florentine *berretta* on his head, he would have been fit to stand by the side of Leonardo da Vinci; but how when he presented himself in trousers which were not what English feeling demanded about the knees? --and when the fire that showed itself in his glances and the movements of his head, as he looked round him with curiosity, was turned into comedy by a hat which ruled that mankind should have well-cropped hair and a staid demeanor, such, for example, as Mr. Arrowpoint's, whose nullity of face and perfect tailoring might pass everywhere without ridicule? One sees why it is often better for greatness to be dead, and to have got rid of the outward man. (I, x)

By domesticating Klesmer and describing him in realistic details - his clothes, spectacles, and so forth - Eliot achieves satire in two directions: she mocks the narrowness of Victorians who would view the inspired artist in this mundane and irrelevant fashion, but she also rejects the overblown literary stereotype of the romantic musician by humanizing him and placing him against a realistic background.

Eliot does admire Klesmer's artistic integrity, talent, and vision and uses her foreign music-master to cast her English philistines into petty insignificance. Klesmer is blunt but kind, impassioned but disciplined. Eliot adds:

> Klesmer was as versatile and fascinating as a young Ulysses on a sufficient acquaintance--one whom nature seemed to have first made generously and then to have added music as a dominant power using all the abundant rest, and, as in Mendelssohn, finding expression for itself not only in the highest finish of execution, but in that fervour of creative work and theoretic belief which pierces the whole future of a life with the light of congruous, devoted purpose. (III, xx)

Although Klesmer exalts the life of the artist and the role of the musician, he realistically observes that the artistic vocation is "a life of arduous, unceasing work, and uncertain praise," and admits, "Genius at first is little more than a great capacity for receiving discipline." Art is a justifiable pursuit only if regarded with serious purpose: "An honourable life? Yes. But the honour comes from the inward vocation and the hard-won achievement: there is no honour in donning the life as a livery" (III, xxiii). In his impassioned defense of the musical profession, Klesmer insists that music has a social role. When the ignorant Mr. Bult remarks of Klesmer, "I was sure he had too much talent to be a mere musician," Klesmer fumes:

> "Ah, sir, you are under some mistake there," said Klesmer, firing up. "No man has too much talent to be a musician. Most men have too little. A creative artist is no more a mere musician that a great statesman is a mere politician. We are not ingenious puppets, sir, who live in a box and look out on the world only when it is gaping for amusement. We help to rule the nations and make the age as much as any other public men. We count ourselves on level benches with legislators. And a man who speaks effectively through music is compelled to something more difficult that parliamentary eloquence."
>
> With the last word Klesmer wheeled from the piano and walked away.
>
> Miss Arrowpoint coloured, and Mr. Bult observed with his usual phlegmatic solidity, "Your pianist does not think small beer of himself." (III, xxii)

The music Klesmer admires - Beethoven rather than Bellini - suggests his artistic seriousness but also a certain rigidity on his part. Klesmer excludes popular tunes and light Italian airs which Eliot admitted in her letters "were a welcome relief from more searching music" (Letters, VII, 344). Klesmer's performances are passionate to an extreme: at the Mallingers', his "torrent-like confluences of bass and treble seemed, like an convulsion of nature, to cast the conduct of petty mortals into insignificance" (VI, xiv); his own composition called "Freudvoll, Leidvoll, Gedankenvoll" (Joy, Sadness, and Thoughtfulness) seems in part intended as a parody of emotional German music:

> Herr Klesmer played a composition of his own, a fantasia called Freudvoll, Leidvoll, Gedankenvoll--an extensive commentary on some melodic ideas not too grossly evident; and he certainly fetched as much variety and depth of passion out of the piano as that moderately responsive instrument lends itself to, having an imperious magic in his fingers that seemed to send a nerve-thrill through ivory key and wooden hammer, and compel the strings to make a quivering lingering speech for him. (I, v)

Throughout Eliot emphasizes the "grandiose" effect of Klesmer's music, its awe-inspiring, formidable quality, but nowhere does she praise its tender beauty or soothing effect. Like Wagner's music, Klesmer's performances seem so emotional that they are wearying. Klesmer's continual emphasis on large sound (He calls on Gwendolen to "Sing now something larger"), his exaltation of the artist as a supramortal being "of another caste," and his desire for the "fusion of races" also suggest Wagner, whose ideas Eliot regarded with considerable reservations. Just as her description of Klesmer's performance emphasizes its effect on "petty mortals," so her comments in "Liszt, Wagner, and Weimar" on Wagner's operas place his music above "ordinary mortals": "*Lohengrin* to us ordinary mortals . . . has a dreamy charm for a little while, but by and bye you long for the sound even of a street organ to rush in and break the monotony" (*Essays*, p. 102). Klesmer, like Wagner, approaches his art and his audiences with unrelenting seriousness.

In her description of Liszt, Eliot notes that "There was nothing petty or egoistic to mar the picture" (Cross, I, 250); her remarks on Klesmer, however, do expose his egotism. After comparing Klesmer to Mendelssohn and admiring his generosity, Eliot adds that his "foibles" are his arrogance and vanity (III, xxii). Mr. Bult's conclusion that Klesmer "thinks no small beer of himself" has validity, for, as Gwendolen notes, Klesmer "admires his own genius" (V, xxxv). Klesmer arrogantly tells his future wife, Miss Arrowpoint, that "Even you can't understand the wrath of the artist: he is of another caste from you." Klesmer's decision to marry Catherine Arrowpoint follows her submissive answer, "That is true . . . He is of a caste to which I look up--a caste above mine" (III, xxii).

Despite Klesmer's grand claims for himself and his profession, he at times seems ineffectual and morally weak; these aspects of his character have been ignored by critics who view him as an artistic paragon. Klesmer willingly endures the patronage of the ignorant Arrowpoints and attends trivial social events, such as the archery meet, where he sits silently, "as taking up his cross meekly in a world overgrown with amateurs" (I, vi). Although Haight reads Klesmer's marriage to Miss Arrowpoint, "despite the disparity of wealth and social position," as "a happy note too often forgotten by the critics who insist on seeing *Daniel Deronda* as a melancholy book," such an interpretation seems debatable. Klesmer's appreciation for Miss Arrowpoint stems from her devotion to his genius, and his marriage, like the rest of his behavior, is a denial of his Judaic heritage. Klesmer's name, Yiddish for musician, signals his Jewishness, as does his description as "a felicitous combination of the German, the Sclave, and the Semite." Why, then, does Eliot provide no further discussion of this aspect of her character in a book so intimately concerned with Judaism? David Kaufmann admires the "fine touch of humour" in Klesmer's name and writes, "He is unmistakably a Jew, but he never betrays himself, although the unfortunate name Julius Klesmer is enough for the initiated." Kaufman's use of "betray" is interesting, for this works in two ways: Klesmer does not dare "betray" his Jewishness if he hopes to receive the continued patronage of and acceptance by aristocratic English society, but by this denial and his subsequent marriage to an Anglican heiress, Klesmer betrays his religion. Like Thackeray's Baroski, who attends church and makes a point of eating pork, Klesmer finds it lucrative to remain vague about his heritage. One cannot assume Eliot applauds this action, since she later attacks a society which forces Jewish singers, such as Mirah Cohen, to change their names before they can perform. Moreover, in her essay "The Modern Hep! Hep! Hep!" Eliot criticizes Jews who, like Klesmer, do not struggle to maintain a separate identity: "If they drop that separateness which is made their reproach, they may be in danger of lapsing into a cosmopolitan indifference equivalent to cynicism."

Klesmer symbolizes not the ideal artist but the foreign artist. Eliot admires Klesmer's artistic integrity, proficiency, and discipline, particularly when placed against a backdrop of English philistinism, but she simultaneously mocks Klesmer's romantic fervor and high seriousness. Klesmer's scornful remarks about his English public ("He can hardly tolerate anything we English do in music," Miss Arrowpoint observes) seem less admirable when one remembers his willingness to profit from this same public. To read Klesmer as Eliot's "perfection" of the "true artist," as Sullivan does, misses Eliot's two-directional satire.20

Much of Klesmer's sense of superiority, however, appears justified when one examines the vast array of snobbish and unmusical Englishmen surrounding him. The only proficient English musician in the novel appears to be his wife, Catherine Arrowpoint, but Eliot's major praise of her musicality is that it is "thorough," a phrase repeated three times in connection with Miss Arrowpoint's performances; as Gwendolen Harleth notes, Catherine has an "exasperating thoroughness" (I, vi). The other English men and women in *Daniel Deronda* cannot even claim this thoroughness.

Gwendolen Harleth, like Rosamond Vincy, prides herself on her musical "accomplishment" but, without disciplined practice and competent instruction, she has only achieved mediocrity. Eliot presents Gwendolen as a parody of the true artist and suggests that the blame lies not only with Gwendolen's moral shortcomings but with a society which expects no more from its women than that they, like Jane Eyre, play "a littie."

Eliot parodies the heroine whose love of music and fondness for nature seem intertwined by showing the vain Gwendolen's cruelty towards a singing bird:

> . . . there was a disagreeable silent remembrance of her having strangled her sister's canary-bird in a final fit of exasperation at its shrill singing which had again and again jarringly interrupted her own. She had taken pains to buy a white mouse for her sister in retribution, . . . inwardly excusing herself on the ground of a peculiar sensitiveness which was a mark of her general superiority. (I, iii)

In the same chapter Eliot achieves irony by showing Gwendolen posing as St. Cecilia, the patron saint of music. Gwendolen sits at an organ and wants to be painted in "an admirable pose" with her hair down: "Here is an organ. I will be Saint Cecilia: someone shall paint me a Saint Cecilia" (I, iii). Gwendolen's concern with her appearance and theatrical pose mock the art whose patron saint she represents. Later Eliot presents Gwendolen in a scene which parodies the Shakespearean notion of music as a restorative force: when Gwendolen poses as Hermione in *The Winter's Tale* and music is called for to awaken her, a panel flies open and discloses the picture of a dead face (I, vi).

Like Rosamond Vincy, Gwendolen soon learns that music can be useful: she bribes her uncle into giving her a saddle-horse by singing to him, and uses her accomplishment "to strike others with admiration." Eliot writes, "About her French and music, the two justifying accomplishments of a young lady, she felt no ground for uneasiness," and Gwendolen delights in the fact that she looks her prettiest while engaged in singing. Because Gwendolen has a "moderately powerful soprano" and good ear, her singing "gave pleasure to ordinary hearers" (I, iv, v).

In *Middlemarch*, when Rosamond Vincy learns that Lydgate will be listening to her music she says to him with false humility, "I will let you hear my attempts. But I shall tremble before you, who have heard the best singers of Paris" (*Middlemarch*, II, xvi). But unlike Lydgate, who lacked musical discernment and was no judge of Rosamond's performance, Klesmer critically listens to Gwendolen's rendition of an air by Bellini and bluntly expresses his disapproval, because "woman was dear to him, but music was dearer":

> "You are not quite without gifts. You sing in tune, and you have a pretty fair organ. But you produce your notes badly; and that music which you sing is beneath you. It is a form of melody which expresses a puerile state of culture--a dangling, canting, see-saw kind of stuff--the passion and thought of a people without any breadth or horizon. There is a sort of self-satisfied folly about every phrase of such melody: no cries of deep, mysterious passion--no conflict--no sense of the universal. It makes men small as they listen to it. Sing now something larger." (I, v)

Klesmer is extreme in his censure of Italian music but quite correctly notes Gwendolen's lack of musical passion and seriousness. She sings "from the drawingroom *standpunkt*," without sincere love or understanding of the works she chooses. Although Gwendolen has artistic potential - she appreciates good music and has an inborn ability to keep in tune - at her age, Klesmer notes, she can "hardly achieve more than mediocrity"; only if she had received qualified instruction beginning in childhood might she have achieved greatness (III, xxiii). Rather than admitting her limitations as an artist but continuing to give and receive pleasure from her music, Gwendolen haughtily renounces the art: "I have given a great deal of time to music. But I have not talent enough to make it worth while. I shall never sing again" (V, xxxiv). Eliot implies that Gwendolen's refusal to continue as a musical amateur is as mistaken as her naive belief that she can become a great musician or actress merely by choice.

Eliot suggests that Gwendolen's faulty musicianship is as much the result of her surroundings as of her own lack of discipline. Gwendolen, "not being one of those exceptional persons who have a parching thirst for a perfection undemanded by their neighbours," has become merely "a charming young lady" (I, vi; III, xxiii). As Gwendolen notes herself, "We women . . . are brought up like the flowers, to look as pretty as we can, and be dull without complaining" (II, xiii) Young women *must* learn music to succeed in Victorian society, despite the fact that "Many of our girls nowadays want lessons not to sing" (V, xxxvi).

Gwendolen's audiences lack musical discrimination and taste. Her uncle, the "sound English" rector Mr. Gascoigne, "would have sung finely if his time had not been too much take up by graver matters." Sir Hugo has turned his choir-room into a stable, symbolizing the degradation of English aristocratic culture. Hans Meyrick, a painter, "can't sing two notes in tune" (V, xxxvii). The archdeacon's classical son Clintok, who prefers croquet to music, finds Klesmer's playing "like a jar of leeches where you can never tell either beginnings or endings" and exclaims, "What extreme guys those artistic fellows usually are!" (I, v, x). Similarly, the expectant peer Mr. Bult ridicules Klesmer as a "mere musician" and frivolous "coxcomb" (III, xxii). Musical amateur Mr. Lush, whose name and corpulence suggest his sensuality, regards his cello playing as a luxury and is "too fond of Meyerbeer and Scribe--too fond of the mechanical-dramatic" (II, xi). Finally, Gwendolen's brutal husband, Grandcourt, hates "fellows wanting to howl litanies" and sneeringly tells Lush to invite to his party "one of your damned musicians. But not a comic fellow" (V, xxxv; II, xi). He silences Gwendolen's attempts to sing by remarking: "I don't see why a lady should sing. Amateurs make fools of themselves. And one doesn't want to hear squalling in private" (VI, xlv). What wonder, then, that in this milieu Gwendolen has not developed her musical potential!

In addition, Eliot shows that devoted artists, despite their talent and vision, occupy a low position in the Victorian social hierarchy. The Arrowpoints are glad enough to exhibit Herr Klesmer to their neighbors, since "to have a first-rate musician in your house is a privilege of wealth," but they are outraged to learn of his plan to marry their daughter and they promptly disinherit her (III, xxii). They mistakenly thought their daughter was as safe with Klesmer in the house as "with the footman," since most musicians would know their place. Mrs. Arrowpoint rejects her daughter's insistence that Klesmer's genius makes him her superior and she cannot accept his eccentricities: "While Klesmer was seen in the light of a patronised musician, his peculiarities were picturesque and acceptable, but to see him by a sudden flash in the light of her son-in-law gave her a burning sense of what the world would say." After futilely insisting that their daughter marry "a gentleman" or "a nobleman," Mr. and Mrs. Arrowpoint hurl insults at Klesmer. He is "a gypsy, a Jew, a mere bubble of the earth," "a mountebank . . . a charlatan"; Mr. Arrowpoint objects, "He won't do at the head of estates. He has a deuced foreign look--is an unpractical man." Though willing to exploit Klesmer's talent, the Arrowpoints have no intention of granting him social equality (III, xxii).

To counter her portrait of the Engiish musical heroine, Gwendolen Harleth, and the musical philistines, Eliot describes a Jewish musician and a Jewish music appreciator. She praises both Mirah Lapidoth's sincere, spontaneous skill, which contrasts with Gwendolen's affected mediocrity, and Deronda's appreciation of music's inspirational power and enjoyment of his own limited talent.

The "Jewess" Mirah, like Scott's Zilia, Meredith's Emilia, and Eliot's Caterina, is musical by nature. Her singing is "like a bird's wooing" and her words are "as spontaneous as bird-notes"; Deronda marvels, "you might imagine her singing all came by nature" (VI, xlv, V, xxxvi). She sings without self-consciousness and without theatricality, and her choice of Beethoven's *Lied*, patriotic songs, German arias, Schubert songs, and Hebrew hymns reflects her sincerity and passion. Eliot describes her voice: "She sang Beethoven's 'Per pieta non dirmi addio,' with a subdued but searching pathos which had that essential of perfect singing, the making one oblivious of art or manner, and only possessing one with the song. It was the art of voice that gives the impression of being meant like a bird's wooing for an audience near and beloved" (IV, xxxii). As a music-master in Vienna informs Mirah, her voice is meant not for ostentatious or grandiose display but for intimate performances: "it will never do for the public: --it is gold, but a thread of gold dust" (III, xx). The tender pathos of Mirah's voice, a far cry from the massive sounds of nineteenth century operas and orchestral symphonies, evokes an earlier age of simplicity. Eliot nostalgically describes Mirah's performance of a Hebrew hymn "of quaint melancholy intervals" and shows the soothing effect of such music on the old-fashioned Mrs. Meyrick: "Her voice is just perfect," Mrs.

Meyrick says, "not loud and strong, but searching and melting, like the thoughts of what had been. That is the way old people like me feel a beautiful voice" (IV, xxxii).

Like Klesmer, Mirah suffers exploitation as an artist. She changes her last name to deemphasize her Jewishness, and at Lady Mallinger's is "remarked on in a free and easy way, as if she were an imported commodity disdainfully paid for by the fashionable public" (VI, xlv). Because artists are regarded in this way, Daniel Deronda chooses not to cultivate his musical talent. Deronda's Jewish ancestry seems to account for his gift, and his "musical instinct" exhibits itself early in childhood. When his guardian Sir Hugo asks him if he would like to develop his "thrilling voice" and become a great singer, Deronda replies, "No; I should hate it," because he realizes such a career would exclude him from the English gentry. Eliot writes of Deronda: "Now, spite of his musical gift, he set himself bitterly against the notion of being dressed up to sing before all those fine people who would not care for him except as a wonderful toy" (II, xvi). Deronda avoids being a "toy"; Klesmer objects to being an "ingenious puppet," and Mirah is treated as "a fashionable commodity":   Eliot reiterates the theme found in Thackeray and Meredith that Victorian society regards the artist as an object and possession.

Deronda chooses not to become a musician; nevertheless, he continues to sing and to appreciate the music of others. The chanted liturgies he hears at a synagogue inspire him with "self-oblivious lifting up of gladness" (IV, xxxii). Rather than giving up music, the way Gwendolen does, Deronda continues to play as a source of personal inspiration: he tells her, "if you are fond of music, it will always be worth while in private, for your own delight. I make it a virtue to be content with my middlingness . . . it is always pardonable, so that one does not ask others to take it for superiority" (V, xxxv). As he reveals to Gwendolen, Deronda finds music to be a fruitful source of metaphor which "answers for all larger things" in life (V, xxxvi).

In a letter to Harriet Beecher Stowe in 1876, Eliot concedes of *Daniel Deronda* that "the Jewish element seems to me likely to satisfy nobody," and adds that she hoped to use antisemitism as an illustration of Victorian prejudice:

> Can anything be more disgusting than to hear people called "educated" making small jokes about eating ham, and showing themselves empty of any real knowledge as to the relation of their own social and religious life to the history of the people they think

themselves witty in insulting? . . . This inability to find interest in any form of life that is not clad in the same coat-tails and flounces as our own, lies very close to the worst kind of irreligion. The best than can be said of it is, that it is a sign of the intellectual narrowness--in plain English, the stupidity--which is still the average mark of our culture. (Cross, III, 294-5)

Eliot also uses musical ignorance and contempt of the musician to illustrate this "intellectual narrownees" which is the "average mark" of Victorian culture, and weaves the two motifs together by making her Jewish characters musical. Eliot's obsession in *Daniel Deronda* with Jewish musicians results in part from her nostalgic regard for Judaism as a culture of greater beauty and "primitive" harmony. By presenting her "Jewess" as innately musical and by describing Mirah's father as a money-grubbing Jew who wants to make a financial profit from his daughter's singing, Eliot seems to echo the very racial stereotyping she hoped her novel would transcend.

In *Daniel Deronda* Eliot's use of music as metaphor finds its most complete exploration. Eliot's final novel is unique among the Victorian novels because of its pervasive preoccupation with music and its insistence that the musician, like any other artist, must practice diligently, receive competent instruction, transcend the shallow taste of his age, set high standards, and be willing to suffer indignities for the sake of his art.

Percy M. Young in "George Eliot and Music" sets Eliot apart from her contemporaries and concludes that her extensive treatment of music compensates for other Victorian novelists' neglect of this art:

> Without George Eliot there would be missing the musical life of the period. In general musicians feel a sense of disappointment with the Victorians, but George Eliot mitigates that disappointment. She assures us that music was by no means a lost art, that village communities enjoyed communal music-making before the era of Rural Music Schools, that the *bourgeoisie* carried on the ancient tradition of domestic music and that the aristocracy still spent money lavishly, if not always wisely, on patronage . . . Music, she postulates, is good for the community, and should be provided for the benefit of the many.[21]

Eliot does far more than just assure us that there was indeed a flourishing "musical life of the period." Her European travels made her painfully aware of the musical shortcomings of her country, and she introduces musical scenes into her novels to illustrate Victorian provincialism and the need for better education. In her final novel she attempts to move beyond the sentimentalism, cynicism, and nostalgia of her contemporaries by realistically depicting her romantic maestro and "accomplished" female as complex characters suffering from the artistic poverty of their environment.

Yet despite Eliot's attempts to transcend the literary stereotype of the musician and vindicate the art of music, she never seems fully comfortable with this art form. By presenting so many musicians in her novels who are foreigners, affected females, or effeminate dilettantes, and by choosing not to develop the character of a professional English musician, Eliot reinforces Victorian suspicion of the art. Like Dickens, Thackeray, and other Victorian novelists, Eliot uses the musician as a metaphor for the artist and uses Victorian amusicality to symbolize the shocking state of aesthetics in England, but like the other novelists, Eliot herself cannot fully escape the prejudices of her time. Although Eliot's novels treat music with a new note of realism, she sentimentally links music with "race," nostalgically describes the simple musicians of the past, and cynically suspects that many who practice music do so to avoid work and social responsibility. To describe her own activity as a writer Eliot finds painting a more appropriate metaphor, as in her famous remarks in *Adam Bede* that her writing resembles the painting of the Dutch realists (see Hugh Witemeyer, *George Eliot and the Visual Arts*[22]). Eliot admires the musician but seems reluctint to embrace his profession without stipulating that he perform a service for the community, select his compositions carefully, and remain free of moral taint. Eliot's multi-faceted attitude towards the musicians of her novels typifies the Victorian uncertainty towards music. Fascinating, inspiring, and soothing though it was to members of Victorian society, music, because of its severance from morality and national identity, remained an unassimilable art.

Chapter VIII: Notes

1 Gordon Haight in *George Eliot: A Bibliography* (Oxford: Claredon Press, 1968), p. 471, notes that Eliot frequently visited Edmund Deutsch, the model for the Jewish Mordecai in *Daniel Deronda*, at his lodgings with the Reverend and Mrs. Haweis.

2 J. W. Cross, ed. *George Eliot's Life, as Related in her Letters and Journals* (N.Y.: Harper Brothers, 1885), I, 18-19. Subsequent references to Cross's work will be indicated by page number in the text.

3 *The George Eliot Letters*, ed. Gordon S. Haight (New Haven: Yale University Press, 1954), I, 13. Eliot letters referred to in the text are from this edition.

4 Ludwig Feuerbach, *The Essence of Christianity*, trans. George Eliot (London: John Chapman, 1854), pp. 3-4, 8.

5 "Worldliness and Other-Worldliness: the Poet Young" (January, 1857), in *Essays of George Eliot*, ed. Thomas Pinney (London: Routledge & Kegan Paul, 1963), p. 379.

6 William J. Sullivan, "George Eliot and the Fine Arts," Ph.D. Diss., University of Wisconsin (1970), p. 41.

7 "Liszt, Wagner, and Weimar" (July, 1955), in *Essays*, pp. 97 ff. Also see Eliot's remarks on Liszt in Cross, I, 243 ff.

8 See chapter II of this study, n. 64.

9 Barbara Hardy, *The Novels of George Eliot* (London: Athlone Press, 1954), p. 117.

10 D. J. Smith, "Music in the Victorian Novel," *Kenyon Review*, 25 (Summer 1963), p. 524.

11 Albert R. Cirillo, "Salvation in *Daniel Deronda*: The Fortunate Overthrow of Gwendolen Harleth," *Literary Monographs, I*, ed. Rothstein and Dunseath (University of Wisconsin Press, 1967), p. 203.

12 Shirley Levenson, "The Use of Music in *Daniel Deronda*," *Nineteenth Century Fiction*, 24 (Dec. 1969), 317-34; Percy M. Young, "George Eliot and Music," *Music and Letters*, 24 (April 1943), 92-100.

13 Levenson, p. 319; Cirillo p. 218.

14 Levenson, p. 317.

15 Sullivan, p. 338.

16 Gordon Haight, "George Eliot's Klesmer," *Imagined Worlds*, ed. Maynard Mack & Ian Gregor (London: Methuen, 1968), pp. 209, 212.

17 Reverend H.R. Haweis, *Music and Morals* (N.Y. : Harper & Brothers, 1871), pp. 272-73.

18 Haight, "George Eliot's Klesmer," p. 205.

19 Ibid.

20 Sullivan, p. 338.

21 Young, pp. 99-100.

22 For a discussion of Eliot and painting see Hugh Witemeyer's *George Eliot and the Visual Arts* (New Haven: Yale University Press, 1979).

Chapter VIII

Conclusion

He. AH, the bird-like fluting
        Through the ash-tops yonder-
Bullfinch-bubblings, soft sounds suiting
        What sweet thoughts, I wonder?
Fine-pearled notes that surely
        Gather, dewdrop fashion,
Deep-down in some heart which purely
        Secretes globuled passion--
Passion insuppressive--
        Such is piped, for certain;
Love, no doubt, nay, love excessive
        'T is, your ash-tops curtain . . .
        Holds earth such a wonder?
Fairy-mortal, soul-sense-fusing
        Past thought's power to sunder!. . .

She. All's your fancy-spinning!
        Here's the fact: a neighbor
Never-ending, still beginning,
        Recreates his labour:
Deep o'er desk he drudges,
        Adds, divides, subtracts and
Multiplies, until he judges
        Noonday-hour's exact sand
Shows the hour-glass emptied:
        Then comes lawful leisure,
Minutes rare from toil exempted,
        Fit to spend in pleasure.

        Out then with--what treatise?
        Youth's Complete Instructor

How to play the Flute. Quid petis?
                    Follow Youth's conductor
On and on, through *Easy*,
                    Up to *Harder, Hardest*
Flute-piece, till thou, flautist wheezy,
                    Possibly discardest
Tootlings hoarse and husky,
                    Mayst expend with courage
Breath--on tunes once bright, now dusky--
                    Meant to cool thy porridge. . .
                    Robert Browning, "Flute-Music,
                              With an Accompaniment"

Browning's "Flute-Music, with an Accompaniment" describes two people listening to a musician: the man views the flautist as a "fairy-mortal" who discloses a realm of enchanted beauty; the woman factually sees him as a neighbor whose performance is wheezy and amateurish. Like Browning, Victorian novelists regarded the musician with a blend of romanticism and realism and used the tension between these two visions to illustrate the changing spirit of their age.

Anthony Trollope writes in his biography of Thackeray, "To be realistic you must know accurately that which you describe."[1] Because most Victorian novelists, like their contemporaries, lacked a thorough grounding in music, they depicted the musician as superhuman, subhuman, or prehuman, an emblem of divinity, demonism, or pastoral innocence. The musician symbolized the allure and danger of romanticism, the attractions and shortcomings of other ages and cultures. Although radically different, the godlike Chevalier Seraphael, sinister Svengali, innocent Florence Dombey, aging Mr. Harding, and Beethovean Klesmer share a common feature: existence outside ordinary society. Their love of music symbolizes this otherness.

Music's fluidity and freedom from words made it an uncontrollable, dangerous, but immensely exciting art form. Victorian novelists likened the musician's ability to sexual power because, like sex, music invaded the emotions and released inhibitions. Also like sex, music simultaneously attracted and repelled Victorians: the irrational nature of both was threatening to a culture which prided itself on its common sense, sobriety, and restraint. The Jewish Svengali and Italian Count

Fosco, however satanic, offer their English listeners new vistas of beauty and magic. Rochester's singing penetrates Jane Eyre, Angel Clare's harp-playing brings Tess erotic pleasure; Stephen Guest's singing reawakens Maggie's dormant sensibility; Klesmer's playing arouses Gwendolen Harleth, whose eyes "become brighter, her cheeks slightly flushed" (*Daniel Deronda*, I, v). Because Victorian prudery made it impossible for novelists to describe explicitly the darker side of human nature - sexual passions, subconscious desires - , music became an important literary tool. The musician offered what Victorian society denied, repressed, and feared, what it yearned for, what it could not understand. Count Fosco's simultaneous charm and horror, Oran Haut-ton's bestiality and divinity, and Catherine Gilfil's innocence and diabolism reveal the Victorian novelists' contradictory emotions towards all that music symbolized. Late Victorian George Moore captured this tension in *Evelyn Innes* (1899) and *Sister Teresa* (1901), the two-part story of an English *prima donna* who abandons her musical profession to become a nun.

Yet novelists also discerned that these musical characters hardly seemed appropriate in British novels which aimed to be realistic. Just as Wordsworth's praise of the innocent child "trailing clouds of glory" and Shelley's celebration of the ethereal marriage between god and goddess bore little resemblance to the squalling toddlers and strife-ridden marriages of Victorian life, so the musicians of the literary past seemed obsolete figments of the imagination. In a scientific climate which fostered Darwinian evolution and Mendelian genetics, nightingales became just birds, not melodious, divinely-inspired artists. The sky, Samuel Butler observed, had been untuned; glorious harmony had changed to reality's discord:

> I saw the world a great orchestra filled with angels whose instruments were of gold. And I saw the organ on the top of the axis round which all should turn, but nothing turned and nothing moved and the angels stirred not and all was as still as a stone, and I was myself also, like the rest, as still as a stone.
>
> Then I saw some huge, cloud-like forms nearing, and behold! it was the Lord bringing two of his children by the hand.
>
> "Oh, Papa!" said one, "isn't it pretty?"
>
> "Yes, my dear," said the Lord, "and if you drop a penny into the box the figures will work."
>
> Then I saw that what I had taken for the keyboard of the organ was no keyboard but only a slit, and one of the little Lords dropped a plaque of metal into it. And then the angels played and the world

turned round and the organ made a noise and the people began killing one another and the two little Lords clapped their hands and were delighted. (*Notebooks*, viii)

Musicians no longer escaped close scrutiny: they were humans with human feelings and needs. Did Keats's belle-dame earn money for her 'faery's song'? asked cynical Victorian novelists. Although an inspiring romantic figure, Meredith's Emilia must watch her weight; despite their rustic innocence, Hardy's Mellstock Quire members must rehearse; however grand, Eliot's Klesmer must earn an income. As Butler conceded of his artistic idols, "was not the Iliad written mainly with a view to money? Did not Shakespeare make money by his plays, Handel by his music, and the noblest painters by their art?" (*Notebooks*, xi).

For Victorian novelists, the intrusion of monetary concerns into the musical sphere illustrated the negative qualities of nineteenth century England. Thackeray's Sir George Thrum counts the guineas he earns from "his little trade," Dickens' Mrs. Briggs and Mrs. Taunton regard their daughters' musical instruments and instruction as shrewd investments, Hardy's Wessex composer switches to a more profitable vocation, and Eliot's Klesmer lacks "that supreme, world-wide celebrity which makes an artist great to the most ordinary people by their knowledge of his great expensiveness" (*Daniel Deronda*, I, x). With great originality, Victorian novelists used musical scenes to ridicule Victorian commercialism and avarice.

Music also offered novelists the ideal means to satirize British affectation and uncouthness. Victorians read novels and looked at paintings in relative privacy and silence, but when attending recitals and concerts they were forced into the public eye. To demonstrate their countrymen's philistinism, novelists showed them applauding in between movements of a symphony, arriving late, talking during performances, thinking of petty concerns while Beethoven's strains engulfed the concert hall. "Igh art won't do in this country . . . It's a melancholy fact," notes Gandish in *The Newcomes* (I, xvii).

As the musician became a metaphor for the artist, novelists began to depict his craft with greater realism and appreciation. Victorian novelists sympathized with the composer's inability to have his works properly executed, the musician's herculean task of gaining the admiration and acceptance of tone-deaf Britishers who regarded him as a fashionable toy. Dickens and Thackeray made their readers see that music requires incessant practice. In her poem "Stradivarius" George Eliot argued for a realistic recognition of musical talent.

> Not Bach alone, helped by fine precedent
> Of genius gone before, nor Joachim
> Who holds the strain afresh incorporate
> By inward hearing and notation strict
> Of nerve and muscle, made our joy to-day:
> Another soul was living in the air
> And swaying it to true deliverance
> Of high invention and responsive skill:
> That plain white-aproned man who stood at work
> Patient and accurate full fourscore years,
> Cherished his sight and touch by temperance,
> And since keen sense is love of perfectness
> Made perfect violins, the needed paths
> For inspiration and high mastery.

When romantic painter Naldo claims that the arts "subsist on freedom - eccentricity - / Uncounted inspirations," Stradivari counters:

> "If thou wilt call thy pictures eggs,
> I call the hatching, work. 'T is God gives skill,
> But not without men's hands: He could not make
> Antonio Stradivari's violins
> Without Antonio. Get thee to thy easel."

As Klesmer tells Gwendolen in *Daniel Deronda*, genius is little more than the ability to receive discipline, the life of a musician one of "arduous, unceasing work."

In a sense, Victorian novelists destroyed the literary convention of the romantic musician by exaggerating their musical characters to ludicrous heights or reducing them to lilliputian stature. Because of their concern that art be moral and useful, novelists viewed musicians with suspicion and depicted them as weak, lazy, or impotent. Victorian novelists also were unwilling to abandon their national pride. Although novelists conceded England's amusicality and used it as a symbol of their country's faults, they seemed reluctant to admit that this proved foreigners' superiority. Wagner's blatant German nationalism, his insistence that concerts be serious, formidable experiences, and his vision of the musician as a priestlike mentor antagonized many Englishmen. In seeking an English replacement for the musicians of German romanticism, Victorian novelists turned to the unschooled but gifted folk-singers of the English countryside. In addition, novelists celebrated the virtues of the hearty, healthy Englishman who refused to pretend appreciation for foreign music: Mr. Pole, Fitz-boodle, Cox, and Tom Tulliver, though unmusical, have redeeming qualities.

It is perhaps too easy to ridicule Victorian novelists' approach to music and to ignore their extraordinary achievements. Dickens, Thackeray, Hardy, Eliot, and other novelists denigrated the hero-musician by domesticating him and showing his monetary motives, but they also did much to elevate the art of music by approaching it with greater accuracy and respect. Though not capable of overcoming the attitudes of their time, Victorian novelists did far more than just mirror the musical life of their period: they used music metaphorically to reveal character and to symbolize change, and turned discussions of the musician into an exploration of how artists should conduct themselves in a world which was increasingly unreceptive to their vocation. Passages on music in the Victorian novel - Fosco defending Italian opera, Mrs. Ponto's rapturous response to her daughters' performances, Mr. Slope's denunciation of church music, Casaubon's disdainful remarks on "measured noises" - reveal that many Victorian novelists transformed music into a fertile symbol. Their unique use of music and varied portrayal of the musician left an indelible impression on novelists, poets, and playwrights of succeeding generations.

Oscar Wilde writes in the Preface to *The Picture of Dorian Gray* (1891), "From the point of view of form the type of all the arts is the musician." Wilde, Pater, and the symbolist poets rejoiced in the musician's lack of moral concentration and in his ability to stimulate the senses. Music was abstract, intangible, its beauty untrammeled by moral concerns or questions of social utility.[2] Because Wilde and others held that "all art is immoral . . . emotion for the sake of emotion is the aim of art," music emerged as "the perfect type of art."[3]

Around the turn of the century, George Bernard Shaw took iconoclastic gibes at the Victorian approach to music. To counter John Ruskin's remark that "True music is the natural expression of a lofty passion for the right cause," Shaw writes, "Music will express any emotion, base or lofty. She is absolutely unmoral."[4] Shaw ridicules Ruskin's "virtuous indignation" towards the "moral degradation" of operatic works such as *Don Giovanni*: and also insists that not *all* Italians are musical. In addition, Shaw attacks the Victorian passion for spreading music to the poor: in 1889 he writes with justifiable indignation, "What we want is not music for the people, but bread for the people, hope for them, enjoyment, equal respect and consideration, life and aspiration, instead of drudgery and despair. When we get that I imagine the people will make tolerable music for themselves."[5]

Although Wilde and Shaw react against Victorian attitudes, their treatment of music is heavily indebted to the Victorian novelists. In *The Importance of Being Earnest*, Wilde mocks the romantic pose by having Algernon play with expression rather that accuracy, and he ridicules philistines like Lady Henry in *Dorian Gray*, an English aristocrat who likes Wagner's music best because its loudness enables her to talk right through the performance. Similarly, Shaw continues Dickens' and Thackeray's expose of English parochialism and shallowness. To Ruskin's remark that young ladies should continue their accomplishments as a "means of assistance to others," Shaw replies a la Thackeray, "The greatest assistance the average young lady musician can render to others is to stop." "Hell is full of musical amateurs," he adds in *Man and Superman* (Act III).

Like Samuel Butler, Thomas Hardy, and George Eliot, later novelists found Wagner's music and philosophy heavy and wearisome, emotionally draining. Wilde challenges the seriousness of Wagner's Ring Cycle by comparing it to the ring of the doorbell.[6] Even Shaw, a "violent Wagnerite," admits, "My favourite way of enjoying a performance of The Ring is to sit at the back of the box, comfortable on two chairs, feet up, and listen without looking."[7] George Moore, another champion of Wagner, suggested in his novels that Wagner's operas could be overwhelming, psychologically disturbing. Like Nietzsche, who changed from adoration of Wagner to violent abhorrence of his work and philosophy, many twentieth century English writers sought to extricate art from overseriousness and dangerous emotionalism. "He has made music sick," wrote Nietzsche of Wagner[8]; similarly, characters in D.H. Lawrence's *Aaron's Rod* (1922) feel like retching when forced to listen to Wagner's music. As in Hardy, relief for Lawrence comes through simple folk melodies or medieval music played on the unaccompanied flute. Margaret in E.M. Forster's *Howards End* speaks for many when she complains, "I wonder if the day will ever return when music will be treated as music . . . the real villain is Wagner. He has done more than any man in the nineteenth century towards the muddling of the arts" (*Howards End*, ch. v).

The Englishman whose zest and sincerity compensate for his lack of musical skill and understanding continues to appear in twentieth century works. In *Aaron's Rod* Lawrence praises his wonderful English colonel who dances a jig during a supposedly serious recital:

> Lady Franks started with a *vivace* Schumann piece. Everybody listened in sanctified silence, trying to seem to like it. When suddenly our Colonel began to spring and bounce in his chair, slinging his loose leg with a kind of rapture up and down in the air, and capering upon his posterior, doing a sitting-down jig to a Schumann *vivace* . . . Rosy and unabashed, he was worthy of the great nation he belonged to. (xiii)

Just as Lawrence's Colonel turns a solemn musical event into an entertaining occasion, so Gilbert and Sullivan's comic operas "in English" reverse and comment on Wagner's deadly serious approach to the operatic form.

D.H. Lawrence writes, "In England, everybody seems held tight and gripped, nothing is left free" (*Aaron's Rod*, xv). George Eliot used Dorothea's hysterical response to an oratorio to suggest her repressed emotions, and Thackeray described Ridley's interpretation of music in order to show his imaginative soul; to an even greater extent, twentieth century writers have seized on music as a vehicle for revealing hidden emotions. A character's response to music, like his dreams, provides a glimpse beyond surfaces to underlying psychological truths. Forster's *Howards End* (1908-10), Virginia Woolf's "String Quartet" (1921), Lawrence's *Aaron's Rod* (1922), James Joyce's *Ulysses* (1922), Aldous Huxley's *Point Counter Point* (1928), and countless other twentieth century British novels and stories employ musical scenes to unlock characters' minds.

In *Howards End*, for instance, Forster describes the audience at a Beethoven concert:

> It will be generally admitted that Beethoven's Fifth Symphony is the most sublime noise that has ever penetrated into the ear of man. All sorts and conditions are satisfied by it. Whether you are like Mrs. Munt, and tap surreptitiously when the tunes come--of course, not so as to disturb the others--; or like Helen, who can see heroes and shipwrecks in the music's flood; or like Margaret, who can see only the music; or like Tibby, who is profoundly versed in counterpoint, and holds the full score open on his knee; or like their cousin, Fraulein Mosebach, who remembers all the time that Beethoven is "echt Deutsch"; or like Fraulein Mosebach's young man, who can remember nothing but Fraulein Mosebach; in any case, the passion of your life becomes

more vivid, and you are bound to admit that such noise is cheap at two shillings.

(*Howards End*, v)

Alex Aronson in *Music and the Novel: A Study of Twentieth Century Fiction* writes of this and other passages in Forster's novels, "In his emphasis on the authentic listener to music as a character endowed with a singular insight into the folly and insensitivity of the socially conditioned concert-goer, Forster reveals himself a faithful disciple of a tradition first established by the French writer in his great novel" [Proust, *Remembrance of Things Past*].[9] Equally important is Forster's indebtedness to Victorian novelists - to Dickens, Thackeray, Hardy, Eliot, and others who receive no mention in Aronson's book. When Forster's Mrs. Munt proudly discusses Elgar and other English composers, "what *we* are doing in music," one thinks of Thackeray's Mrs. Newcome or Dickens' Mr. Podsnap. In *Aaron's Rod* Lawrence's descriptions of Englishmen arriving late at operas and patronizing the professional musicians, his ironic assertion that a nightingale's singing is "entirely unaesthetical," and his portrait of female performers thinking of domestic concerns while playing classical music suggest his familiarity with nineteenth century novels. Lawrence's exploration of the link between the musician and sexual power (Aaron's flute is a phallic symbol) continues an association made by Hardy and other Victorians. Similarly, James Joyce draws on methods of earlier novelists when he uses music to demonstrate Stephen's disillusionment with romanticism in *Portrait of the Artist as a Young Man*, to delineate the older generation's strong sense of nostalgia in "The Dead," or to gauge Leopold Bloom's mood in *Ulysses*.

Like their predecessors, twentieth century novelists found and continue to find the musician to be a rich source of metaphor, musical scenes an ideal forum for artistic commentary. The relationship between composer, performer, and listener offers a unique opportunity to explore the process of creating, interpreting, and responding to art. Music's non-mimetic quality fascinates writers interested in abandoning Victorian realism; many share Wilde's belief that, "As a method, realism is a complete failure."[10] Twentieth century writers draw on Victorian musical symbolism but go beyond the earlier novelists in their use of music to reveal the depths of man's subconscious and to analyze the nature of artistic form.

Victorian novelists were for the most part denied musical education, they lived in an age which produced no distinguished English composers, and they inherited a literary tradition of musical imagery which held little in common with their own experience. What is striking is not that the novelists of "das Land ohne Musik" treated the musician with occasional sentimentality, affected nostalgia, or cynical suspicion, but that they often transcended the biases of their age and brought music into their novels in dramatically new ways.

Walter Houghton writes of the Victorians, "nearly every fault and failing of the Victorian mind was exposed by the Victorians themselves . . . The worship of material progress, the anti-intellectualism, the dogmatism, the commercial spirit, the exaltation of force, the marriage market, and the insincerities of conformity, moral pretension, and evasion - all of these Victorian weaknessess were recognized and attacked."[11] The Victorian novelists' treatment of the musician illustrates this admirable capacity for self-analysis and criticism. Ironically, England's dearth of music inspired a wealth of literature.

Chapter VIII: Notes

1 Anthony Trollope, *William M. Thackeray* (N.Y.: Harper & Brothers, 1901), p. 182.
2 See, for instance, Walter H. Pater, "The School of Giorgione" (1877), in *The Renaissance* (London: Macmillan, 1910), pp. 130-54. Music, Pater writes, is the "ideally consummate art" (pp. 134-5).
3 Oscar Wilde, "The Critic as Artist," *The First Collected Edition of the Works of Oscar Wilde*, ed. Robert Ross (London: Dawsons, 1969), VIII: 175, 152-3.
4 George Bernard Shaw, "Ruskin on Music," *Shaw on Music*, ed. Eric Bentley (N.Y.: Doubleday, 1955), p. 50 ff.
5 Shaw, *London Music in 1888-89 as Heard by Corno di Bassetto* (N.Y.: Dodd, Mead and Co., 1961), p. 138 (May 31, 1889).
6 Wilde, *The Importance of Being Earnest*, Act I.
7 Shaw, Preface to the 4th Edition of *The Perfect Wagnerite*, in *The Collected Works of Bernard Shaw* (N.Y.: Wise, 1931), XIX: 167.
8 Friedrich Nietzsche, *The Case of Wagner*, trans. Walter Kaufmann (N,Y.: Random House, 1967), p. 166.
9 Alex Aronson, *Music and the Novel: A Study in 20th Century Fiction* (N.J.: Rowman & Littlefield, 1980), p. 79.
10 Wilde, "The Decay of Lying: An Observation," *Works*, VII: 25.
11 Walter Houghton, *The Victorian Frame of Mind*, 1830-70 (New Haven: Yale University Press, 1957), p. 424.

Bibliography

Primary Sources

The primary sources listed below include not only the novels, short stories, plays, and poems discussed in my study but also those prose works written before 1900 which I used to reveal attitudes towards music during or prior to the Victorian period.

Addison, Joseph. *The Spectator.* Ed. Robert Bisset. London: Cawthorn, 1799.

Ascham, Roger. "The Scholemaster." *The Whole Works.* Ed. Rev. Giles. London: John Russell Smith, 1864. Vol. III.

Austen, Jane. *Persuasion.* New York: New American Library, 1964.

---------- *Pride and Prejudice.* New York: New American Library, 1961.

---------- *Sense and Sensibility.* New York: New American Library, 1961.

Avison, Charles. *An Essay on Musical Expression.* 2nd ed. London: C. Davis, 1753.

Balzac, Honore de. *Gambara. The Novels of Balzac.* Trans. Ellen Marriage. Philadelphia: Gebbie Publishing Co., 1899.

Beattie, James. "Essay on Poetry and Music, as they affect the Mind." *Essays.* Edinburgh: William Creech, 1776.

Beethoven, Ludwig von. *Letters, Journals, and Conversations.* Ed. and Trans. Michael Hamburger. New York: Pantheon, 1952.

Bentham, Jeremy. *Works.* Edinburgh: William Tait, 1843. Vol. II.

Boswell, James. *The Life of Samuel Johnson.* New York: Modern Library, 1952.

Bronte, Charlotte. *Jane Eyre.* Ed. Richard Dunn. New York: Norton, 1871.

Browning, Robert. *The Complete Poetic and Dramatic Works of Robert Browning.* Cambridge, Mass.: Riverside Press, 1895.

Burgh, A. *Anecdotes of Music, Historical and Biographical: in a series of letters from a Geneltman to his Daughter.* London, 1814.

Burney, Charles. *A General History of Music: From the Earliest Ages to the Present Period.* (1789) New York: Harcourt, Brace, 1935.

Burton, Robert. *The Anatomy of Melancholy.* London: J.M. Dent, 1621.

Busby, Thomas. *Concert Room and Orchestra Anecdotes of Music and Musicians, Ancient and Modern.* Lonson: Clementi and Co., 1825.

Butler, Samuel. *The Notebooks.* Ed. Henry Festing Jones and A.T. Bartholomew. Lonson: Capte, 1926. Vol. XX.

---------- *The Way of All Flesh.* New York: Random House, 1950.

Byron, George Gordon, Lord. *Poetical Works.* Ed. Frederick Page. London: Oxford University Press, 1970.

Calvin, Jean. *Commentary on the Book of Psalms.* Trans., Rev. James Anderson. Grand Rapids, Mich.: Eerdmans, 1949.

Carlyle, Thomas. *Critical and Miscellaneous Essays.* 5 vols. New York: Scribner's, 1903.

---------- *Heroes and Hero-Worship. The Works of Thomas Carlyle.* 30 vols. New York: Scribner's, 1903. Vol. V.

---------- *Sartor Resartus. Works.* Vol. I.

Chesterfield, Lord. *The Letters of Phillip Dormer Stanhope, Earl of Chesterfield.* Ed. Lord Mahon. 5 vols. Philadelphia: Lippincott, 1892. Vol.

Coleridge, Samuel. *The Complete Poetical Works of Samuel Taylor Coleridge.* Cambridge Edition. Ed. Andrew George. Boston: Houghton, 1932.

Collier, Jeremy. "On Musick." *Essays on Several Moral Subjects.* London: Brown, 1709.

Collins, William Wilkie. *The Woman in White.* Ed. Harvey Sucksmith. London: Oxford University Press, 1975.

Cooper, Thomas. *The Life of Thomas Cooper, Written by Himself.* London: Hodder & Stoughton, 1879.

Cowper, William. *The Correspondence of William Cowper.* Ed. Thomas Wright. 4 vols. New York: Harper & Bros., 1904

Cross, J.W., Ed. *George Eliot's Life as Related in her Letters and Journals.* 3 vols. New York: Harper & Bros., 1885.

Curwen, J. Spencer. *Studies in Worship-Music.* London: J. Curwen & Sons, 1880.

Dickens, Charles. *Bleak House. The Works of Charles Dickens.* 30 vols. N.Y.: Collier, 1895. Vols. XXII-III.

---------- *Christmas Stories. Works.* Vol. XXIV.

---------- *Dickens's Correspondence with John Hullah.* Hitherto Unpublished from the Collection of Count de Suzannet. Walter Dexter: private printing, 1933.

---------- *David Copperfield. Works.* Vols. II-III.

---------- *Dombey and Son. Works.* Vols. XIV-V.

---------- *Edwin Drood. Works.* Vol. XXX.

---------- *Great Expectations. Works.* Vol. XXX.

---------- *Life and Adventures of Martin Chuzziewit. Works.* Vols. IX-X.

---------- *Nicholas Nickleby. Works.* Vols. XI-XII.

---------- *Old Curiosity Shop. Works.* Vols. XVI-XVII.

---------- *Our Mutual Friend. Works.* Vols. IV-V.

---------- *Pickwick Papers. Works.* Vols. XX-XXI.

---------- *Sketches by Boz. Works.* Vol. XIX.

Disraeli, Benjamin. *Tancred. The Bradenham Edition of the Novels and Tales.* Lonson: Constable, 1927. Vol. X.

Du Maurier, George. *Trilby.* New York: Harper, 1895.

Eliot, George. *Adam Bede. Works.* Boston: Estes, 1893-95. Vols. I-II.

---------- *Daniel Deronda. Works.* Vols. XI-XIII.

---------- *Essays of George Eliot.* Ed. Thomas Pinney. London: Routledge & Kegan Paul, 1963.

---------- *The George Eliot Letters.* Ed. Gordon S. Haight. New Haven: Yale University Press, 1954.

---------- *Middlemarch. Works.* Vols. XIV-VI.

---------- *The Mill on the Floss. Works.* Vols. XIX-XX.

---------- "The Modern Hep! Hep! Hep!" *Works.* Vol. X.

---------- *Poems of George Eliot. Works.* Vol. XVII.

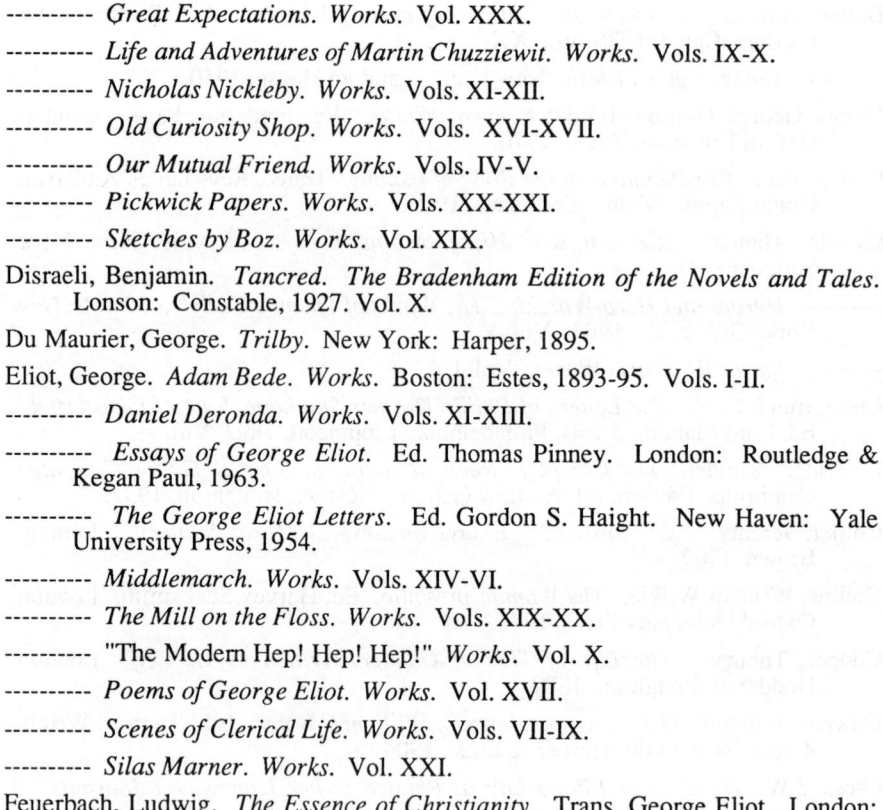

---------- *Scenes of Clerical Life. Works.* Vols. VII-IX.

---------- *Silas Marner. Works.* Vol. XXI.

Feuerbach, Ludwig. *The Essence of Christianity.* Trans. George Eliot. London: John Chapman, 1854.

Forster, E.M. *Howards End.* New York: Alfred Knopf, 1946.

Gardiner, William. *The Music of Nature; or, an attempt to prove that what is passionate and pleasing in the art of singing, speaking, and performing upon musical instruments is derived from the sounds of the animated world.* Boston: Oliver Ditson & Co., 1832; rpt. 1837.

Gothe, Johann Wolfgang von. *Conversations with Eckermann.* New York: Dunne, 1901.

Grant Duff, Sir Moutstuart E. *A Victorian Vintage.* Ed. A Tilney Bassett. London: Methuen & Co., 1930.

Hanslick, Eduard. *Music Criticism, 1846-99.* Trans. Henry Pleasants. Baltimore: Penguin, 1950.

Hardy, Thomas. *Collected Poems of Thomas Hardy.* New York: Macmillan, 1953.

---------- *Far from the Madding Crowd. The Works of Thomas Hardy in Prose and Verse.* Wessex Edition. 21 vols. London: Macmillan, 1912-14. Vol. II.

---------- *Jude the Obscure. Works.* Vol. III.

---------- *Mayor of Casterbridge. Works.* Vol. V.

---------- *Return of the Native. Works.* Vol IV.

---------- *Tess of the d'Urbervilles. Works.* Vol. I.

---------- *Under the Greenwood Tree. Works.* Vol. VII.

Haweis, Reverend Hugh Reginald. *Music and Morals.* New York: Harper & Bros., 1871.

---------- *My Musical Life.* London: Longmans, 1902.

Hazlitt, William. *The Complete Works of William Hazlitt.* 21 vols. Ed. P.P. Howe. London: J.M. Dent, 1930. Vols. V, XX.

Hagel, Georg Friedrich Wilhelm. *The Philosophy of Fine Art.* Trans. F. Osmaston. London: George Bell & Sons, 1920.

Hoffman, E.T.A. "Beethoven's Instrumental Music." *Source Readings in Music History.* Ed. Oliver Strunk. New York: Norton, 1950.

Hogarth, George. *Musical History, Biography, and Criticism.* London: John W. Parker, 1838.

Hogarth, William. "The Enraged Musician." *Marriage a la Mode and Other Engravings.* New York: Lear, 1947.

Hueffer, Francis. *Half a Century of Music in England, 1837-87.* London: Chapman & Hall, 1889.

Hullah, John. *The History of Modern Music.* 4th Ed. London: Longmans, 1884.

Hunt, Leigh. *Musical Evenings, or Selections, Vocal and Instrumental.* Ed. David R. Cheney. Columbia, Missouri: University of Missouri Press, 1964.

---------- *The Poetical Works of Leigh Hunt.* 2 vols. Boston: Tickner & Fields, 1857.

Huxley, Aldous. *Point Counter Point.* New York: Modern Library, 1930.

Johnson, Samuel. *Johnsonian Miscellanies.* Ed. G.B. Hill. New York: Harper, 1897.

Joyce, James. *Dubliners.* New York: Viking Press, 1961.

---------- *A Portrait of the Artist as a Young Man.* Ed. Chester Anderson. New York: Viking Press, 1968.

---------- *Ulysses*. New York: Vintage Books, 1961.

---------- *The Letters of John Keats,.1819-21*. Ed. Rollins. Cambridge, Mass.: Harvard University Press, 1958.

Keats, John. *Selected Poems and Letters*. Ed. Douglas Bush. Boston: Houghton Mifflin, 1959.

Knox, Vicesimus. "On Music as an Amusement." *Essays Moral and Literary*. 9th Ed. 3 vols. London: Charles Dilly, 1878. Vol. II

Lamb, Charles. *The Essays of Elia*. New York: A.L. Burt, 1885.

Lawrence, D.H. *Aaron's Rod*. New York: Thomas Seltzer, 1922.

Locke, John. "Some Thoughts on Education." *The Works of John Locke*. London: Ward, Locke, & Col, n.d.

Macaulay, T.B. *The Letters of Thomas Babington Macaulay*. Ed. Thomas Pinney, 4 vols. London: Cambridge University Press, 1974.

Mann, Thomas. *Doctor Faustus*. Trans. H.T. Lowe-Porter. New York: Vintage Books, 1948.

Meredith, George. *Sandra Belloni*. *The Works of George Meredith*. Memorial Edition. New York: Scribner's, 1910. Vols. III-IV.

---------- *Vittoria*. Works. Vols. VII-VIII.

Mill, John Stuart. *Autobiography and Other Writings*. Ed. Jack Stillinger. Boston: Houghton Mifflin, 1969.

Moore, George. *Evelyn Innes*. Carra Edition. New York: Boni & Liveright, 1923. Vol. VI.

---------- *Sister Teresa*. Carra Edition. Vol. VII.

More, Hannah. *Strictures on the Modern System of Female Education*. Philadelphia: Budd & Bartram, 1800.

Newman, Cardinal John. *On the Scope and Nature of University Education*. Ed. Wilfrid Ward. London: Dent, 1915.

Nietzsche, Friedrich. *The Birth of Tragedy and The Case of Wagner*. Tr. Walter Kaufmann. New York: Random House, 1967.

Ovid. *Metamorphoses*. Trans. Rolfe Humphries. Bloomington, Ind.: Indiana University Press, 1955.

Parratt, Walter. "Music." *The Reign of Queen Victoria: A Survey of Fifty Years of Progress*. 2 vols. Ed. Thomas Humphry Ward. London: Smith, Elder, 1887. Vol.II.

Pater, Walter Horatio. "The School of Giorgione." *The Renaissance*. London: Macmillan, 1910.

Peacock, Thomas Love. *Critical and Other Essays. The Works of Thomas Love Peacock.* London: Constable, 1926.

---------- *Peacock's Novels.* New York & London: Scribners, n.d.

Philipson, David. *The Jew in English Fiction.* Cincinatti: Robert Clarke, 1889.

Plato. *Five Great Dialogues.* Trans. B. Jowett. New York: Walter Black, 1942.

Rousseau, Jean Jacques. *A Concise Dictionary of Music.* Trans. William Waring. London: Murray, 1709.

Rubinstein, Anton. *Autobiography.* Trans. A. Delano. Boston: Little, Brown & Co., 1890.

Ruskin, John. "Essay on the Relative Dignity of the Studies of Painting and Music." *The Complete Works of John Ruskin.* London: George Allen, 1905.

---------- "Traffic." *Complete Works.* Vol. XVIII.

Schopenhauer, Arthur. *The World as Will and Idea.* Trans. Haldane and Kemp. London: Routledge & Kegan Paul, 1883; rpt. 1957.

Schumann, Robert. *On Music and Musicians.* Trans. Paul Rosefeld. New York: Pantheon, 1948.

Shaw, George Bernard. *London Music in 1888-89 as heard by Corno di Bassetto (Later known as Bernard Shaw) with some further Autobiographical Particulars.* New York: Dodd, Mead & Co., 1961.

---------- *The Perfect Wagnerite. Collected Works of Bernard Shaw.* New York: Wise, 1931. Vol. XIX.

---------- *Shaw on Music.* Ed. Eric Bentley. New York: Doubleday, 1955.

Shelley, Percy B. *Poetical Works.* Ed. Thomas Hutchinson. London: Oxford University Press, 1970.

Sheppard, Elizabeth. *Charles Auchester.* London: J.M. Dent & Sons, 1911.

Spencer, Herbert. "On the Origin and Function of Music." *Essays on Education, Etc.* Lonson: J.M. Dent & Sons, 1911.

Steele, Richard. *The Spectator.* Ed. Robert Bisset. London: Cawthorn, 1799.

Thackeray, William Makepeace. *The Book of Snobs. Complete Works.* 26 vols. New York: Harper, 1904. Vols XI-XII.

---------- *Cox's Diary. Works.* Vol. V.

---------- *The History of Henry Esmond. Works.* Vols. XII-IV.

---------- *The Memoirs of Barry Lyndon, Esquire. Works.* Vol. VII.

---------- *The Newcomes. Works.* Vols. XV-VI.

---------- *Ravenswing. Men's Wives. Works.* Vol. VIII.

---------- *Vanity Fair. Works.* Vols. I-II.

Trollope, Anthony. *Barchester Towers.* New York: New American Library, 1963.

---------- *The Warden.* New York: Doric Books, 1950.

---------- *William M. Thackeray.* New York & London: Harper Bros., 1901.

Wackenroder, W.H. *The Remarkable Life of the Musician Joseph Berglinger. Source Readings in Music History.* Ed. Oliver Struck. New York: Norton, 1950.

Wilde, Oscar. "The Critic as Artist." *First Collected Edition of the Works of Oscar Wilde.* Ed. Robert Ross. London: Daswons, 1969. Vol. V.

---------- *The Importance of Being Earnest.* New York: Avon Books, 1965.

---------- *The Picture of Dorian Gray.* Middlesex, England: Penguin Books, 1891; rpt. 1976.

Woolf, Virginia. "The String Quartet." *The Haunted House and Other Stories.* New York: Harcourt, Brace, 1944.

Wordsworth, William. *The Complete Poetical Works of Wordsworth.* Cambridge Edition. Ed. Andrew George. Boston: Houghton, 1932.

Wyclif, John. *The English Works of Wyclif.* Ed. F.D. Matthew. London: Trubner & Co., 1866.

Secondary Sources

Abrams, M.H. *The Mirror and the Lamp.* London: Oxford University Press, 1953.

Altholz, Josef, Ed. *The Mind and Art of Victorian England.* Minneapolis: University of Minnesota Press, 1976.

Arendt, Hannah. *The Origins of Totalitarianism.* N.Y.: Harcourt, Brace & World, 1966.

Aronson, Alex. *Music and the Novel: A Study in 20th Century Fiction.* New Jersey: Rowman & Littlefield, 1980.

Barzun, Jacques. Introduction to *The Pleasures of Music.* New York: Viking, 1951.

---------- *Race: A Study in Superstition.* Revised ed. New York: Harper & Row, 1965.

Bayliss, Sue. "Hazlitt at the Opera." *Chesterian,* 26 (April 1952), 80-84.

Bentley, Eric Russell. *A Century of Hero-Worship.* Philadelphia & New York: Lippincott, 1944.

Berdoe, Edward. *The Browning Cyclopaedia.* Aberdeen: University Press, 1949.

Brewer, Luther. *Leigh Hunt and Charles Dickens: The Skimpole Caricature.* Iowa: private printing, 1930.

Bronson, Bertrand. "Some Aspects of Music and Literature in the 18th Century." *Music and Literature.* U.C.L.A.: Clark Memorial Library, 1953, pp. 22-25.

Brown, Steven. "Browning and Music." *Browning Society Notes,* 6 (1976), ii: 3-7.

Buckley, Jerome Hamilton. *The Victorian Temper.* Cambridge, Mass.: Harvard University Press, 1951.

Butwin, Joseph. *The Artist as Actor in English Fiction.* Ph.D. Diss. Harvard, 1971.

Buston, John. *Elizabethan Taste.* London: Macmillan, 1963.

Carlton, William J. "Fanny Dickens, Pianist and Vocalist." *Dickensian,* 53 (1957), 133-43.

Cirillo, Albert R. "Salvation in *Daniel Deronda*: The Fortunate Overthrow of Gwendolen Harleth." *Literary Monographs.* Ed. Eric Rothstein and Thomas Dunseath. Madison, Wisconsin: University of Wisconsin Press, 1967. II: 203-240.

Connolly, Thomas. "Swinburne on 'The Music of Poetry'." *PMLA,* 72 (1951), 680-88.

Dent, Edward J. "Music." *Early Victorian England, 1830-65.* Ed. G.M. Young. London: Oxford University Press, 1934. II: 251-64.

Dodds, John W. *The Age of Paradox. A Birography of England, 1841-1851.* New York: Rinehart, 1952.

Donakowski, Conrad. *A Muse for the Masses: Ritual and Music in an Age of Democratic Revolution (1770-1870).* Chicago: University of Chicago Press, 1972.

Einstein, Albert. *Music in the Romantic Era.* New York: W.W. Norton, 1947.

Ellis, Havelock. *A Study of British Genius.* London: Hurst & Balckett, 1904.

Felton, Felix. *Thomas Love Peacock.* London: Allen & Unwin, 1973.

Ford, Ernest. *A Short History of English Music.* New York: McBride, Nest & Co., 1912.

Fuller-Maitland, J.A. *English Music in the Nineteenth Century.* London: Grant Richards, 1902.

---------- "Music and Letters." *Essays and Studies.* Oxford: Clarendon Press, 1932, pp. 44-45.

Gay, Penelope. "Browning and Music." *Robert Browning.* Ed. Isobel Armstrong. Athens, Ohio: Ohio University Press, 1975, pp. 211-230.

Greene, Herbert E. "Browning's Knowledge of Music." *PMLA*, 62 (1947), 1095-98.

Grout, Donald. *A History of Western Music.* Revised ed. New York: Norton, 1973.

Grundy, Joan. *Hardy and the Sister Arts.* London: Macmillan 1979.

Haight, Gordon S. *George Eliot: A Biography.* Oxford: Clarendon Press, 1968.

---------- "George Eliot's Klemser." *Imagined Worlds.* Ed. Maynard Mack and Ian Gregor. London: Methuen, 1968, pp. 205-14.

Hardy, Barbara. *The Novels of George Eliot.* London: Athlone Press, 1954.

Hardy, Florence Emily. *The Life of Thomas Hardy. 1840-1928.* New York: St. Martin's Press, 1962.

Harvey, William John. *The Art of George Eliot.* London: Chatto & Windus, 1961.

Hollander, John. *The Untuning of the Sky: Ideas of Music in English Poetry, 1500-1700.* Princeton: Princeton University Press, 1961.

Holloway, John. *The Victorian Sage.* London: Macmillan & Co., 1953.

Houghton, Walter, E. *The Victorian Frame of Mind, 1830-70.* New Haven: Yale University Press, 1957.

Hutton, James. "Some English Poems in Praise of Music." *English Miscellany*, 1951, pp. 1-64.

James, Burnett. *Beethoven and Human Destiny*. London: Phoenix House, 1960.

Jensen, H. James. *The Muses' Concord: Literature, Music and the Visual Arts in the Barouqe Age*. Bloomington, Ind.: Indiana University Press, 1976.

Johnson, Charles. "Lost 'Chord', Wrong 'Chord', and other Musical Anomalies in 'A Toccata of Galuppi's'." *Studies in Browning and His Circle*, 4 (1976), i: 30-40.

Kivy, Peter. "The Child Mozart as an Aesthetic Symbol." *Journal of the History of Ideas*, 28 (June 1962), 249-58.

Lang, Paul Henry. *Music in Western Civilization*. New York: Norton, 1941.

Levenson, Shirley Frank. "The Use of Music in *Daniel Deronda*." *Nineteenth Century Fiction*, 24 (Dec. 1969), 317-34.

Lightwood, James T. *Charles Dickens and Music*. London: Charles Kelly, 1912.

Lipking, Lawrence. *The Ordering of the Arts in 18th Century England*. Princeton: Princeton University Press, 1970.

Loesser, Arthur. *Men, Women, and Pianos*. New York: Simon & Schuster, 1954.

Longyear, Rey M. *Nineteenth Century Romanticism in Music*. Englewood Cliffs, N.J.: Prentice-Hall, 1969.

Love, Frederick R. "Nietzsche's Quest for a New Aesthetic of Music." *Nietzsche Studien*, 6 (1977), 154-94.

Mackerness, Eric D. *A Social History of English Music*. London: Routledge & Kegan Paul, 1964.

Mardon, J. Vera. "Thomas Hardy as a Musician." *Monographs on the Life of Thomas Hardy*. Ed. J. Stevens Cox. Beaminister, Dorset: Toucan Press, 1964. XV: 5-24.

Nettel, Reginald. *The Englishman Makes Music*. London: Dennis Dobson, 1952.

Palacio, Jean de. "Music and Musical Themes in Shelley's Poetry." *Modern Language Review*, 59 (1964), 345-59.

Peckham, Morse. *Beyond the Tragic Vision: The Quest for Identity in the 19th Century*. New York: Briller, 1962.

Peters, Robert. "The Poetry of the 1890's: Its Relationship to the Several Arts." *Summaries of Doctoral Dissertations*, University of Wisconsin, 14 (1954), 442-43.

Pinion, S.D. "Music." *The Hardy Companion*. New York: St. Martin's Press, 1968.

Praz, Mario. *The Flaming Heart*. New York: Doubleday, 1958.

Pulver, Jeffrey. *Paganini, the Romantic Virtuoso*. London: Herbert Joseph, 1936.

Rainbow, Bernarr. *The Land Without Music: Musical Education in England 1800-1860 and its Continental Antecedents*. London: Novello, 1967.

Raynor, Henry. *Music and Society since 1815*. New York: Schocken Books, 1976.

Ridenour, George M. "Browning's Music Poems: Fancy and Fact," *PMLA*, 78 (Sept. 1963), 369-77.

Rosenberg, Edgar. *From Shylock to Svengali: Jewish Stereotypes in English Fiction*. Stanford: Stanford University Press, 1960.

Rosenthal, Harold. *Two Centuries of Opera at Covent Garden*. London: Putnam, 1958.

Routley, Erik. *The Musical Wesleys, 1703-1876*. New York: Oxford University Press, 1968.

Salz, Paulina. "Peacock's Use of Music in his Novels." *Journal of English and Germanic Philology*, 54 (1955), 370-79.

Scholes, Percy A. *The Mirror of Music, 1844-1944*. London: Oxford University Press, 1947.

---------- *The Oxford Companion to Music*. Second ed. London & New York: Oxford University Press, 1943.

---------- *The Puritans and Music in England and New England*. London: Oxford University Press, 1934.

Schoolfield, George C. *The Figure of the Musician in German Literature*. Chapel Hill: University of North Carolina Press, 1956.

Schueller, Herbert M. "Correspondences Between Music and the Sister Arts, According to 18th Century Aesthetic Theory." *Journal of Aesthetics and Art Criticism*, 14 (1955), 218-47.

---------- "Immanuel Kant and the Aesthetics of Music." *Journal of Aesthetics and Art Criticism*, 14 (1955), 218-247.

---------- "Literature and Music as Sister Arts: An Aspect of Aesthetic Theory in 18th Century Britian." *Philological Quarterly*, 26 (July 1947), iii: 193-205.

---------- "The Use and Decorum of Music as Described in British Literature, 1700-1780." *Journal of the History of Ideas*, 13 (1952), 73-93.

Smith, D.J. "Music in the Victorian Novel." *Kenyon Review*, 25 (Summer 1963), 517-32.

Smith, Preserved. *The Life and Letters of Martin Luther*. Boston: Houghton Mifflin, 1914.

Sorgatz, Heimfried. *Musiker und Musikanten als Dichterisches Motiv.* Germany, 1939.

Stevens, John. *Music and Poetry in the Early Tudor Court.* London: Methuen, 1961.

Strunk, Oliver, Ed. *Source Readings in Music History: The Romantic Era.* New York: Norton, 1955.

Sullivan, William J. *George Eliot and the Fine Arts.* Ph.D. Diss. University of Wisconsin, 1970.

Tamm, Merike. *Inter-Art Relations and the Novels of Jane Austen.* Ph.D. Diss. University of Wisconsin, 1976.

Taylor, Ronald. *Hoffmann.* New York: Hillary House, 1963.

Thomson, Patricia. *The Victorian Heroine: A Changing Ideal, 1837-73.* London: Oxford University Press, 1956.

Walker, Ernest. *A History of Music in England.* Oxford: 1907; revised 1952.

Warwick, Alan R. *A Noise of Music.* London: Queen Anne Press, 1968.

Watson, J. Arthur. "Thackeray and Music." *Monthly Musical Record*, 82 (March-April 1952), 60-66.

Weber, William. *Music and the Middle Class.* New York: Holmes & Meier, 1975.

Witemeyer, Hugh. *George Eliot and the Visual Arts.* New Haven: Yale University Press, 1979.

Young, Percy M. "George Eliot and Music." *Music and Letters*, 24 (April 1943), 92-100.

Gisela Argyle

GERMAN ELEMENTS IN THE FICTION OF GEORGE ELIOT, GISSING, AND MEREDITH

European University Studies: Series XIV (Anglo-Saxon Language and Literature). Vol. 74
ISBN 3-8204-6500-6   252 pages   paperback US $ 40.50*

*Recommended price – alterations reserved

George Eliot, Gissing and Meredith are the nineteenth-century British novelists who, in their fiction, made the most significant and substantial use of German material. The function of this material is twofold, relating both to the life presented and to the presentation. An elucidation of the German references adds not only to a fuller understanding of the individual novels, but also of the author's theory and practice of fiction, and of one of the experimental tendencies in the 'wide' tradition of the English novel.

Contents: George Eliot. 'Middlemarch'. 'Daniel Deronda'. Gissing. The 'Double Art'. The 'Double Life'. Meredith. An 'Alpine Affinity'.

PETER LANG PUBLISHING, INC.
62 West 45th Street
USA – New York, NY 10036

Alan D. Perlis

A RETURN TO THE PRIMAL SELF
Identity in the Fiction of George Eliot
New York, Bern, Frankfurt/M., Paris, 1989.

American University Studies: Series 4, English Language and Literature. Vol. 71
ISBN 0-8204-0637-6   221 pages   hardback US $ 35.50/sFr. 49.50

Recommended prices – alterations reserved

A Return to the Primal Self addresses the neglected theme of wholeness of self in George Eliot's fiction. Arguing that the preponderance of Eliot criticism has focused on how Eliot's characters achieve a social identity, Alan Perlis emphasizes how these characters seek to realize an integrated sense of the elements of their own being. Drawing on sources as diverse as Plato and Wordsworth, the author demonstrates that Eliot's most sympathetic characters return to primal scenes from their own childhood and manage to align them with the adult self, thus attaining a new maturity of vision.

Contents: Character development in George Eliot's fiction – Critical analysis of the novels.
"By way of a study of character and characterization from a variety of perspectives, Perlis reaffirms George Eliot's position in British fiction as a profound and innovative psychological novelist." (Joseph Wiesenfarth, University of Wisconsin, Madison)

PETER LANG PUBLISHING, INC.
62 West 45th Street
USA – New York, NY 10036

Phyllis C. Ralph

VICTORIAN TRANSFORMATIONS
Fairy Tales, Adolescence, and the Novel of Female Development
New York, Bern, Frankfurt/M., Paris, 1989.

American University Studies: Series 4, English Language and Literature. Vol. 96
ISBN 0-8204-1039-X   176 pages   hardback US $ 31.95/sFr. 48.95

Recommended prices – alterations reserved

Why do fairy tales and myths have universal appeal? Is it because they have happy endings? Or perhaps because their heroes and heroines set out on their own and overcome great obstacles before achieving their goals? Psychologists tell us that tales of transformation can provide paradigms of the process of growing up to guide and support their readers at a subconscious level. *Victorian Transformations* examines the psychological implications of these tales as their motifs were used by Jane Austen, Charlotte and Emily Brontë, and George Eliot in their creation of female protagonists who grow and change through their own initiative. Their adventures correspond to those of the fairy tale heroines in transforming not only themselves, but also their prospective husbands.

Contents: Contents include discoussions of selected fairy tales and myths, their psychoanalytical interpretations, adolescent development, and nineteenth-century British novels by and about women focusing on their growth and development.

PETER LANG PUBLISHING, INC.
62 West 45th Street
USA – New York, NY 10036